Seep Garden of Monkeyflowers and Fireweed near Truckee River

Explorer's Gentian on trail to Lake Fontanillis

Mariposa Lily in Sherwood Forest

Pinedrops near Benwood Meadow

Arnicas on Galena Creek

Bridge's Gilia at General Creek

HIKING TAHOE'S *Wildflower* TRAILS

Written by
JULIE STAUFFER CARVILLE

Illustrations by
STEPHANIE BARBONI-SEPPA

LONE PINE

The Publisher: Lone Pine Publishing

206, 10426-81 Ave.	202A, 110 Seymour Street	16149 Redmond Way, #180
Edmonton, Alberta	Vancouver, British Columbia	Redmond,Washington
Canada T6E 1X5	Canada V6B 3N3	USA 98052

Canadian Cataloguing in Publication Data

Carville, Julie Stauffer.
   Hiking Tahoe's wildflower trails

   Previous ed. has title: Lingering in Tahoe's wild gardens
   ISBN 1-55105-101-X

   1. Wild flowers—Tahoe, Lake, Region (Calif. and Nev.) 2. Hiking—Tahoe, Lake, Region (Calif. and Nev.)—Guidebooks. 3. Botany—Tahoe, Lake, Region (Calif. and Nev.)—Guidebooks. 4. Tahoe, Lake, Region (Calif. and Nev.)—Guidebooks. I. Title. II. Title: Lingering in Tahoe's wild gardens.
QK149.C37 1997   582.13'09794'38   C97-910227-8

Illustrations: Stephanie Barboni-Seppa
Photography: Julie Stauffer Carville
Cover photo: Mike Carville
Cover inset photos: Laird R. Blackwell
Cover design: Jun Lee
Printing: Best Book Manufacturers, Toronto, Ontario, Canada

The publisher gratefully acknowledges the support of Alberta Community Development and the Department of Canadian Heritage.

Contents

Foreword

To a naturalist, a book that combines a warm appreciation of the beauty created by Nature's wild gardens with a genuine regard for the scientific value of these beauty spots is a rare treasure. Yet this is what Julie Carville offers to those nature lovers who are fortunate enough to explore the kaleidoscopic mosaic of beauty in the wild lands that surround Lake Tahoe. As a do-it-yourself guide to these and similar spots, *Lingering in Tahoe's Wild Gardens* is unequalled anywhere in our western states.

Mrs. Carville has a genuine love of wild lands, based upon her profound knowledge of them. She is equally aware of the desires and limitations of budding amateur naturalists who wish to see and learn more. After an overview of the modern aspects of systematic botany as they relate to botanizing in wild areas, she describes a series of hikes of varying degrees of difficulty. In precise language, that is nevertheless permeated with appreciation, in wonder and awe, of the natural tapestry that can be recognized easily by those whose eyes are opened to it, she describes to the reader the flowers that any hiker or stroller can see. Since enthusiasm is catching, this book will be particularly valuable to young people or to those, who, young in spirit, but hitherto city-bound wish to make a hobby of exploring and understanding the never ending beauty and complexity that Nature has evolved in the world of plant life.

G. Ledyard Stebbins
Professor of Genetics, Emeritus
University of California, Davis

1

Acknowledgements

Our journeys through life and the accomplishments along the way are never achieved alone, therefore I wish to give special thanks to the following: to my husband, Phil, for his valuable editorial input, for so gently bringing me into the computer age and for his beautiful, supportive love; to my son, Michael, and my daughter, Jennifer, for the gift of their wonderful individuality, joy and spirit; to Stephanie Barboni-Seppa, for her dear friendship and for adding such richness to this book; to my parents, Gert and Perry Stauffer, for their years of love and support; to my brother, Brett Stauffer, and his wife, Maggie, for generously lending me their ocean home so I could simplify my days, quiet my mind and get started; to Nancy Zacher, for sharing the peacefulness of Bolinas; to Wilma McPherson, who reminded me that the "gift" is not the knowledge of wildflowers but the expression of love for them; to the Tahoe Chapter of the California Native Plant Society, for the wild, crazy and fun beginning; to Lela Joslin, for helping with the early load with such joy; and to my students, who helped me to stretch and grow as they shared my love of the flowers.

I am also very grateful to: Dawn Anderson, Candy Badiner, Laird Blackwell, Sherman and Jean Chickering, Tonja Pearce, Carl Sharsmith, Bill Shriver, Gladys Smith, G. Ledyard Stebbins, and Myron Stollaroff, for so generously sharing their precious time to read part or all of the manuscript and for giving me their valuable perspective, inspiration and input.

Finally, I want to give special thanks to the wildflowers, themselves, for showing me the way back to myself and for making the process so much fun!

A Note from the Author

"It is possible to know a flower, root,
and stem and all the processes of growth,
and yet have no appreciation
of the flower fresh bathed
in heaven's dew."

Helen Keller

T he snow is falling outside my cabin window, covering the woods in a blanket of white. I feel excited by winter as I watch the flakes drift slowly downward through the trees, but I must confess that my thoughts are on the thousands of little flowers sleeping away the winter beneath this protective covering.

Fifteen years ago I moved to Tahoe. Although I had back-packed for many years in the Sierra while living in the Bay Area, I had no idea how beautiful its gardens could be until I began living among them. Then one brisk morning in June, I walked out my back door down through the woods and came upon a meadow of solid yellow buttercups. As I knelt down to inhale their sweet fragrance, I discovered tiny rainbows sparkling on little silver-haired leaves.

That morning changed my life because it was the beginning of my commitment to myself to make the backcountry, and other such wild places, an integral part of my life. Now after many years of writing a wildflower hiking column for Tahoe's local newspapers and after many more years as an instructor of wildflower photography and botany field classes, I have lived that commitment, and it has filled my life with richness.

During this time I have taken many people into the special

gardens that I have discovered since that first morning among the buttercups. Over the years my readers and students have asked me to collect my writings and experiences into a book, but for just as many years I resisted. I was afraid such a book might bring too many people into "my" gardens. But through the caring responses of my readers, and through the wonderful people that I have met in my classes, I have come to realize that it is by sharing such gardens that we protect them. For wild places will only be saved if others know they exist and if they are cherished by many people. I believe it is through ignorance that we destroy what should be precious to us.

And so I am sitting in my cabin, putting the final touches on my book, so that we can travel together through Tahoe's backcountry, sharing stories about the flowers, the animals and the insects, and about the ways in which Native Americans appreciated the plant world.

I have called my book, *Lingering in Tahoe's Wild Gardens* because I believe it is important to take the time to pause along the way. If we climb a mountain without ever lingering along the way, or if we learn a plant's name without appreciating that it is an exquisite expression of the life force, then what have we really achieved?

And so, I look forward to our journey together, for as Goethe once said "A joy shared is a joy doubled."

Julie Stauffer Carville
Lake Tahoe,
January 14, 1989

A Blooming Overview

L ingering in Tahoe's Wild Gardens takes the reader as an active partner into hundreds of the region's most beautiful wildflower gardens, within a format of 30 scenic hikes. It offers short hikes for little children and other "zen souls," who wish to concentrate on the flowers and streams along the way without the goal of arriving somewhere, and longer hikes for those who want to reach the mountain top and feel the joy of their muscles working. And there are overnights for those who wish to remain on the mountain after sundown to experience the transcendence of merging with a special person under a star-filled night-time sky.

Highlighted Wildflowers

Each hike begins with a list of the flowers that are most beautiful or most interesting along the trail. If you want to find the hikes that feature your favorite flowers, check the index. Since it is not the intent of this book to go into botanical detail for every flower mentioned, I recommend that you carry an illustrated, botanical field guide to aid you in identification. I feel the best choice for the Tahoe region is *A Field Guide to Pacific States Wildflowers* by Theodore F. Niehaus and Charles L. Ripper. It has excellent illustrations, covers the greatest number of species and is readily available at most book stores. (Other recommended flower books are listed in the Appendix.) For the sake of consistency, all botanical names used are based on *A California Flora and Supplement* by Philip A. Munz and David D. Keck.

5

The Effect of Snowpack on Blooming

The beginning of each hike specifies the general blooming season for that trail. This assumes a normal snowpack the preceding winter, as well as normal spring temperatures. Since both can vary considerably from year to year, the blooming times I have given will also vary, as will the abundance of their displays. After a heavier than normal snow year, the flowers may bloom several weeks later than the times I have given, or in a light snow year they may bloom several weeks earlier. So use my descriptions as a general guide. If the flowers are less spectacular than described, come back another time to enjoy their beauty. If they are more spectacular, then you have received a gift from the Gods!

Sequence in a Normal Blooming Season

Spring generally arrives at Tahoe in May with the appearance of the first buttercups at the 6,200 foot lake-level. The height of the wildflower season is June through August, when a myriad of color flows and cascades over granite boulders, winds its way along narrow ledges or brightly follows the courses of meandering creeks. Other flowers can be found gently cradled in tiny alpine meadows, where high peaks form rugged and powerful backdrops as they lovingly provide shelter for their clustered treasures.

One of the joys of mountain wildflowers is that specific flowers don't come and go in only a few weeks, as they often do in coastal or desert areas where there is little elevation change. In the mountains, flowers continue to bloom throughout the season as conditions of sunshine, moisture and temperature change — with these displays generally moving up the mountains as the days become warmer and the snow melts. So if you miss your favorite buttercups at lake-level in May, you will still be able to enjoy them 2,000 feet higher in July during "our" summer and "their" spring.

The height of Tahoe's wildflower season may be June through August, but May is still beautiful for lake-level buttercups, camas lilies and violets, and September for blue gentians and red fuchsias. The season doesn't end in September but rather announces the beginning of another stage in a wildflower's life, that of the bright reds and golds of berries and changing leaves. With October comes the height of fall color in golden aspen, red mountain ash and clusters of red elderberries.

By November, the world begins to quiet down. Gentle snow storms dust gardens and turn them into monochromes of buff yellow and brown. Soon the ground is frozen, and the gardens become rumpled and listless reminders of once glorious days. This time of year used to sadden me until I realized that the end of the flower season need not be lamented, for it is merely a necessary step in a re-occurring cycle, which will bring new and dazzling displays of wildflowers in the coming spring!

A Diverse Community of Plants

Tahoe hosts a rich botanical community within a state known for its great diversity of plants and animals. It has been recorded that there are more native plant and animal species in California than in the northeastern and central United States combined and that fifty per cent of California's species are found no where else on earth.

The great variety of plants at Tahoe is due in part to the complex mixture of granitic, volcanic and metamorphic rocks that have decomposed to create a variety of soil types. The botanical diversity is also due to the fact that Tahoe is a meeting place for species that have migrated up from the western flanks of the Sierra, and from the eastern Great Basin, to offer us a wonderful mixture of flowers that could take a lifetime to explore and enjoy.

Tahoe's Rare Plant Species

Within this abundance, there are the rare plants. The Truckee Barberry *(Berberis sonnei)*, a shrub similar in appearance to the Oregon Grape, was considered extinct until it was recently found growing on the banks of the Truckee River in Truckee. Only a few plants still survive out of a perhaps once large population. Some botanists believe that the introduction of beavers to the Sierra may have been the cause of its demise.

The Tahoe Cress *(Rorippa subumbellata)*, a Federally and State Listed Plant, grows nowhere else in the world but at Tahoe. It has small, yellow mustard flowers and can be found growing in the sand along the shores of Lake Tahoe.

Of course, it will probably not be the rare plants that will most excite your senses, but rather the wonderful color, fragrance and wide variety of species that cover the hillsides and meadows, that snuggle on the mountain tops or that line the shores of Lake Tahoe.

The Beauty of Lake Tahoe

Lake Tahoe, itself, is an exquisite, turquoise body of water 22 miles long and 12 miles wide, that lies in a basin surrounded by majestic mountain ranges. It was once described by Mark Twain, after he first hiked to its shores from Carson City on a hot summer day in the early-1860's, "...at last the Lake burst upon us — a noble sheet of blue water lifted six thousand three hundred feet above the level of the sea, and walled in by a rim of snow-clad mountain peaks that towered aloft a full three thousand feet higher still.... As it lay there with the shadows of the mountains brilliantly photographed upon its still surface, I thought it must surely be the fairest picture the whole earth affords!"

The Washo Indians of western Nevada also saw Tahoe as the earth's great gift, honoring it as a sacred, life-giving body of water. There have been many names for the lake, but the one that we use today was the name given it by the Washos and means "a great, spiritually powerful body of water."

A Word about Picking the Flowers

The wildflowers that you will find at Tahoe are lovely, and I know it will be tempting to pick them, but it is so much better to leave them for others to enjoy. One day as I hiked down a trail, I came upon a forlorn-looking pile of wildflowers that someone had picked and then later discarded after the flowers had wilted. Domestic flowers may be bred to withstand picking, handling and "life in a vase," but most wildflowers, plucked from their wild gardens, are like caged animals in a zoo — they soon wither in spirit and body.

If you want bouquets of wildflowers, grow them in your garden. If you want to examine a flower that grows along the trail, don't pick it, but rather get down on your hands and knees and meet it at its own level on its own terms. When we enjoy flowers in this way, we honor the preciousness of all life. Flowers, like us, are living breathing expressions of the life force. Just as we do, they deserve to complete their life cycles unmolested.

Judging the Hike

In planning your hike, look at the beginning of each hike for the trail mileage, elevations, recommended maps and directions to the trailhead. The net gain is the difference in elevation between the beginning and the end of the hike. The total gain is the approximate number of feet climbed on the ups and downs of the trail. Look at these numbers carefully, as they will indicate how easy or strenuous the trip may be.

I strongly recommend that you carry a topographic map and compass, because from time to time trail signs change or disappear. This can make decisions at trail junctures confusing, unless you have a map and compass to help you head in the right direction.

The ⚲ symbol, given at a hike's beginning, highlights the trip as especially suitable for small children, the elderly or the physically challenged. The ♿ symbol indicates there is wheel chair access. If, in the past, you have thought of yourself as unable to experience such back-country areas, I hope this book will change your mind and bring a new richness into your life.

In judging how long a hike will take, allow about two miles an hour. This takes into account ups and downs but not stops. This rate, of course, does not apply to the very young or the elderly, who have their own special pace. In judging the difficulty or timing of a hike, you will need to know if the trails are free of snow. In some years, the higher elevation trails may be under snow through July. In other years, they may be free by late-June. Contact the U. S. Forest Service at Tahoe's north or south shore for the latest seasonal information.

Specific hiking times have not been included with the mileage of each hike because that is too personal for flower hikers (besides it can be estimated from the mileage). Just be sure to take into account that with a wildflower book or camera in hand, a mile may take many hours and with love in the heart, a whole day!

9

Botany Or...
How Do They Do It!

"You soon realize that in strolling in the
meadows in the merry month of May you are
witnessing an orgy of sex beside which
La Dolce Vita is like a bishop's garden party."
Adrian Bell

Adrian Bell's comment on the sex life of plants is a light-hearted reminder that flowers are just glorious collections of reproductive organs, brightly and unabashedly announcing their availability to neighborhood insects or carelessly casting their fate to the wind.

The flowery process of self-perpetuation is delightfully similar to that of humans. Pollen, which is analogous to sperm, is produced in little sacs called anthers. When the pollen combines with the female egg cell in the womb-like ovary of the flower, fertilization (conception) takes place. Pollen is distributed from one flower to another by the wind or by birds and insects as they search the plants for nectar. Sometimes (or in some species) flowers self-fertilize, but over the long haul this does not generally create the healthiest populations. Sexual reproduction, where genetic material is combined from two different parents, insures the greatest variety in the gene pool. This tends to create healthier more viable seed and plants that are more able to respond to environmental changes or to come up with new ways to more successfully adapt to a given environment.

Flowers evolved nectar, along with bright petals and elaborate reproductive structures and mechanisms, in order to entice insects

11

and birds to help insure pollination. This magnificent process is discussed in more detail on the Sagehen East hike, where you will have a chance to sit in front of a camas lily, with its "color coded" reproductive parts, to "see" and understand the cycle of flower to seed.

Plants, the Foundation of All Life

Through the miracle of flowers plants may reproduce themselves, but through the miracle of photosynthesis, plants convert the energy of sunlight into sugar and in doing so sustain not only themselves but all other forms of life on this planet.

In the process of photosynthesis the leaves of plants consume carbon dioxide and release oxygen. Thus over millions of years, billions of leaves have converted the poisonous, carbon-dioxide-rich atmosphere of ancient times into the oxygen-rich air that man and animals need to survive. Take away the plants and all other forms of life would soon come to an end. Plants also have the ability, as Brendan Lehane so beautifully expressed it in his book, *The Power of Plants,*

"...[to] break rocks, staunch floods, precipitate rain, or knit sand to resist the buffets of the sea. After catastrophes of fire, eruption, hurricane, and avalanche they can rise again, like the phoenix, to retrace their patient progress across the land. To procreate their species they have enslaved whole races of insects. To spread themselves they enlist wind, sea, and animals as porters. No man can garner sunbeams, or commit his off-spring to the wind for a journey of a thousand miles. A dandelion can. Science has far to go before it matches the ingenuity of a wayside weed."

So whether we find ourselves in a home garden or a wild one, let's never forget to stand in awe and respect before all plants, as we honor them for their wonderful ingenuity as sustainers of all life. Let's also never forget that the dancing of wildflowers gives form to the wind and joyful delight to our hungry souls.

The Evolution of Botany

Botany, or the study of plants, has grown gradually for thousands of years. Since prehistoric times, man has named and organized plants into categories. Early man grouped plants by their uses for food, medicine, shelter and clothing.

Early physicians became botanists to study plants for medicinal preparations. This led the Greeks to a system of classification based upon the medicinal qualities of plants. Theophrastus, a student of Aristotle who lived from 370 to 285 B.C., was the first person known to have left written records of systematic plant classification. For the next 2,000 years written plant knowledge was preserved in herbals according to their economic and medicinal uses.

After the startling discovery that plants reproduced sexually (a concept that took some time to be accepted) Carl Linnaeus, a Swedish naturalist, developed a system of classification based upon the number of sexual organs in a flower. Linnaeus' discovery that flowers reproduced sexually horrified many in the religious community. One outraged minister claimed such a concept could only come from a "grossly prurient mind," but the scientific community recognized the truth of his observations and, in time, honored him as an outstanding scientist.

Linnaeus knew his approach to plant categorization was only a convenient way of grouping plants and that a more detailed and accurate system would be developed as man learned more about the plant world. His thinking went far beyond the times for we do now try to name and categorize plants according to their own natural relationships. This marks a change in man's thinking away from the man-centered, limited viewpoint of the past, which saw plants in terms of their usefulness to man, to the present appreciation of Nature's plan.

Since we now categorize plants to understand the relationship of each plant to all other plants in the world, families and other such plant groupings are based upon natural criteria. Thus plants are grouped by shared evolutionary development, as well as by similar genetic structure, chemical composition or embryonic development. They are also grouped by observable flower structures, which scientists believe are manifestations of the above concepts.

Plants have always been given names to help categorize them, but it was Linnaeus who came up with our presently-used system of binomial Latin names, or the use of two words in the naming of each plant.

For instance, there are many violets throughout the world, but there is only one type of violet with the name, *Viola glabella*. The first word, *Viola*, is a genus grouping of closely related species which have certain characteristics in common, such as similarity of flowers and fruits. The binomial, *Viola glabella*, is the species name of one type of violet, with the second word, *glabella*, being the epithet of the binomial. A species is defined as a recognizable and self-perpetuating system of populations that is generally isolated genetically or environmentally.

Plants are also grouped more broadly by family. A family is made up of one or more genera based upon a shared evolutionary history as judged by the above-mentioned characteristics.

There are at least 335,000 known species of plants throughout the world, and there are perhaps thousands of plants, mainly in the tropical climates or other remote areas, that have not yet been found or categorized. To name all these plants has been a formidable task, and prior to Linnaeus there was no consistent nomenclature. Many plants carried cumbersome names of five or more words. His system of two Latin names for each plant enabled botanists throughout the world to share knowledge with one another in a systematic and easily understood language. This became the basis for the development of modern botany.

The Naming of Wildflowers

Learning the names of wildflowers can help you to become better acquainted with them. When first learning plant names most people have **no** intention of **ever** learning the Latinized botanical names. They are content with common names because such names are usually charming and easy to remember. But common names can be confusing because the same plant may be given different names in various regions, or different plants in different regions may have the same common name. For instance "Dogtooth Violet" in some botany books refers to a little, blue violet and in other books to a white lily.

Even with such confusion, most flower lovers will be content with the common names, but for botanists from different regions or countries this confusion would make it very difficult to discuss plants and exchange knowledge; therefore, as one might expect, they always use botanical names.

Scientific plant nomenclature is in the form of Latinized words, because this was the language of scientists when Linnaeus (and others) first developed the system we now use. Botanical names seem complicated because Latin is unfamiliar to us, but once we become acquainted with them, they are easy to use. For example, geranium, which is a Latin genus designation, has become a household word.

Latin names can also be helpful because they can be both descriptive and interesting, telling us of the flower's structure, habitat or other aspects of the plant. For instance, the botanical name for the buttercup genus is "*Ranunculus*," a word derived from Latin for "little frog" because many members of this genus share wet habitats frequented by frogs. The Snow Plant, which is bright red and looks like a large fleshy asparagus, is called "*Sarcodes sanguinea*." *Sarcodes* comes from Greek for "flesh-like" and *sanguinea* means "blood red."

The concept of plant families and genera based upon observable structures was appreciated by many cultures, including the Egyptians, Eskimos, Aztecs and Native Americans. Knowing the general characteristics of family or genera will bring a satisfying familiarity into your interpretation of the plant world by helping you to easily see similarities and differences. It will also help make the identification of new flowers easier because if you know the family or genus of a flower just by looking at it (as you can easily do in most cases after minimal study), you can skip that part of the key and go directly to the species' key.

A Word about Botanical Keys

A "botanical key" is a binary system used for finding the name of a wildflower. Many botany books carry such keys for identifying flowers in the field. Such a key is wonderfully simple: one is presented with two choices that distill down to two additional choices and so on until the flower is identified.

Though it sounds clear-cut, the actual process, even for a trained botanist, can be frustrating. There are many reasons for this, but it mainly has to do with the way keys are created. Most keys are drawn from herbarium specimens. These are dried, pressed flowers (often preserved with stinky chemicals) that are placed in enclosed racks in a huge collection room.

To go into the field to prepare a book and key for thousands of flowers, that live in many different environments throughout the world, would be a long and laborious task. Thus many botanists use herbarium specimens to prepare their books. The problem with such specimens is that, with the many years of handling and storage (some were gathered as long ago as the late 1800's), they have become damaged and the colors have faded. A shriveled-up flower, with faded broken parts, is a far cry from the lovely colors and

15

structural beauty of a flower in the field.

Problems also arise because a particular flower in the field, that you may be looking at, may deviate in some way from the flowers used by the person(s) who authored the key. Without field experience, it is easy for the beginning botanist to believe the key, rather than his or her own observations. I often come across books that definitively say a flower grows only in a certain environment, up to a certain elevation or to a certain height, while in front of me sits the same little flower deviating from all three norms.

It is also important to remember that dynamic and fluctuating plant populations will not always be interpreted the same way by different botanists, no matter how competent they may be. The flower world is full of infinite variety, and botanists are individuals, so while there may be enough consistency that we can develop and use keys fruitfully, there is also enough variety that we must leave our minds open and, with experience, begin to trust our own observations.

Another problem for the beginning botanist is the seemingly complicated terminology of most plant keys which, though usually precise for the experienced botanist, is couched in a wholly new language for the amateur. Many a beginner has been frustrated by a description like "lvs. canescent, pinnatifid with linear-filiform subterete divisions" or confused by the 22 different terms botanists use just to describe the shape and growth patterns of hairs on a leaf.

I have often thought how delightful it would be if the books would just describe what we can easily observe in the field like, "five, lovely, little, 1/4 inch long, pink petals with bright yellow filaments and gorgeous blue anthers." Botanists too often leave out the soul of the flower, but then I suppose that is how some define science — objectivity with emotions left behind.

This is not to say that I don't appreciate scientific objectivity when appropriate, or that I don't use and actually love flower keys, for I do. In fact, they seem like magic to me. Imagine finding a totally new flower, sweetly staring up at you with divine innocence, and in a few minutes with the key you know its family, genus and species. With that knowledge you can search out all the information written about your flower, such as how it got its name, medicinal and edible uses, how it reproduces, details of its structure and its environmental range, and thus come to a greater understanding of it than if you only saw it as a cute, little, pink flower with blue anthers.

Another problem arises when the newer botany books list family, genus or species names that are different from the older books. This happens because these groupings are not cast in stone. They are revised when necessary as botanists gain new understanding of plant structures and processes. While this may at times be frustrating to the new student (and old botanist), it is a reminder that botany is a living science and that botanists are flexible enough to re-organize their way of interpreting plants when better, more logical ways present themselves.

Monocots and Dicots

You may also have heard botanists bounce around the terms "monocot" and "dicot." These words may seem complicated, unless you realize that they are merely shortened forms of the words monocotyledon and dicotyledon, that refer to two major sub-groups within the flowering world. Botanists believe that these two groups split and evolved separately from a common ancestor millions of years ago. It is important to be able to tell the difference between these two groups in the field, if you want to key out flowers, because many books separate flowers into these two categories before they further break them down into families, genera and species.

The terms monocotyledon and dicotyledon refer to the number of tiny leaves that form inside a seed before it sprouts. Some plants have one leaf at this early stage and are thus called monocotyledons. Mono, of course, means "one," and cotyledon means "seed leaves." Other flowering plants have two leaves at this stage and are thus called dicotyledons. Di is from the Greek word for "two." Next time you plant a seed, look for the leaves that first appear (since these are the ones that were formed inside the seed casing), and you can determine whether it is a monocot or a dicot.

When keying out plants in the field, it is usually easy to look at a mature plant to determine whether it is a monocot or dicot. The monocots generally share the traits of three petals and three sepals, which are often the same shape and color. Its stamens also come in multiples of three, and the plants carry simple leaves that are smooth-edged and parallel-veined. Some books suggest that the monocots may have appeared more recently on the evolutionary scale, but botanists disagree on this point. While the monocots have successfully covered the earth in vast numbers, they carry fewer family groups than do the dicots. The monocots include the grasses, orchids, onions, palms and lilies. The dicots generally include all other flowering plants that share the traits of petals and sepals that number four to five, (or multiples thereof), with these parts often differing in shape and color. Their leaves can be simple but are often compound and variously shaped, with leaf veins that form a patterned network. As you begin to look at plants in this way, it will become easy to categorize them into dicots or monocots.

A Personal Approach to Botany

The study of flowers is an enriching journey if we remember to approach plants in a way that makes us feel deeply connected to them and to the life force, for it is not what we know that counts but how we use it. If learning the Latin names and understanding the processes of flowers helps you to more deeply connect, that's wonderful. If your way is to daydream in a meadow of flowers and never learn a name, then that is fine too. My way is to combine knowledge and daydreaming. Through this I have found my greatest enrichment and connection, for I believe that "knowledge" without soul is empty, while soul with knowledge helps give form and thus expression to the emotions.

Flowers are only one of the many ways to take this exciting journey into the mystery of life, but they are a wonderful way for their incredible variety and exquisite forms are awe-inspiring expressions of life's love for itself. When we take the time to explore the mystery, we become more aware of the richness of life around us. Just as a painter becomes sensitized to form, color and light, so does the student of botany become sensitized to the intriguing and exquisite forms and processes of plant growth, survival and reproduction.

Studying wildflowers in the field is an exciting reminder that botany is more than just book-learned "facts" and that a formal education is not a prerequisite to becoming a competent botanist. The only prerequisite is an inquisitive mind, and the real keys to learning are love, enthusiasm, wonder and spontaneity. In *Lingering in Tahoe's Wild Gardens,* we will approach botany from these perspectives so that the process of studying wildflowers is both meaningful and fun.

- Plainleaf Fawn Lily
  (Erythronium purpurascens)
- Macloskey's Violet
  (Viola macloskeyi)
- Western Long-spurred Violet
  (Viola adunca)
- Crimson Columbine
  (Aquilegia formosa)
- Torrey's Monkeyflower
  (Mimulus torreyi)
- Creeping Phlox
  (Phlox diffusa)
- Mountain Pride
  (Penstemon newberryi)
- Smooth Yellow Violet
  (Viola glabella)
- Nuttall's Violet
  (Viola praemorsa)
- Anderson's Lupine
  (Lupinus andersonii)
- Crest Lupine
  (Lupinus arbustus)

The Loch Leven Lakes

For Violet Lovers, Swimmers and Loafers

One day/overnight	
One way 3 miles	
Trail begins/ends 5600'/6920'	
Net gain/total gain 1320'/1520'	
Topo maps USGS Donner Pass, Calif.	
USGS Emigrant Gap, Calif.	
Wildflower Season Late-May through August	

T he Loch Leven Lakes are alive in July with gardens of wildflowers, and unlike most Sierran lakes, their waters are "warm." The grassy banks and granite slabs along the shorelines offer excellent camping and fishing and provide wonderful spots for loafing, while small islands on several of the lakes "beg" to be swum to and explored. Along the steady uphill trail, a small wooden bridge crosses a creek where the waters peacefully flow under the boughs of red-stemmed dogwoods. Among damp alder gardens hidden clusters of wild violets bloom in purples, yellows and pure whites, while on conifered-covered slopes in June thousands of satiny white lilies come into bloom heralding the annual return of spring.

Plainleaf Fawn Lily

Trailhead Directions

Heading west on Interstate 80 out of Truckee, take

19

the Big Bend exit, about 9 miles west of the Castle Peak rest station. Go left under the freeway, then turn right and head westerly for about 2 miles to the roadside parking area which is .1 mile beyond the Big Bend Visitor's Center. There you will see a U. S. Forest Service sign that reads, "Private Road, Public Trail, Loch Leven Trail 1/4." Heading east on Interstate 80, take the Big Bend exit. Take a left at the stop sign on Hampshire Rocks Road, at the bottom of the exit, and drive about .1 mile to the off-road parking, where you will see the Forest Service sign mentioned above.

Be sure to park on the shoulder of the paved road, not on the private dirt road that leads into the trailhead. On a power pole along the dirt road is a weathered sign reading "Old Wagon Road." This sign is a nostalgic reminder that this was once part of the Over-

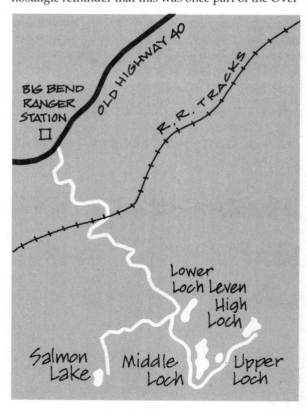

land Emigrant Trial used by pioneers in the late 1840's. As many as 30,000 settlers came to California on this trail in 1849 alone.

To find the trailhead, walk along the private road that leads south from the roadside parking for about 1/4 mile. After passing several homes and wonderful patches of pussy paws that bloom in early-July, you will arrive at another sign reading, "Loch Leven Trail." The trail from that point to all the lakes is easy to follow. The first lake is reached in about 2 miles, the last one in about 3.

The Trail Begins in Spring among Carpets of Fawn Lilies

Spring at Lake Tahoe, and along the Loch Leven Lakes trail, usually arrives in late-May. It is then that the snow is just completing its retreat from the mountainsides, and tiny suggestions of the Plainleaf Fawn Lily *(Erythronium purpurascens)* are beginning to peek out of the dampened soil.

If you hike the trail in late-May, you will find the emerging lilies just a few feet past the trailhead sign. Since they usually come into full bloom anywhere from early- to mid-June and are in full bloom for only a week or so, it is best to begin visiting the trail weekly in late-May. That way it will be easy to anticipate the full bloom. It is a sight not to be missed; in a good season after plenty of snow, the hillsides are carpeted with its lovely white blossoms.

Each flower carries 6 white petals that are yellow at the base and resembles the little "pin wheels" that we, as children, played with at the county fair. Its floppy blossoms catch even the gentlest of breezes with a fluttering that looks, to me, like a community of bobbing heads gathered to celebrate the arrival of spring. Every year they make my heart dance with excitement in anticipation of the coming wildflower season.

This lily closely resembles another called the Fawn Lily, a plant that has markings on its leaves like the markings on a fawn. Since "our" lily has plain green leaves, it is called the Plainleaf Fawn Lily. If you find it slightly past the peak of its bloom, look closely and you will see that after fertilization, it "symbolically" turns pink then purple. This color change in the petals led to its species name, *purpurascens*.

As you climb up the trail in June, you will be able to see the fawn lily's cycle of change from bud, to flower, to seed, although in reverse order, since the lower elevation plants will be swelling with seed as the higher ones are just coming into bud. Sharing these stages with a child is a wonderful way to help him or her understand the cycle of a flower's life, that a flower is not a static thing that dies when it fades, but rather that it is a part of a process of life, with the flower just as alive when swollen with seed as when in full bloom.

Within a few days after fertilization, its purplish petals drop off to reveal an intriguing, 3-sectioned, green ovary. With 6 petals and a 3-sectioned ovary, would you expect this flower to be a moncot or dicot? (See the Botany section if you are unsure.) If you hike the trail after the fawn lily has gone to seed, all is not lost because the ovary, in its own subtle way, is as lovely as the flower, as it swells with the maturing seeds. Don't pass it by without getting down on your hands and knees to peer at one of the ovaries. Be sure to angle yourself so that the sun shines through the ovary, and you will be treated to little rows of seeds, neatly housed in each translucent chamber.

Though it annually produces seed, the fawn lily is a perennial, with a bulb that is tucked away all winter, under a heavy blanket of snow, to protect it from the cold. In spring, the supply of nutrients stored in the bulb during the winter sustains new growth, until the plant begins to draw nourishment from warming soils to once again manufacture its own food.

Nests of Wild Violets

If you return a few weeks later in early-June, you'll find other harbingers of spring — nests of wild vio-

Macloskey's Violet

lets that greet you soon after you set foot upon the trail. In all of Tahoe, I have never found so many species of violets in one area, so I especially recommend this hike for violet lovers.

The first violets you will come upon are the white Macloskey's *(Viola macloskeyi)* and the bluish purple Western Long-spurred Violets *(Viola adunca)* blooming in lush delight in shaded, wet gardens. The white Macloskey's Violet grows only a few inches tall with the same heart-shaped leaves typical of most garden violets. Both its flowers and leaves rise directly out of creeping rootstocks, and it spreads by sending out leafy runners which give rise to scores of new little plants. Because of this, it is usually found growing in carpets, where it blooms profusely — its white blossoms contrasting in seeming innocence against the deep green of its leaves and the mossy greens of its wet habitat.

A Roadsign for Insects

When you come upon this violet, take a moment to sit down and view its beautiful flower detail through your hand lens. Purple lines radiate from the flower's center on the 3 lower petals. These lines, or other such markings on petals, are thought to be nectar guides for insects — a kind of "road sign" pointing the way to the nectar at the flower's center. Botanists believe that plants developed nectar to keep insects from over-consuming the pollen which is needed to produce next year's new plants.

As you hike along the trail, look at the detail in other flowers. Some have brightly colored spots, rows of soft hairs or strangely shaped petals to entice insects. Being sensitive to the markings and shapes of petals will awaken you to the amazing variety of expression in the flower world.

The Western Long-spurred Violet

You will also find the Western Long-spurred Violet *(Viola adunca)* in similar wet environments. Though it occurs infrequently along the trail, it is easy to

Western Long-spurred Violet

23

identify because of its prominent petal spur, which is often hooked at the end. (If you have difficulty finding it, look in shaded, wet areas under the Old Wagon Road sign that you passed on the way in.)

The Western Long-spurred Violet varies from a deep violet to a bluish violet color and looks like the typical garden variety that I grew up with as a child. Because of this resemblance, it somehow seems too vulnerable to me or "too far from home" to be able to survive Tahoe's harsh winters. But it is a hardy little plant, with the widest distribution of any native North American violet. It occurs throughout the Pacific States, from the mountains to the coast, and all across the northern part of North America. Botanists believe it migrated 1,000 miles south of its previous range in Canada and Alaska with the advance of glaciers in the Ice Age. When the glaciers retreated 10,000 years ago, it was content to remain and to spread its gentle beauty across the United States, from the mountains to the seashore.

When you find this violet, look closely at its flowers. You will see that the 3 lower petals are white at the base and are marked with contrasting, dark-violet nectar lines, while the 2 lateral petals carry soft white hairs. These white hairs and dark nectar lines attract both bumblebees and moths, which are its main pollinators. The white hairs on both the petals and the stigma (female part) also act as combs to scrape pollen off the insect's body as it enters the flower. In this way, pollen comes into direct contact with the stigma, and fertilization can take place. (See the Sagehen East hike to review the mechanics of fertilization.)

If you visit this area in July, look for these violets in seed. When mature, the seed cases split into 3 little canoe-shaped sections. As these "little boats" dry, their sides slowly move together to create a pressure that thrusts the seeds out onto the ground.

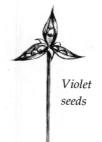

Violet seeds

An Uphill Climb through Nodding Columbines
On this early section of the trail, you may feel winded

by the steady uphill climb, but the initial steepness soon gives way to a gentle uphill which eventually levels out. As you begin your climb, you will pass beneath a canopy of conifers where in mid-June to July in sunny damp areas, you will find wonderful gardens of the red and yellow flowers of Crimson Columbine *(Aquilegia formosa).*

Its intricate flowers nod gracefully atop stems that are about a foot or more tall, and in some spots you will find it growing quite densely forming gardens of delicate beauty. Its leaves show the same grace as they create a verdant garden beneath the nodding blossoms.

Look closely at the flower and you will see that the petals are yellow at the base and extend upward to form 5 crimson, round-tipped, nectar spurs. The red "petals" that flare outward are actually colored sepals that enclose the flower in bud. Be sure to locate the buds while you are looking at the flowers. They are intricately beautiful and will help you to understand the flower parts when in full bloom.

The reproductive parts, or cluster of yellow stamens, hang down from the flower's center and surround the 5 styles. The columbine is lovely in the fall when its 5 ovary chambers, that housed the ripening seeds, split open and flare outward forming a brittle, tan "star flower."

The Crimson Columbine is common throughout the Tahoe area on stream banks and in wet, grassy environments. It graces such areas throughout most of western North America, from sea level to timberline. It does well in home gardens, sowing its seed in abundance to carpet moist areas with lacy leaves and lovely, nectar-filled flowers that attract hummingbirds — a simple reminder that beauty attracts beauty.

Columbine flower and bud

Columbine Pollinators and Robbers
While hiking the trail, take a few minutes to sit by a columbine garden to observe who pollinates it. Hummingbirds are drawn to its red flower and have no

25

trouble reaching up the tip of the spur, with their long feathery-tipped "tongues," to sip the sweet nectar. A bumblebee can unfold its long proboscis to do the same. Both hummingbirds and bumblebees pollinate the flowers by brushing against the ripened anthers as they reach up the spur for the nectar.

A honeybee approaches the flower differently. Because of its short proboscis it can't reach all the way up the spur to gather nectar, so it has devised a way of sipping the nectar without performing its pollinating duty. If you have a chance to observe one, watch as it flies up to the spur, grabs hold and bites a tiny hole in the side to effortlessly steal the flower's sweet gift. If you look carefully, you will often find these tiny holes near the tips of the spurs.

Ants also attempt to gather nectar but are usually prevented from reaching the flower by the sticky guard hairs that grow along the stem. You will find these hairs on other plants as well; they act to discourage ineffective pollinators from reaching the flower. Effective pollinators have wings and can fly from plant to plant with minimum pollen loss, while insects like ants lose too much pollen in their ground travels from flower to flower. Ants are also less effective as pollinators because, unlike bees, they do not concentrate on one species of flower during each gathering session.

The Crimson Columbine has always been a favorite of mine. In my early years of flower identification its uniquely beautiful flower made it easy to recognize. This familiarity first awakened in me the feeling that my return to the flowers each spring and summer was a return to old and treasured friends.

The Shrubs of Dry Open Slopes
As the trail climbs higher, you'll enter open sunny areas of dry, chaparral-covered slopes where in June and July, you will find several prominent shrubs in full bloom. They are individual enough that you can easily tell them apart.

The shrub that grows leafy and dense up to about

4 feet tall with clusters of tiny, white flowers is called White Thorn *(Ceanothus cordulatus)*. It is a member of the Buckthorn or Wild Lilac Family and can be easily identified by its thorns that usually grow near the tips of its branches. You can also identify it by its typical lilac-shaped flowers that grow in a rounded form with tiny, radiating, spoon-shaped petals.

The shrub that grows less compactly and up to about 5 or 6 feet tall with scraggly-looking, white-petaled flowers is called Serviceberry *(Amelanchier pallida)*. Later in the season, it carries dark purple berries which are an important food source for small animals. In the past, the berries were gathered by Native Americans and eaten raw or left to dry in the sun for later use.

You will also find a shrub, 6 feet or more tall, that grows in an open form with delicate, white, fuzzy-looking flowers called Bittercherry *(Prunus emarginata)*. Taste the shiny red berries in the fall and you'll see how this plant received its name!

Bittercherry and Serviceberry are both members of the Rose Family, a family characterized by 5 petals with numerous reproductive parts and with leaves that grow alternate to one another along the stem. If you compare the flowers of the 2 shrubs, you'll find that the Serviceberry has 5 linear, twisted petals that are about twice as long as the rounded petals of the Bittercherry. Check out the distribution of the flowers and you will see that those of the Serviceberry bloom loosely along the end of the stems, while those of the Bittercherry bloom in tight clusters right at the branch tips.

You can also tell them apart by comparing the leaves. Those of the Serviceberry are flat and oval with roughly serrated tips, while those of the Bittercherry are oblong, very finely serrated along the entire edge and folded in half along the mid-vein.

Huckleberry Oak *(Quercus vaccinifolia)* also grows in profusion along the trail. This evergreen shrub, with its horizontally spreading branches, reaches a height of about 4 feet. Huckleberry Oak is easy to identify because of its dull, gray-green leaves that are smooth-edged and pale beneath. In June, yellowish male flowers hang downward from the branches in pendulous, slender catkins. The female flowers are born in the axils of the leaves and, after fertilization, take two years to produce mature acorns. Most flowers carry male and female reproductive parts in the same flower, but some plants, like the oaks, willows and conifers, have separate flowers that house either male or female parts.

Hiking through Other Dry Environment Flowers

Also on these dry slopes, which are within 1/4 mile of the trailhead, you will find a wide range of herbaceous plants like the golden flowered Single-stemmed Senecio *(Senecio integerrimus)*. This plant is easy to identify because its scraggly-petaled, 1 inch wide, daisy-like flowers bloom atop sturdy stems that are usually a foot or more tall. When I first discovered this senecio, I thought it must be at the end of its blooming season because the flowers looked so bedraggled, but regardless of how fresh they are, they always look weary.

Its genus name, Senecio, comes from the Latin word senex for "old man," which is a reference to the white, hairy-like pappus that surrounds each seed. The pappus is most easily seen later in the season after the seeds have matured, for it is then that the pappus opens up like a little parachute to catch the air currents and distribute the seed away from the parent plant. Most of you are familiar with this pappus in the dandelion seed head.

Single-stemmed Senecio

Fuchsia-pink Flowers Carpet Sandy Flats

When you arrive at sandy flats in open, sunny areas and see an intense fuchsia-pink created by delicate little flowers, you will have found one of Tahoe's prettiest monkeyflowers. The Torrey's Monkeyflower *(Mimulus torreyi)*, in this area, is usually found growing only about 2 to 3 inches tall, and its dainty flowers sweetly look up at you as if unaware that they seem to be defying the odds by living in such dry, barren soil.

Look closely and you will see that each tubular blossom has 5 flaring petals. The 3 lower petals are marked with 2 yellow ridges that are outlined in red along the sides and ends. Its herbage is glandular and hairy as can easily be seen through a hand lens - look for a tiny rounded blob, like a drop of honey, at the tip of each hair.

Its reproductive parts lie hidden in the flower tube, but if you gently pull the petals back you can look at their delicate beauty. If you use a ten-power hand lens, you will be able to see that each little, glabrous anther looks like a single, ruffly, white flower.

Tahoe's Tiniest Monkeyflower

Torrey's Monkeyflower is not the smallest monkeyflower found along the trail. There is another one that usually grows here only an inch or so tall with flowers that are about 1/8 inch wide. It is called Brewer's Monkeyflower *(Mimulus breweri)*, and though it is also pink, its shade is lighter. Its 2 upper petals are deep pink, and its 3 lower ones are light pink, with each petal carrying a central, dark pink line surrounded by dots. Its yellow throat has ridges also spotted in deep pink.

Its narrow, gray-green leaves are hairy, while its fused sepals form a tube that is hairy, glandular and unequally lobed. If you spot this one, you have excellent eyes or a botanical sixth sense. It grows in damp, wooded areas in sandy soils, nestled at the base of Jeffrey Pines, or in great masses in sunshine along the trail.

A Dry Environment Violet

Also in areas of sunshine on sandy, dry slopes alongside the trail in June and July, you will find another violet, called the yellow Mountain Violet *(Viola purpurea)*. Its 3 lower petals have purplish brown nectar lines, and if you look at the back of the upper 2 petals, you will see that they are a brownish purple.

This coloring is an easy way to identify this species and the basis for its botanical name, *purpurea*.

The Mountain Violet's lemon-colored flower looks too vulnerable to exist in such a dry and barren spot. But it is a tenacious little survivor that sends down a long taproot covered with millions of microscopic root hairs that search out scarce moisture, thus allowing it to survive in environments that seem inhospitable to us.

Fragrant Rock Gardens by a Creek Crossing

As the trail climbs higher, you will arrive at large rock outcroppings carpeted with two of Tahoe's prettiest rock garden flowers — the wonderfully fragrant Creeping Phlox and the vivid-pink Mountain Pride.

Creeping Phlox *(Phlox diffusa)*, which begins blooming in early-June, has 3/4 inch wide tubular flowers with flaring petals. It blooms in white or in pastel shades of pink and lavender. Look closely and you will find soft orange anthers peeking out at you from the center of the flower. On a warm day its sweet fragrance floats everywhere, but on a cooler one you may need to get down on your hands and knees to enjoy its fragrant gift.

In late-June through July, one of the brightest of all wildflowers in these rock gardens is Mountain Pride *(Penstemon newberryi)*. Its deep pink flowers are tubular with 5 flaring petals. White fuzzy ridges on the lower petals invite insects into the flower to enjoy the sweet nectar that sits at the base of the tube. This is only one of several species of penstemon that blooms here — at least 10 grow in the Tahoe Sierra and 90 different species grow throughout California.

Mountain Pride's species' name, *newberryi*, is in honor of John Newberry, who botanized in California in the mid-1880's. Its genus name, *Penstemon*, comes from the Greek words *pente* for "five" and *stemon* for "stamen." This refers to the fact that penstemons have 5 stamens, which are the male reproductive parts.

In penstemons, one of these stamens is sterile,

which in this case means it has no anther or pollen-producing sac on the end of the filament. Its sterile stamen is easily seen when examining the flower and is important when keying out different species, for one of the major divisions between species is based on whether this sterile filament is hairy (bearded) or smooth (glabrous).

If you look at the flower's toothed leaves, you will see that they are leathery. This tough, waxy coating is an important environmental adaptation which helps reduce evaporation in its sunny, dry environment. This is a great wildflower to include in dry areas in domestic gardens. It requires little care once established and will bring beauty, insects and hummingbirds to your garden. It is available through local nurseries that specialize in natives.

Mountain Pride grows abundantly at Tahoe, from lake level at 6200 feet up to 11,000 feet. It is usually at its fullest bloom at both Donner Summit and Loch Leven from early- to mid-July, during which time you will also see it blooming profusely all along Interstate 80 and along old Highway 40, which parallels Interstate 80 to the south.

After enjoying this rock garden, which is within 3/4 mile of the trailhead, you will arrive at an alder-lined creek with a small bridge. The creek is wonderful to explore because it changes every few feet from little pools and open slabs to rounded boulders shaded by alders and dogwood in the narrow bends. The rocks by the small cascades below the bridge often come alive in the late afternoon light, going from shades of gray to a glowing rusty-gold. Be sure to save your hike out for late afternoon to enjoy the creek's changing moods.

An Enchanted Mossy Garden

After crossing the creek, you will enter a cool, lush garden of humid fragrances. Dense leafy growth lines the trail, and 15 foot tall alders droop to shade the path. Within a couple hundred feet, a small creek crosses the trail, its moisture nourishing more tiny carpets of violets.

This creek is fed by a spring that runs clear and cold until late-fall. Looking up the creek beneath the canopy of leafy shrubs, you will find an enchanting mossy garden that remains moist and inviting, all summer, with columbines, alpine lilies, orchids and violets lushly blooming along its banks.

This little spot along the trail is especially beautiful because 3 violets bloom here: the white Macloskey's, the bluish violet Western Long-spurred and the Smooth Yellow *(Viola glabella)*. The Smooth Yellow Violet can be identified by its large, yellow flowers and deep green, heart-shaped leaves. Its petals are a rich yellow, and its 2 lateral ones are softly bearded. The botany books say only the 3 lower petals are veined in purple, but most of those in this little garden are veined on all 5 petals.

The unusual growth pattern of the leaves also makes this violet easy to identify — the stem is leafy just below the flower and then naked for at least 6 inches down to the ground. Though its species' name, *glabella*, should indicate that its leaves are glabrous (hairless), they are often finely hairy. This could confuse you when closely checking the leaves with a hand lens. The leaves of violets are high in Vitamin C and, along with the flowers, are a lovely addition to salads. Because of their edibility and beauty, I always have several species of violets growing in my vegetable garden.

A Violet that Never Opens

If you hike the trail in late-summer, you will find an intriguing flower bud rising out of the axils of the leaves of these and other violets — intriguing because this bud never opens like the early-season ones do. Most flowers follow a "rule" of Nature — that of producing flower forms, blooming sequences or placement of parts that avoid or reduce the chances of self-pollination. Self-pollination, or in-breeding, can weaken a plant species by reducing the number of variables in the gene pool.

Smooth
Yellow
Violet

32

Variations come from cross-pollination (pollen from a different plant of the same species). Without these variations to "choose from," plants are less likely, over the long haul, to adapt to environmental changes or to come up with improvements to enhance their chances of survival in relatively stable environments. But many violets deviate from this "rule" by producing two kinds of flowers — one that blooms early in the season and depends upon cross-pollination, and one that is formed later in the summer that is cleistogamous (self-pollinating).

The word, cleistogamous, comes from Greek and means "closed marriage." Since this second flower never opens, but rather remains tightly closed in bud, it self-pollinates as its reproductive parts ripen and come into contact. Though these flowers rise out of the axils of the upper leaves of the Smooth Yellow Violet, in some violets you will find them close to the ground hidden under the leaves.

Cleistogamy is an interesting environmental adaptation since violets bloom in early-spring, when it may still be too cold for the insect population to be out pollinating, this mechanism acts as a kind of backup system for seed production, in case the early-season flower is not pollinated. This strange flower offers us a valuable lesson, for it shows us that Nature is willing to take many different paths to arrive at the same end, even if it means deviating from the "norm."

Violets hybridize frequently, so don't be frustrated if you find in keying out your flower that it has characteristics of 2 different species. By botanical definition, different species do not hybridize (mate to create viable seed), but of course some do, so I guess this just goes to show that Nature often defies our attempts to narrowly categorize her, which is of course part of her charm! It is also a reminder that the categorization of plants was created by man, not Nature, as a sort of grid system put upon the plant world to help reduce its complexity to an understandable order.

cleistogamous violet

Continuing along Open Sunny Slopes

After this little creek, the trail enters open sunny slopes of bracken fern, where you will pass shrubs of honeysuckle *(Lonicera conjugialis)*, currants *(Ribes nevadense and R. viscosissimum)*, mountain maple *(Acer glabrum)* and bittercherry. You will also find damp slopes of aspen trees *(Populus tremuloides)*, with their lovely quaking leaves, and, alongside them, hundreds of bright yellow Arrowleaf Senecios.

The Arrowleaf Senecio *(Senecio triangularis)* has flowers similar to its relative, that we saw earlier, the Single-stemmed Senecio, but its leaves are very different; they are arrowhead in shape and grow thickly along the usually hairless stem. The Arrowleaf Senecio is a showy plant growing sometimes up to 5 feet tall (even 7 feet in coastal regions), with clusters of yellow flowers blooming atop each stem.

In these damp areas, only a couple hundred feet beyond the little creek, you will also find the tall, purple flowers of Horsemint *(Agastache urticifolia)* with fragrant leaves that can be steeped for tea, though for me its flavor is a bit too intense.

In other areas, lodgepoles and white firs tower above large-leaved Thimbleberries *(Rubus parviflorus)*. Since the Thimbleberry is a member of the Rose Family, you will find that it has 5 petals and lots of reproductive parts. They bloom with 1 inch wide, white, crinkly-petaled flowers. Later in the season the flowers will have turned into bright red clusters of tiny berries that sit in a flat receptacle. They are usually sweet but rather seedy.

Also, along these sunny, open wooded areas in July, look for a fifth violet, Nuttall's Violet *(Viola praemorsa)*, which blooms with bright yellow flowers that appear on the tops of stems, at about the same height as the vertical leaves. The lower leaves are long-stemmed and clustered, while the leaf shape itself is lance-like to oval. Its leaves are usually smooth edged but are sometimes toothed. The lower 3 petals are veined in purple; its flower face is one of the happiest of all our violets. Look at the back of the flower and you will see the tiny flower spur that holds the nectar for visiting insects.

I was surprised in my early days of botanizing to learn that, of the 25 species of violets that grow in the western states, most are yellow, while only about 1/4 are violet-colored, with a few being white or combinations of these colors. East of the Rockies the color changes, for there, most species are blue to violet. The name violet is a derivative of the Greek word for the color and the flower. Pansies, which are similar though larger than violets, come from Europe and Asia and are also members of the Violet Family.

Crossing the Railroad Tracks

In less than a mile from the trailhead, and after a short uphill climb, you will cross the Southern Pacific Railroad tracks and continue along the trail until you arrive at a series of switchbacks and boulder-strewn slopes. On a hot summer day, the shade of the tall conifers along this part of the trail is a welcome relief from the heat.

As you hike through these wooded areas, you will cross a creek whose meandering is controlled by a small concrete spillway. Just beyond, on both sides of the trail beneath the conifers, look for the plants of the Spotted Coral Root *(Corallorhiza maculata)*. This plant is discussed on the Summit Lake hike. It blooms under conifers all along the trail but is easy to spot here, as it grows in large clusters, blooming from mid-June through July.

Look too in wooded areas from late-May through July for a plant called Pinewoods Lousewort *(Pedicularis semibarbata)*. It has "fern-like" leaves that are crinkly and deeply divided with thin, purple-colored edges. The leaves lie flat on the ground, radiating outward from a central point. If you kneel down and look beneath the leaves at the base of the plant, you will find inch-long, yellowish, tubular flowers. Their 2 upper petals form a curved beak and the lower lip is divided into 3 petal lobes.

Trailside Lupines

As you continue along the wooded trail in late-June through July, you will be treated to the heavenly, sweet fragrance of the Crest Lupine *(Lupinus arbustus)*. Its lavender flowers grow along the upper part of the stem, above leaves that radiate outward from a central point, like the fingers from the palm of the hand — a leaf shape that is typical of lupines.

Lupines, as members of the Pea Family have the characteristic pea-flower shape of a vertical petal, called the banner, 2 side petals, called the wings, and 2 fused petals, called the keel, which house the reproductive parts. The Crest Lupine can be distinguished from other similar-looking species by the tiny spur on the upper part of the sepal tube.

Another lupine that grows shrub-like along the trail is Anderson's Lupine *(L. andersonii)*. It blooms with long clusters of lavender to white flowers. After pollination, the flowers fade to brown and then form fuzzy, green pea pods that turn brown as they age. Unlike our garden peas, the seeds and herbage of all wild lupines are toxic to humans and if eaten can cause convulsions and paralysis.

Also in this area, along the trail, look for the flowers of the Giant Red Paintbrush *(Castilleja miniata)* that bloom in June and July, in damp to dry areas, among the lavender lupines and yellow senecios. Later in the season (late-July to early-August) the gorgeous bright pink flowers of Fireweed *(Epilobium angustifolium)* decorate the slopes. Both plants/rise several feet tall among the other plants.

Hot dry areas and dense wooded groves alternate with lush sunny flower gardens as you pass by several more small creeks where you will find the unusual green flowers of the Sparsely Flowered Bog Orchid *(Habenaria sparsiflora)* and Brewer's Mitrewort *(Mitella breweri)*. The bog orchid grows among alders along one of the creeks, while the mitrewort can be found nestled at the base of large boulders that extend into another creek to form a small, gentle cascade. Both flowers are discussed in detail on other hikes and can be located in the index.

Reaching the Summit above Lower Loch Leven Lake

Soon you will pass a 1.5 mile marker — an indication that you are almost to the summit above Lower Loch Leven Lake. After a final short climb through an open forest, the trail levels out and the first lake comes into view. When you reach this spot, you will be on a small summit, among big boulders, where you'll look down upon the blue waters of Lower Loch Leven. Here the trail begins a steep, but short, descent to the lake.

In July, this dusty slope is usually colored with the blue-to-purple flowers and yellow buds of the Azure Penstemon *(Penstemon azureus)*. Look closely at the flower and see if you can find the sterile stamen. Is it bearded (hairy) or glabrous (bald)? Remember to look for this characteristic in each penstemon that you meet to help you key out the flower. (It is usually glabrous in this species — there is no such word as "always" in botany!)

In a few hundred yards, you will arrive at the beginning of the Loch Leven Lakes area, a series of five lakes — Lower, Middle, Upper, and High Loch Leven, and Salmon Lake — which are scattered along the trail, like a broken necklace, whose beads have rolled away to find their own little niches. Around the lakes in springtime in early-June, Red Mountain Heather *(Phyllodoce breweri)* and white Cassiope *(Cassiope mertensiana)* bloom in profusion. Nearby, among the rocks, look also for carpets of Creeping Phlox, pink tufts of Pussy Paws and the delicate Three-leaved Lewisia *(Lewisia triphylla)*.

Later in the season (the end of June through July), coarse white Corn-lily *(Veratrum californicum)*, white flowered Labrador Tea *(Ledum glandulosum)* and bright pink stalks of Fireweed *(Epilobium angustifolium)* appear at the water's edge, while pinkish White-veined Mallows *(Sidalcea glaucescens)* bloom in dry areas near the lake.

Passing the Salmon Lake Junction

After stopping along the shore of Lower Loch Leven, you may want to continue along the trail around the south side of the lake. As you do so, look for the flowers of the yellow Pond Lily *(Nuphar polysepalum)* floating on the water's surface. At the south end of the lake, you'll also find the junction with the Salmon Lake trail, which heads off to the west. You can follow this trail to warm Salmon Lake or continue east, along the end of the lake, where you'll find several good campsites. From here continue south along the trail away from the lake toward Middle Loch Leven.

After a slight downhill, there is a short climb to the next lake, Middle Loch Leven. This lake has several small islands which are a delight if you want to spend the day sunbathing in privacy. Red Mountain Heather bloom along its shores in June, and lavender Anderson and Crest Lupines bloom on the dry slopes above, in late-June through July. At this point the trail climbs to the western shore of Middle Loch Leven. It then curves around the southern tip of the lake and crosses several ponds before it traverses large slabs of rock where the trail has been marked with tacky-looking blotches of orange paint.

After this point, the trail travels through dense, fragrant groves of Mountain Spiraea *(Spiraea densiflora)*. These 3 to 4 foot tall shrubs carry fuzzy clusters of hundreds of tiny, pink flowers in late-June and July. These plants do well in home gardens and are available, along with a white species, in local nurseries. Before moving on, be sure to stop a moment to inhale the sweet fragrance of these lovely flowers of the Rose Family.

After crossing a small creek, look for masses of little flowers that grow only about 4 inches above the ground. The Bud Saxifrage *(Saxifraga bryophora)* blooms in July and because it blends in with the soil, it is often hard to see until you spot the first one, then you will notice that others abundantly cover the ground. They are easy to identify because of the way the flowers grow; lateral flowers bloom at the ends of downward-hanging pedicels, beneath the single terminal flower.

You'll need to get down on your knees and look at the flowers through your hand lens to truly appreciate their intricate beauty. Each white petal has 2 yellow spots, and if you look closely at the center of the flower, you will see the 2-beaked ovary that is typical of members of the Saxifrage Family. The 2 beaks of the ovary are very easy to see, after fertilization, when the ovary begins to swell. Its small leaves are glandular-hairy and grow in basal clusters.

After about 1/4 mile, the trail begins to climb steeply through large boulders. At this point, off to your left, you will spot Upper Loch Leven Lake. There is usually no one at the lake because no obvious trail leads to its shores, probably because its shoreline falls too abruptly to offer good campsites. But it is a pretty lake with steep granite walls and carpets of Red Mountain Heather in June.

The Rock Gardens of High Loch Leven

After continuing along the trail, through the short, steep, bouldered part, you will pass through the woods for about 1/4 mile, until you arrive at High Loch Leven Lake. This lovely alpine lake is made more lovely by the wonderful, flower-filled rock gardens that bloom near its shores.

In July and August, the gardens come into full bloom with the blues of Azure Penstemon, the yellows of Sulphur Flower (*Eriogonum umbellatum*) and the reds of Wavy-leaved Paintbrush (*Castilleja applegatei*). You will also find the whites of Bud Saxifrage along with a myriad of other hues and shapes created from sedums, sandworts, phlox and other treasures. It would be easy, and delightful, to spend a whole day keying out and just enjoying these colorful gardens. High Lock Leven Lake is tranquil, since it is the farthest from the trailhead, and so is a wonderful place to spend several serene days in close contact with Nature and yourself.

A Moonlight Swim in Warm Waters

The Loch Leven Lakes are a particularly nice area to spend time because their warm waters make them some of the most swimmable lakes in the Sierra. I once hiked to Lower Loch Leven with my husband, Phil, and our friends Candy and Bill Badiner to sleep out under the stars and to enjoy a full moon. As the moon appeared over the ridges, we swam out to an island that was bathed in golden light. Later that night clouds moved in, releasing droplets of rain that made sweet music on the water's surface but less sweet music on our faces and sleeping bags!

That night we felt richly connected with all of life as we immersed ourselves in warm waters, enjoyed the fragrance of damp pine needles and soil, and gazed up at the full moon. It was a beautiful experience that reminded me once again that life is a treasured gift to be enjoyed and shared with those dear to us.

Castle to Round Valley

Exploring Two Flowery Meadows

杰夫&

One day/overnight	
One way 3 miles	
Trail begins/ends 7200'/7700'	
Net gain/total gain 500'/ 800'	
Topo map USGS Donner Pass, Calif.	
Wildflower Season Late-June through August	

Highlighted Flowers

- Smooth-leaved Gilia
  (Gilia capillaris)
- Glandular Willow Herb
  (Epilobium glandulosum)
- Large-leaved Avens
  (Geum macrophyllum)
- Primrose Monkeyflower
  (Mimulus primuloides)
- Arrowleaf Senecio
  (Senecio triangularis)
- Bolander's Yampah
  (Perideridia bolanderi)
- Pretty Face
  (Brodiaea lutea)
- Rock Fringe
  (Epilobium obcordatum)
- Soft Arnica
  (Arnica mollis)
- Lemmon's Paintbrush
  (Castilleja lemmonii)

Castle Peak is one of the best kept secrets in the Sierra. The volcanic extrusions that form the ridgeline along her jagged summit look like the turrets of an ancient medieval castle, a form that glows in exquisite beauty when bathed in the golden light of an afternoon's setting sun. On the western side beneath the rugged peaks, open meadows lie green and lush while gently flowing creeks meander through the meadows, forming ribbons of color from the flowers that line its grassy banks.

Trailhead Directions

Heading west on Interstate 80, take the Boreal Ridge exit (just past the Castle Peak Rest Station). At the off-ramp stop sign, take the black-topped road to the right uphill a few hundred feet to where it turns into a dirt jeep road. Heading east on Interstate 80, take the Boreal Ridge/Castle Peak Area exit (just

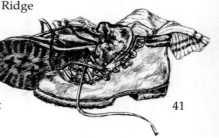

41

past the Norden exit). Drive past the Boreal Ridge ski area, turn left at the stop sign and head north under the freeway to the blacktopped road.

The Trail Begins

After parking at the end of the blacktopped road, head north along the old jeep road which is on the east side of Andesite Ridge. Within about a hundred yards of the trailhead, a dirt road leads off to the left. Ignore that spur and continue along the main road for about one level mile, until you arrive at Castle Valley.

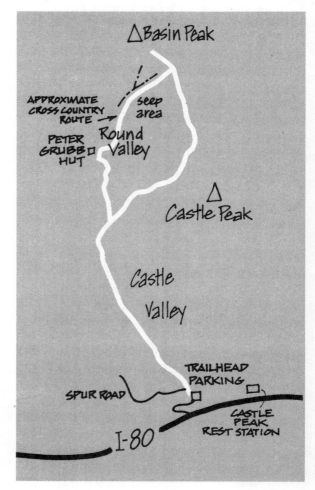

If you are one who moves about in a wheel chair, you will appreciate the valley as an easily accessible and beautiful place to spend the day. The jeep road can be driven in a passenger car; there is a small parking turnout in the trees next to the meadow.

Exploring the Creek's Edge in Castle Valley

Castle Valley is a quiet place to picnic, to spend hours with canvas and paints or to photograph in the late afternoon light, when the lichen-colored cliffs of Castle Peak form a dramatic backdrop to the meadow's rich color.

The valley is also a wonderful introduction to the many gorgeous, wet environment plants that grow at Tahoe. If you wander along the creek in the meadow in mid-July, which is usually the height of the bloom, look for nodding red columbines (*Aquilegia formosa*), purple stalks of lupines (*Lupinus polyphyllus*) and pink elephant heads (*Pedicularis groenlandica*). Look also for 3 to 4 foot tall red paintbrushes (*Castilleja miniata*), yellow senecios (*Senecio triangularis*) and blue-purple larkspurs (*Delphinium glaucum*).

As you walk along the creek's edge, notice what these wet environment plants all share in common, and ask yourself how their leaf shapes help them to adapt to their surroundings. Notice that because there is plenty of water, leaves can be large and transpire freely. In a moist, sunny, soil-rich environment, leaves don't need to conserve and so they grow lushly. Like humans, plants don't limit their consumption if it's not necessary!

When you climb higher to the dry, rocky areas on Castle Peak, compare the leaves of these two environments to see what differences you find. What conclusions can you draw from the various leaf shapes and growth patterns of wet versus dry environment plants?

In exploring the flowers near the creek, look also for those that grow close to the ground. The Smooth-leaved Gilia (*Gilia capillaris*) has linear leaves that are about an inch long and 1/8 inch wide, and its white-to-pink blossoms grow on stems up to about 2 inches tall.

You'll have to get down on your hands and knees to appreciate the beauty of its tiny flower. If you take out your hand lens, you will be amazed at the detail. Look closely at the 5 petals and you'll see that they're lined with lavender veins, while the flower tube (which may be white or yellow), gives rise to a white style that carries a blue, 3-lobed stigma. Royal blue anthers surround the pistil, and tiny black-to-clear colored glands sit upon the tips of the hairs that cover the thread-like stems.

Another flower, that blooms at the creek's edge in July, is the Glandular Willow Herb *(Epilobium glandulosum)*. It is also lovely when viewed with a hand lens. The willow herb grows about 1 to 3 feet tall. Its leafy stems are glandular and hairy near the top of the plant but are without hairs near the base. Its oval to lance-oval leaves are finely toothed and crowd around the clusters of pink-to-rosy purple flowers at the top.

Notice too that some of the stems are red, while others are green. Notice also that the leaves have a lovely, dark-red mid-vein. Look closely at the flower and you will see that its petals are veined in purple and are bi-lobed at the tips, while its green sepals are edged in red-purple. With your hand lens check out the detail of the flower parts. Its lavender-to-purple filaments carry creamy white anthers, and its stigma is rounded and also creamy white.

After fertilization, the long ovary (the narrow, tube-like swelling below the petals) elongates with red ribs that spiral around the ovary. As the seeds mature and the casing begins to dry, the tension created by the spiraling causes a counter rotation that bursts the pod open to allow the seeds to float away on "feathery wings."

I'm constantly amazed by the miraculous beauty and function in the details of flowers and in the plant world. We've looked closely at just two plants, and yet every plant in the meadow, as well as those along the rocky mountain sides or among the conifered forests, offers its own exquisite magnificence.

Wandering through the Meadow

As you leave the creek to wander farther into the meadow, look for the plants of the Large-leaved Avens *(Geum macrophyllum)*. They grow up to about 4 feet tall and can be found blooming from late-June through July, with pale yellow, 5-petaled flowers that resemble the flowers of the cinquefoil. Though the avens is closely related to the cinquefoils of the *Potentilla* genus, it is in a separate genus. It can be distinguished from the *Potentillas* by its clasping leaf stems and by its styles, that persist on the ovary after fertilization. In the *Potentillas,* the styles are deciduous and leave tiny depressions in the ovary after falling off.

Since the styles persist in the Geum, you'll have a chance to look at their interesting and intricate structure. Take a moment to find several plants. If you compare the flowers, you'll see that after fertilization the petals drop off, and the ovary swells into a green ball that is covered with the red styles. Use your lens and you will be able to see that each delicate style is curved at the tip and supports a green, horizontal, beak-like structure. The silvery-white hairs that cover the top of the ovary, the style, and the stigma add a shining radiance to the whole exquisite structure.

Its species' name, *macrophyllum,* refers to the large terminal leaflet which is 3-lobed, serrated and very noticeable even at a distance, while the leaflets that grow beneath this terminal leaflet come in various odd sizes and shapes. Once you key in on its leaves, you will never have any trouble identifying this plant.

The Graceful Cinquefoil *(Potentilla gracilis)* also blooms in the meadow at the same time as the *Geum,* and those of you who are interested may want to compare these two plants. This species of cinquefoil has 5 to 7 palmate, fan-shaped, serrate leaves with flowers that are a deep-yellow. It grows about 2 feet tall and can be found in the same area as the Geum.

See if you can spot the tiny depressions left by its deciduous styles.

If you wander through the meadow, in July through September, you'll find the purplish, daisy-like flowers of the Alpine Aster *(Aster alpigenus)*. Its stems, and the leafy receptacles that hold the petals are covered with woolly white hairs, while the solitary flower heads rise out of tufts of linear leaves. After enjoying these, and the many other flowers that bloom in the meadow, you can head west to rejoin the jeep road. After climbing over Castle Pass, you will drop down into Round Valley.

Observing an Animate Stigma with Your Child

In the seeps and creeks that flow off Andesite Ridge, down along the road on the way to Castle Pass, one of Tahoe's prettiest flowers blooms in July. The Lewis' Monkeyflower *(Mimulus lewisii)* is also our largest monkeyflower, with inch long tubular blossoms topped with 5 flaring petal lobes. The flowers bloom on shrub-like plants, which grow up to about 4 feet tall. The bright yellow, hairy ridges and red lines on the lower petals and throat form an enticing trail for insects, leading them to the nectar in the flower's center.

This lovely plant was named after Meriwether Lewis who gathered specimens across the United States from 1804 to 1806, as a member of the famous Lewis and Clark expedition. Its genus name, *Mimulus*, is from the diminutive of the Latin word *mimus* which means "comic actor" or "mime." In naming it, others saw the face of a little monkey, happily smiling out at life. I must confess I don't see either image very clearly, but I do feel its joy.

Lewis' Monkey-flower

Find a comfortable spot and take a moment to look closely at the flower's center. A white hinged structure, parted into 2 flat lobes, sits just above the opening. This is the stigma, the female part which receives pollen for fertilization. (See the Sagehen East hike for details on flower reproduction.) It is interesting because it demonstrates an easily observable mechanism of fertilization. When the stigma is touched by an insect, the 2 lobes close and move tightly against the top of the flower throat. If the stigma has received pollen from another plant of the same species, it remains closed and fertilization takes place. If the stigma receives no pollen, or the wrong kind, it re-opens within a few minutes to await the arrival of appropriate pollen.

This closure is fun to observe with a child, because the response is immediate. Touch the stigma with a blade of grass to watch it close, and then within a few minutes watch it re-open.

Some botanists believe that this temporary closure may act to reduce the chance of self-pollination which could occur during the time when an insect rummages about the flower in search of nectar. Plants usually try to avoid self-pollination, because over many generations this can weaken plant viability.

The Yellows of the Primrose Monkeyflower

Near the Lewis' Monkeyflower, at the edge of slowly moving creeks and in boggy areas, look for the yellows of the Primrose Monkeyflower (Mimulus primuloides). The flower face is spotted in reddish brown on the lower petals, and its small yellow flowers look as if they are trying very hard to be dignified, as they sit upon leafless stems that are about 4 inches tall.

The species' name, primuloides, means "primrose-like." Although this monkeyflower is not a true primrose, it does resemble a primrose's growth. At the base of the thread-like stem you will find a rosette of small, oval leaves that are covered with long, white hairs. If you are here early in the morning, you just might find tiny rainbows sparkling in the morning dew on its little leaves.

Hillsides of Color

If you hike the trail in July and August, after a year of heavy snowfall, you will find great wet fields of bright yellow Arrowleaf Senecios (Senecio triangularis) and white Corn Lilies (Veratrum californicum). In dryer areas between the seeps, you will find some of Tahoe's most spectacular displays of Bolander's Yampah *(Perideridia bolanderi)* and Pretty Face *(Brodiaea lutea)*.

Yampah blooms in umbel form with lacy, white flowers on plants that grow about a foot tall. Pretty Face blooms with 3 petals and 3 sepals that are yellow with a dark mid-vein. It too blooms in umbel form, meaning the flower stems radiate outward from a central point like the spokes of an umbrella. Look closely at the anthers of Pretty Face and you'll see that they sit on a forked filament that is flat, ribbon-like and colored a lovely shade of blue.

Along damp hillsides, you'll find the shrubs of the fragrant, pink Mountain Spiraea *(Spiraea densiflora)*. If you look closely at a single flower, within each cluster of flowers, with a hand lens, you will see the individual rose-flower structure of 5 petals and many reproductive parts.

While you are checking out the flower detail of the Spiraea, be sure to inhale its sweet perfume. You might even want to check out the fragrance of every flower you meet along the trail. The fragrance of flowers floats on the air like music, in a song no less beautiful because it is silent.

You'll also be amazed at the variety of scents. Checking them out will help you to develop a personal relationship with each flower, while toughening up your knees a bit, which is a must for wildflower photographers!

As you continue along the trail, you will arrive at a point where it branches off toward the meadow. Pass the fork and continue along the main road, heading north, until you arrive at the sign indicating the road is closed to motorized vehicles. Here you will climb up to the saddle, where the logging road merges with the Pacific Crest Trail, by the "Castle Pass 7880 feet" sign.

Descending into Round Valley

At the sign, hike north, or downhill, toward Round

Mountain Spiraea

Valley. (The trail to the right, along the saddle, will take you to Castle Peak and is described in the next hike.) After about 1/4 mile of downhill trail, begin looking for patches of the pink, tubular flowers of Mountain Pride *(Penstemon newberryi)* blooming in late-June and July. Later in July and early-August, look for the gorgeous, 4-petaled, pink flowers of Rock Fringe *(Epilobium obcordatum)* cascading over rock slabs, lining the trail or blooming along the edge of the creek.

As you continue along the trail, you will arrive at a magnificent, towering Western White Pine. At this point take the trail to the left, passing through groves of young Red Fir. When the trail divides again, take the right fork, to where the trail descends among the lodgepoles, past dense bloomings of lavender daisies, white yampahs and purple penstemons.

After a mile or so, you will arrive at the big meadow of Round Valley. As you enter the meadow, you will see the Peter Grubb Hut. This old wooden cabin is partially hidden among the pines, near the western edge of the meadow. The hut was built years ago by Sierra Club members. There are four such huts in the backcountry at Tahoe, available to Sierra Club members or to those in an emergency.

Several years ago, we reserved the cabin for a New Year's eve gathering of a few friends. It wasn't fancy, but it was lots of fun to greet the new year in this remote setting. As midnight came we put on our skis and went out to connect with the beauty of the night. There in the snow, we found millions of tiny "rainbows" sparkling on the tips of the hoar frost. It was a magical night and a beautiful way to celebrate a new beginning.

The cabin is equipped with some old, but useable, mattresses, a wood burning stove and, usually, plenty of firewood. The trail into the cabin is a popular and easy cross-country ski route. Those interested should contact the Sierra Club's Clair Tappaan Lodge at Donner Summit for further information.

A Meadow of Rich Flower Color

Lower Castle Creek and other small creeks flow into Round Valley bringing the moisture needed to create a lush meadow of yellow arnicas and monkeyflowers, pink elephant heads and shooting stars, and purple asters. But one of the prettiest flowers that blooms in Round Valley in July is Lemmon's Paintbrush *(Castilleja lemmonii)*. It covers the meadow with swaths of a vivid red-pink. Its leafy flower bracts are 3-lobed, while those housing the tubular flower are a bright red-pink along the upper edges. Its lance-like leaves grow vertically along a stem that grows up to about a foot tall.

If you wander through the meadow up the slopes to the east, you should find wonderful creek gardens of orchids and other wet environment flowers. I hope you visit this flower-filled area before sheep pass through. There is no way to accurately forecast when this will be, as the timing varies from year to year depending on the snow. Sheepherders still graze their stock throughout the Sierra in the summer months, on permits issued by the U. S. Forest Service or by permission from private land owners. The damage left by the grazing can be severe. Hopefully in time this program, which is subsidized by the taxpayer, will no longer be permitted in recreational areas or in areas of such fragile beauty.

This meadow is particularly gorgeous in the late-afternoon light and is a wonderful place to camp throughout the summer and fall. Those who are itching to see more can follow the trail north along the Pacific Crest Trail into the backcountry for miles of solitary travel.

Castle to Basin Peak

Hiking through Ridgetop Gardens

One day	
One way	4.5 miles
Trail begins/ends	7200'/8800'
Net gain/total gain	1600'/1600'
Topo map USGS Donner Pass, Calif.	
Wildflower Season July through August	

T he saddle between Castle and Basin Peaks is a dividing point between the western and eastern side of the North Tahoe Sierra. If you were to sit wedged in among its orange and yellow lichen-colored rocks near the summit, you could begin the day watching the sun rise in pink splendor over shadowed eastern ridges, or end the day watching it sink in the late-afternoon alpenglow far to the west. The 360 degree view on a clear day, from the craggy summit of Castle Peak, is breathtaking. Desolation Wilderness rises to the south, and Mt. Diablo and the Coast Range loom into view.

Castle Peak's craggy, volcanic rocks will guide you toward the top of its 9,103 foot summit with eroded extrusions that take on a variety of forms — from an old man patiently awaiting eternity, to a resting dog peacefully surveying the landscape. Brightly colored flowers burrow in among these craggy rock forms to seek protection from the wind and solar intensity,

Sulphur Flower

51

while flowers in the meadows 2,000 feet below bloom in wild abandon.

Trailhead Directions
See the directions for the previous hike.

Picking up the Trail
Follow the trail description for the previous hike. When the trail splits at the saddle by the Castle Pass sign, head straight (or east) along the saddle toward Castle Peak. An alternative route would be to wander through Castle Valley and then find your way

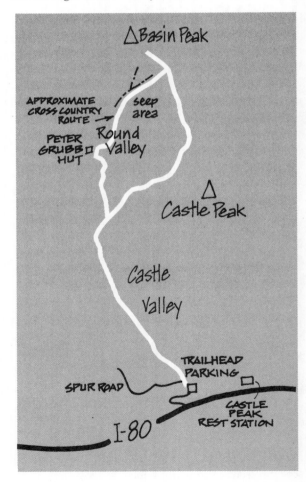

cross-country up to the saddle, using Castle Peak and a topo map as your references.

Finding White Anemones and Pink Primroses

One of the best times to enjoy Castle Peak, and the saddle between Castle and Basin Peaks, is late-June to early-July when the snows have just melted from the slopes. At this time, you should find carpets of fragrant Creeping Phlox *(Phlox diffusa)* and clusters of pink Mountain Pride *(Penstemon newberryi)* growing on the gravelly slopes that lead toward the summit.

If you want to hike the mountains even earlier, and don't mind hiking over patches of snow, you may find a flower that blooms before all the others. Drummond's Anemone *(Anemone drummondii)* grows at the edges of slowly melting snow banks and is often especially abundant along the saddle between the two peaks. Its inch-wide, ruffly flowers bloom close to the ground decorating the soil with white, petal-like sepals that are a gorgeous florescent blue beneath. Yellow pistils and stamens cluster in the flower's center, optimistically awaiting a visit from the few insects that dare to venture this high, so early in the season.

A few weeks later, from early- to mid-July, the Sierra Primrose *(Primula suffrutescens)* comes into full vibrant flower among the rocks. A lavish garden of these flowers blooms along the trail, mid-way between the Castle Pass sign and the craggy rocks, near the summit. Its rose-pink flowers have bright yellow centers and sit at the top of leafless stems, that are about 6 inches high. It is a smaller, and I think, prettier version of the domesticated primroses sold in nurseries. Each stem supports several dazzling little beauties, which are all the more striking because they usually grow amidst exposed, gray, rocky alpine slopes or snuggle below stony ledges, where they are nourished by slowly dripping snow banks.

Its botanical name, *Primula,* is derived from the Latin word for spring, while *suffrutescens* means "woody at the base." This name fails to take notice of its feminine beauty, but aptly describes the growth of this tough little perennial. A perennial is a plant that lives for more than a year. If you check out the stem close to the ground, you will see that it has a woody texture like a shrub. This will tell you that it is a perennial rather than an annual. An annual grows from a seed, creates flowers and sets seed all in one year. Annuals are usually green at the base, because they don't live long enough to build up woody tissue. Often times, in keying out flowers, the species of a particular genus will be divided into annuals and perennials, so you will need to determine the status of your plant by looking at the stem, down low where it meets the soil, to see if it is woody or herbaceous (green).

A Symbiotic Union of Two Plants

As you hike among the volcanic extrusions that lead to Castle Peak, you will see splotches of bright orange, yellow and black on the rocks. Although these splotches of color appear lifeless, they are actually an intriguing plant form, called lichen. They are created by the union of two separate plants, algae and fungi, that live together in mutual support.

The fungi form the structure that encloses and protects the usually single-celled algae. The fungi also put out the thread-like fungal rhizoids, called hyphae, that allow the lichen to adhere to rocks. These hyphae produce strong acids which decompose the rocks, making the minerals available to the green algae for photosynthesis. It is also the job of the fungi to absorb moisture from the air. The algae then uses the moisture in photosynthesis to produce the carbohydrates that sustain life in both the fungi and algae. This is a relationship that seems to suit both plants, with the fungi providing the home, and the algae putting dinner on the table.

In carrying out their life processes, lichens also benefit other forms of life. By decomposing the rocks, the fungi help to create precious soil which gathers in small cracks where tiny plants can cling to begin life. Lichen also acts as a direct food source in the far north, where it is a mainstay in the diet of caribou and reindeer and thus called reindeer moss. Biologists have found that, when conditions are severe, these lichens provide as much as 95 per cent of the animals' diet.

Lichen also acts to directly benefit man as well. Because of its sensitivity to pollutants, English scientists have found that they can employ certain species of wild lichens to warn of excessive concentrations of sulphur dioxide in the air.

The Reproduction of Lichen

Lichen are hardy plants able to withstand extreme differences in temperature and moisture. The Ramalina Lichen in the Negev desert can continue to survive in temperatures over 80 degrees Centigrade, in a dry dormant state, or photosynthesize even when partially frozen, at minus 10 degrees Centigrade.

When conditions are intolerable many lichen simply go dormant to wait for better days. Though these plants go into suspended animation during long days of drought, they are ready when moisture comes, for they can quickly take advantage of it by absorbing up to 50 percent of their body weight in about 10 minutes. If temperatures are warm enough they will begin to photosynthesize.

You can observe this change, in the lichen, by pouring water over an apparently lifeless, gray splotch on one of the rocks. Within minutes it will turn a deep green as the algae become activated and ready to photosynthesize. Such responsiveness is important in areas where moisture is rare and short lived, as is the case on the face of a rock. It is amazing how many different environments plants have colonized, from the ocean's floor, with little sunlight, to sun-drenched, exposed rock faces on the tops of the highest mountains.

Because of the unusually severe conditions in which they live, and the resultant long periods of dormancy, lichens grow and reproduce at a very slow rate. Reproduction is carried out by three different processes. Broken pieces of plant tissue may be spread by the wind during storms. If they fall on receptive surfaces, they begin to grow and colonize. In other cases, the fungi may produce microscopic spores which are carried by the wind. If these spores are able to combine with free algae, they begin a new union. Lichens also produce tiny packets, called sore-dia, that contain both hyphae and algae. The hyphae, or thread-like parts, cling to the rock and, with the algae as partners, begin the process anew.

Hiking Castle Peak in Mid-summer

If you climb the slopes up to Castle Peak, from early-July through early-August, you will usually find flower-filled hillsides of Crest Lupine *(Lupinus arbustus)*, Mountain Mule-ears *(Wyethia mollis)*, and Scarlet Gilia *(Ipomopsis aggregata)*. You will also find the shrubs of Dwarf Sagebrush *(Artemisia arbuscula)*. They resemble the common Sagebrush *(Artemisia tridentata)*, with gray-green leaves that are 3-lobed at the tip, but they grow as a smaller version.

After exploring the rocks near the summit of Castle Peak, head back down and onto the saddle that runs north toward Basin Peak. As you walk along this level juncture, between the two peaks during early-July, you will find many flowers in bloom, even though this exposed, ridgetop environment looks barren from a distance. Among them will be the tightly clustered flowers of Butterballs *(Eriogonum ovalifolium)* with their dense mats of white-woolly, oval leaves. As is typical of members of the Buckwheat Family, its flowers lack true petals. Their sepals, in performing the function of petals, are white and shaped like petals and decorated with green-to-red mid-veins.

These flowers are interesting because they are an example of an important, high elevation adaptation. Butterballs grow at elevations of from 7,000 to 12,000 feet. As the flowers age, they

Whitney's Locoweed

turn a deep-red. At first it may seem odd that a flower would become brighter after it has been pollinated, and no longer needs to attract insects. In this case the color does not function to attract insects. Instead the darker pigment, with its greater ability to absorb warmth, helps the plant to retain heat, so the seeds in the flower head are protected until they mature. In an alpine environment, where winter is long and summer is short, flowers must bloom and set seed very quickly. So, any ability to retain precious warmth gives the plant an advantage.

Also growing in the saddle between the two peaks is Whitney's Locoweed (*Astragalus whitneyi*). Its small pea-flowers bloom in late-June through early-July. Each flower is rose-purple with white wing tips and grows in crowded groups along the tips of the stems. This prostrate little plant lounges on the sandy soil with soft, hairy, pinnate leaves.

If you miss the flowers in bloom, you can easily identify the locoweed by its unusual looking seed pods that appear by late-July. They are tan with rust-colored spots, about an inch or more long and are inflated like little oval-shaped balloons. They lie on the ground in prominent clusters along the stems. Shake one of the pods and you will hear the seeds rattling inside. This led to its other common name, Rattle-weed.

Locoweed is a name given to this plant and to the genus as a whole because the leaves and stems of certain members contain a toxic substance which causes animals that eat them to go *loco*. (*Loco* is the Spanish word for crazy.) This substance affects the optic nerve, causing visual disorientation, lack of coordination and frantic movements. Apparently even very small objects look large and threatening to the animal or it may see objects that don't exist and frantically try to escape.

Arriving at Basin Peak
You may find many other flowers along the saddle, between Castle and Basin Peaks, and on the slopes

along the saddle. As you continue on through the lupines, buckwheats and delicate lavender and pink belly flowers, you will soon arrive at the flanks of Basin Peak. Although not as dramatic as Castle Peak, Basin Peak is more easily maneuvered and also offers beautiful views from its slightly higher 9,115 foot summit.

Many little flowers find shelter among its rocks, which will give you a chance to key them out while you enjoy lunch on the summit. Later you may head back cross-country down to Round Valley, through lush hillsides of orchids, lilies and monkeyflowers as were described in the previous hike. I usually return along the saddle to a point about midway between Castle and Basin Peak and then drop cross-country down the gentlest slope area, through groves of trees. As you do so, keep your eyes open for small ravines that house lush creek gardens. Stay away from any rocky, steep areas that could lead to cliffs.

The hike up to Castle and Basin Peaks is especially nice, because it offers the experience of an above-timberline alpine garden, with some of the least strenuous hiking at Tahoe, although the hike is strenuous enough that you'll feel tired, but pleased, at the day's end.

Summit Lake

Gardens of Pink and a Warm Swimmable Lake

🚶‍♂️🚶

One day/overnight	
One way 1.5 miles	
Trail begins/ends 7200'/7400'	
Net gain/total gain 200'/200'	
Topo map USGS Donner Pass, Calif.	
Wildflower Season Late-June through August	

Highlighted Flowers

- Crest Lupine
  (Lupinus arbustus)
- Alpine Lily
  (Lilium parvum)
- Mountain Spiraea
  (Spiraea densiflora)
- Mountain Pride
  (Penstemon newberryi)
- Fendler's Meadow Rue
  (Thalictrum fendleri)
- Alpine Shooting Star
  (Dodecatheon alpinum)
- Elephant Heads
  (Pedicularis groenlandica)
- Corn Lily
  (Veratrum californicum)
- Spotted Coral Root
  (Corallorhiza maculata)

The trail to Summit Lake, on the east side of Castle Peak, meanders uphill through silent red fir forests and past wet meadows of vibrant color. Along the way it crosses creeks which sparkle brightly over mossy rocks or course swiftly through dark depressions under mud-laden, grassy banks. Summit Lake is reached after passing a small wet meadow of pink shooting stars and elephant heads and traversing a flowery rock garden. The lake is a wonderful place to camp and fish with young children. It sits shallow, muddy and warm amidst dense groves of lodgepoles, while above its surface, iridescent damsel flies flit about in wild courtship.

Trailhead Directions

Heading west on Interstate 80, take the Boreal Ridge exit just past the Castle Peak rest area. At the off-ramp stop sign, turn right and take the blacktopped road up

Alpine Shooting Star

59

the hill until it dead ends by the Castle Valley trail sign. (You could be towed if you park at the rest station, because it is reserved for cars traveling along the highway only, not for those who desire to stop along the way to enjoy the beauty!) Heading east on Interstate 80, take the Boreal Ridge exit, turn left at the off-ramp stop sign and go under the freeway to pick up the blacktopped road referenced above.

The Trail Begins

The height of the bloom, along the eastern side of Castle Peak, usually occurs in early- to mid-July, although this will certainly vary with snow pack. After parking at the end of the blacktopped road, pick up the trail that heads east through the woods (parallel to the freeway). At times the trail fades away, but if the freeway noise is to your right, you will be heading in the correct direction.

After passing through rock gardens of penstemon, paintbrush and aster, that bloom from July through August, you will come to a creek. Just before the creek, look among the ferns, in August and September, for the white, papery flowers of Pearly Everlasting *(Anaphalis margaritacea)* that grow atop stems that are about 2 feet tall. (In dry years they can be found blooming in July.) Looking like small white pearls *(margaritaceus* means "of pearls"), the flowers cluster in tight heads about 2 inches wide, with the true flowers being the tiny yellow structures in the center of the papery bracts.

Soon after crossing the creek, begin looking for gorgeous stands of orange Alpine Lilies *(Lilium parvum)* and pink Lewis' Monkeyflowers *(Mimulus lewisii)*; they usually can be found in full bloom by early-July to mid-July. Look for them in the sunlit groves, among the lodgepoles and bracken fern.

Within 1/2 mile, you will arrive at the pond by the Castle Peak Rest Station. You may pick up the Pacific Crest Trail there, by the sign on the tree, and hike uphill through lovely rock gardens of yellow Sulphur Flowers *(Eriogonum umbellatum)*, white Mari-

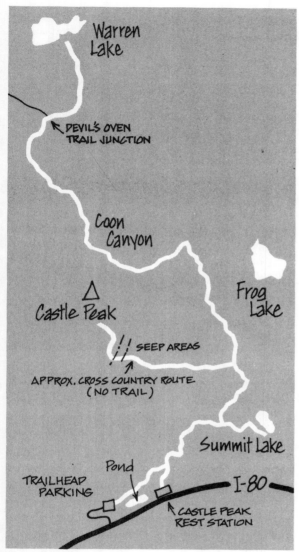

posa Lilies (*Calochortus leichtlinii*) and Red Mountain Heather (*Phyllodoce breweri*). Alternatively, you may continue heading east a few hundred yards more, until you connect with the Summit Lake Trail sign.

If you continue east, alongside the pond, you'll find a trail that heads north up the mountain (after it has left the rest station parking lot). The trail out of the rest station, which is marked by a sign directing the way to Summit Lake, is damper and will take you, in July, past sunlit glens of alpine lilies, columbines and lupines and past the nodding flowers of the One-sided Wintergreen *(Pyrola secunda)*. Its shiny, dark green leaves nestle in little patches of soil among the roots of old conifers. If you hike this section of the trail in late-July through August, look for lovely patches of pink Fireweed *(Epilobium angustifolium)* right near the trail's beginning.

Comparing Simple and Compound Leaves
It doesn't matter which trail you take, since both merge within about 1/4 mile at another Pacific Crest Trail sign that again points the way to Summit Lake. As you wander along either trail, you will pass by the sweetly fragrant Crest Lupine *(Lupinus arbustus)*. It blooms pale lavender above gray-green palmate leaves; palmate means the leaflets radiate outward from a central point, like fingers from the palm of a hand.

In damper and more shaded wooded areas, look for the blue-purple flowers of Jacob's Ladder *(Polemonium californicum)*. These bell-shaped flowers have white to yellow throats, with extruding reproductive parts, and bloom in clusters at the end of hairy, pinnate leaves. Pinnate refers to leaves with leaflets arranged along both sides of the leaf stem in parallel rows.

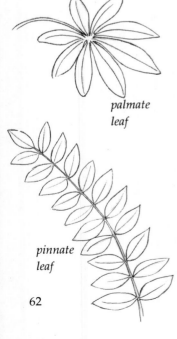

palmate leaf

pinnate leaf

Botanically speaking, leaves are defined as either simple or compound. Simple refers to a single leaf attached to the main stem. Compound refers to a simple leaf, that has become so deeply lobed (either palmately or pinnately) over millions of years, that the original leaf is now made up of many small leaflets.

The Merging of the Two Trails
Soon you will arrive at the second Summit Lake sign. At this point the two trails merge, and the sign reads "Summit Lake 1 1/2 mile." In the damp gardens near your feet, the dainty, white flowers of Macloskey's

Violet *(Viola macloskeyi)* bloom from late-June through early-July. If you kneel to look at the lovely flower more closely, you will have a better appreciation for the beauty of a violet. Georgia O'Keeffe once said, "...in a way - nobody sees a flower - really - it is so small - we haven't time - and to see takes time, like to have a friend takes time." When we take the time to care, our lives become fuller, whether it is with a friend or a little violet.

Make your life fuller by checking out this little violet! All violets have 5 petals—2 upper and 2 lateral, which are often bearded or lined with nectar guides, and 1 that is larger and extends backward to form a spur which holds the nectar. The pistil sits in the throat of the violet and is surrounded by 5 stamens. The 2 lower stamens have little parts which project into the flower spur, on which are formed drops of nectar. Because of where the nectar is located, it is a good guess that its pollinator must have a proboscis that can reach down into the spur. This is the case, since its main pollinators are bees and butterflies who carry such mouth parts.

Granite Gardens and Creek Crossings
As you continue along the trail, you'll cross several small creeks and wander beneath granite walls, softened by vibrant pink sprays of Mountain Pride *(Penstemon newberryi)*. You will also pass through rock gardens of yellows, pinks and purples from sedums, phlox and buckwheats. In these rock gardens, take a moment to look for a little mustard flower that is a dark purple or a creamy yellow and is called Jewel Flower *(Streptanthus tortuosus)*. Its tiny, urn-shaped blossoms, or "jewels," have sepals that twist outward at straggly angles. The flower is followed by long, narrow, horizontal seed pods. Its leaves clasp the stem, like a shield, which led to its other name, Shieldleaf.

If you take a moment to check out the leaves of these dry environment plants, you will find that each has evolved its own way of conserving precious water. The leaves of the jewel flower and the penstemons have a waxy, tough coating on their surfaces to reduce evaporation, while the needle-like leaves of the phlox reduce evaporation by minimizing leaf surfaces. The succulent sedums save water for future use by storing this precious commodity in little leaf-reservoirs.

After these dry gardens, you will cross another creek with slopes that bloom with columbines, lilies and larkspurs. Above the flowers, the shrubs of white flowering Creek Dogwood *(Cornus stolonifera)* spread their lovely branches. In July, clusters of tiny flowers bloom at the tips of the branches, while out of each flower's center, yellow anthers protrude in fuzzy curiosity.

The deeply veined leaves and red bark of these dogwoods will help you to identify them. In winter they take on a special beauty as the branches and stems contrast in bright red against the white of the snow. Native Americans and other mountaineers of the past smoked the inner bark of the branches, while Native American women used the sturdier stems to form cradle boards for carrying their babies on their backs.

An Intriguing Little Flower

*female
meadow rue
flower*

After the creek, a short uphill climb will take you, in early-July, to an opening on the right, with a boggy meadow of pink shooting stars, pink elephant heads, yellow monkeyflowers and blue-purple monkshood. Just before entering this meadow, be sure to look for the flowers of Fendler's Meadow Rue *(Thalictum fendleri)* in the rocks to the right of the trail. Its leaves have a delicate ferny appearance, similar to the columbine, and its inconspicuous flowers bloom on slender stems that are about 3 to 4 feet tall.

If you move in closely and check out several plants, you will discover something interesting. Some of the plants have little green, star-shaped, "5-petaled" flowers, and others have little pinkish tassel-like "things." Take a moment to determine what these structures might be.

What you have discovered is that the meadow rue has two types of flowers, and each type grows on a separate plant. The star-shaped structure is the female flower, while the tasseled one is the male. Thus each flower, in the meadow rue, houses either the male or female reproductive parts. A flower's function, besides that of creating joy in our hearts, is reproduction. The stem, leaves and root serve to support and nourish the flower as it goes about its important business of creating new little bundles of life.

Although most plants have a flower that houses both the female and male reproductive parts in the same flower, some plants, like those of the conifers and meadow rues, have separate flowers. While in the conifer, individual male or female flowers bloom separately on the same tree, in the meadow rue they bloom on separate plants. Thus, one meadow rue plant may bloom with only male flowers, while another one nearby, may bloom with only female flowers. A meadow rue garden is a happy spot where eager females await the attention of neighboring males. Find female flowers and you're sure to find the males nearby!

A Flower without Petals

Before moving on, take another moment to bend down and look more closely at each flower; using your hand lens will help. The star-shaped "petals" on the female are really not petals but sepals. All flowers are enclosed in the bud stage by sepals. When the buds open, the petals inside are exposed, forming a ring of color, like a crown, above the usually green ring of sepals below. (Corolla, the collective word for petals, comes from Latin and means "little crown"). In the meadow rue, you will see only one ring of green, formed by the sepals, with the petals absent.

If you look closely at the male flower, you will see that the "tassels" are formed by pink, silky, thread-

close-up of male meadow rue flower

like filaments that carry yellow anthers. You will also see that the male flower is without petals. You may ask yourself why a flower would lack petals. Botanists believe that brightly colored petals evolved from leaves, because plants with those colored structures were more likely to attract insects, due to the greater display of color. Studies have shown that insects have trouble finding their favorite flowers when the petals are removed.

A flower without petals may seem odd until we realize that these plants are not pollinated by insects but by the wind. The production of petals would be a waste of precious energy as well as a liability, because petals would only act to block wind-deposited pollen. Instead, the meadow rue puts its energy into producing massive amounts of very fine pollen. If you find a ripened anther, look at the pollen grains through your hand lens and you will see that they are like powder. Wind-carried pollen must be as light as possible to be carried by the wind. Botanists have actually found that some types of pollen travel as far as 3,000 miles in their wind-born journeys.

A Meadow of Satiny Pink Shooting Stars

If you arrive at the boggy meadow just past the meadow rue in early- to mid-July, you'll see masses of pink created by Alpine Shooting Stars (*Dodecatheon alpinum*) and Elephant Heads (*Pedicularis groenlandica*). This early in the season, the meadow will be very wet and easily damaged, so if you want a closer look, be sure to stay at the meadow's edge, walking only on rocks and drier ground. This fragile environment cannot take the pounding of many feet, no matter how lovingly we may tread.

As the name suggests, shooting stars resemble those special stars that soar through the night sky with a tail of blazing light. Only the shooting star's "tail" is made by pink reflexed petals. With the petals bent back, the dark purple stamens (below the yellow and maroon rings) are exposed, as is the single pistil which hangs down and outward from the center.

Notice that, after fertilization, each nodding flower points upward, as if to celebrate its fulfillment! The sepals, which have been hidden until now by the reflexed petals, become visible as the petals gradually fall off. The sepals then move upwards around the maturing seed capsule, like protective hands cradling a treasure.

The scientific name *Dodecatheon* comes from the Greek word *dodeka* meaning "twelve" and *theos* meaning "gods." It was named by Pliny, a Roman naturalist and writer, who lived from 23 to 79 A. D. He thought the umbelled cluster of flowers, each bearing a crown of reflexed petals, looked like an assembly of the twelve important gods of the Roman world. Think how long this lovely flower has been admired and cherished!

Soon after the shooting stars begin blooming, the meadow is invaded by elephants — Tahoe style. Stems appear that carry stalks of tiny, pink, elephant head-like flowers with floppy ears, rounded foreheads and outstretched trunks. The Elephant Heads are wonderful flowers to introduce to children and are discussed in more detail on the Tahoe Meadows hike.

Continuing on to Summit Lake

After enjoying this meadow and the gorgeous drier one just beyond it of lupine, paintbrush and corn lilies, follow the trail uphill through the forest a couple hundred yards, until you arrive at a sign that reads, "Summit Lake One-half Mile."

The short walk to the lake passes clusters of Creeping Phlox *(Phlox diffusa)*, blooming in June, and carpets of tiny Torrey's Monkeyflowers, that bring pink to the sandy soils in early-July. Later, in mid-July through early-August, the splashy blue-purple flowers and wonderful yellow buds of the Azure and Showy Penstemons *(Penstemon azureus and P. speciosus)* appear among the rocks.

The Orchid Flowers of Spotted Coral Root

Upon approaching the lake, look among the dense

stands of conifers for different types of plants from those you saw along the trail growing in full sunlight. Here you will find plants that are adapted to live in low light levels. Some of these plants will lack green leaves and so cannot carry out food production through photosynthesis. In order to survive, they must consume other organic matter. If a plant lives dependent upon soil fungi, it is saprophytic; if it directly consumes living matter, it is parasitic. Though the names appear simple, the relationships of these plants to their environments are complex and only beginning to be understood by scientists.

One such plant can be found blooming in mid-June through July in the woods just before the lake. The reddish brown, saprophytic orchid called Spotted Coral Root *(Corallorhiza maculata)* takes its name from the shape of its root. It is not a true root because it lacks the rootlets and root hairs necessary to directly absorb moisture and nutrients from the soil.

Because it lacks these rootlets, the coral root lives totally dependent upon mycorrhizal fungi, that coat its root to perform the absorption function of rootlets. These soil fungi parasitize neighboring roots and gather carbon and other nutrients from the soil, which they then make available to the coral root. In exchange, the coral root provides sugar needed by the fungi.

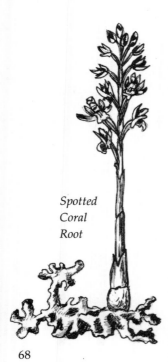

Spotted Coral Root

Even before the coral root's "roots" appear, these soil fungi are important to the life of this orchid. Its seeds are too tiny to carry the nutritive matter needed to sustain them in germination, so the fungi must be present in the soil to provide the nutrients necessary for germination to occur. For this reason, orchids do not disperse their seeds with the wind, or in the socks of people, but rather drop them directly onto the ground below the parent plant to insure that the necessary soil fungi will be present.

In searching for the coral root, look first for its reddish brown, leafless stems that grow up to about 2 feet tall. Then you will spot its 1/2 inch wide flowers, growing loosely along the stem. Its sepals and upper petals are a purplish red, while the 3 lower lobes are white and spotted with red. Its yellowish, thick stigma protrudes out of the flower's center. It is intricately beautiful through a ten-power hand lens, and with such magnification you can clearly make out its tiny orchid form. Its flowers are followed later in the season with elongated brown seed pods that droop along the stem before releasing their seeds to the soil at the base of the plant.

Arriving at the Lake

The lake, which is just beyond the orchids, is easily reached even by young children. I once hiked it with a 2 year old who never complained during the uphill climb for there was enough variety of terrain and flower life to maintain her enthusiasm until the lake was reached. Once there, we found the water buzzing with blue damsel flies and busy water-skeeters.

This warm, swimmable lake is a pleasant place to stop for lunch and to enjoy the remainder of the day. Its muddy bottom is not for the squeamish, but nothing as yet has grabbed my toes, although I'm always ready just in case!

Unfortunately the lake is not very private, because a logging road provides easy access to it, but since it is an easy hike for young children, it is a good place to introduce them to camping.

For those who enjoy fishing, Eastern Brook and Rainbow Trout are supposed to be plentiful. Best of all, the shoreline is shallow and level, making it safe for young fishermen. So if fishing isn't something you love, but your child does, you can relax nearby while your youngster safely fishes to his or her heart's content!

Moonlight on Castle Peak

Hiking through Summit Gardens

One day	
One way 4 miles	
Trail begins/ends 7200'/8800'	
Net gain/total gain 1600'/1600'	
Topo map USGS Donner Pass, Calif	
Wildflower Season July through August	

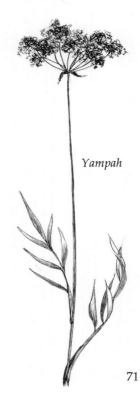

Yampah

H ave you ever sat on the top of a mountain at nighttime, among gardens of wildflowers, watching the full moon rise, or have you wandered cross-country through sweeping hillsides of golden daisies, like in a scene from "The Sound of Music?" The east side of Castle Peak offers these delightful experiences, along with gardens of white lacy yampah, that float above a sea of pink gilias, shoulder-high flowery gardens, that form jungles of growth at the edges of tiny streams, and small pink flowers, that mimic sun-bleached steer's heads on a sandy desert floor.

Trailhead Directions
Follow the Trailhead Directions for the previous hike.

Picking up the Trail
Check out the trail description for the previous hike and then, instead of heading to the right at the sign

71

toward Summit Lake, continue straight uphill along the Warren Lake trail, for about 1/4 mile. As you do so, you'll pass through red fir forests, cross over open

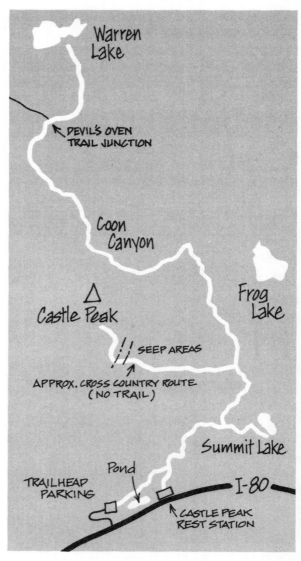

slopes of penstemon and pennyroyal and climb up a rocky, short, steep trail. As the trail tops out, you will find yourself surrounded by hillsides of the daisy-like flowers of Mountain Mule-ears (*Wyethia mollis*) and Arrow-leaved Balsam Root *(Balsamorhiza sagittata)*.

Balsam roots begin their blooming cycle in mid-June and are soon joined by the flowers of Mountain Mule-ears in late-June through early-July. Both plants carry coarse, 3 inch wide, golden flowers on top of stems that are about 3 feet tall. These plants are so similar that they are often mistaken for one another, but once you understand the differences, they can be easily distinguished, even at a distance. The balsam root's large leaves are a velvety green and are arrowhead shaped, as opposed to the more rounded, oblong shape of the large, whitish-green leaves of mule-ears. The flower heads of balsam root usually rise well above the leaves, while the mule-ears' flowers barely clear the tops of the vertical leaves.

The genus name for Mountain Mule-ears, *Wyethia*, honors Captain Nathaniel Wyeth, a trapper and explorer, who "first" discovered them as he traveled across North America in 1834. The species name, *mollis*, means "soft" and refers to the downy leaves in spring.

The scientific and common names for Arrow-leaved Balsam Root come from the Greek words *balsamos* for the aromatic resin in the tap roots and *rhiza* which means "root." The species name is derived from the Latin word *sagitta* for "arrow" and refers to the shape of the leaves.

In the spring the young leaves and stems of the balsam root were eaten raw or cooked by native peoples. The roots were peeled and baked, and the seeds were roasted and eaten (tasting like popcorn), or they were ground into flour for mush. The Paiutes made a chewing gum from the root, and its large leaves were used to cover the camas lily bulb when it was roasted in earthen ovens, as discussed on the Sagehen East hike.

A Plant Gathered by the Shoshonis
As you stand above this golden expanse, beneath a royal blue sky, with puffy, white clouds and look out

toward the distant, snow-capped peaks of Desolation Wilderness, you might just feel that you've been swept away to a scene from "The Sound of Music." You may want to break out into song — let the moment capture you — who cares if you are a little off tune. I'm sure the insect community will buzz with new delight as you add your voice to theirs!

As you sing, depart the trail and head left toward Castle Peak's summit, finding your own path through this golden garden. When the mule-ears begin to thin out, you'll come upon dryish areas covered with the delicate flowers of Bridge's Gilia *(Gilia leptalea)* blooming in pink-purple beneath the white, lacy blossoms of Yampah *(Perideridia bolanderi).*

Yampah is easy to spot because its clusters of tiny, white flowers seem to float in space atop its slender stems. The word yampah is the Shoshone name for this plant. Many native peoples collected both its seeds and its small, sweet, tuberous roots which were either eaten raw or dried and pounded into a flour and then cooked in baskets with hot rocks. Water was added later to form a thickened, soup-like dish.

Sacajawea, the Shoshoni woman who traveled with the Lewis and Clark expedition from 1804-06, gathered the roots of another species of yampah *(Perideridia gairdnerii)* and prepared them for the expedition. It was well received according to the journals of Lewis and Clark, "Sahcargarweah geathered a quantity of the roots of a speceis of fennel which we found very agreeable food, the flavor of this root is not unlike annis seed."

In the same dry areas with the yampah and gilia, you will find a member of the Rose Family, the Downy Avens *(Geum canescens).* Its nodding, reddish flowers are followed by feathery pistils after fertilization.

Look too for the salmon-colored, tubular flowers of the Giant Collomia *(Collomia grandiflora).* Its blossoms form clusters in bowl-shaped, inch-wide receptacles and bloom with blue anthers that are lovely in contrast with the petals.

The vivid pink of Copeland's Owl's Clover (*Orthocarpus copelandii*) and the red, Wavy-leaved Paintbrush (*Castilleja applegatei*) also bring bright color to the dry hillside.

Shoulder-High Creekside Gardens

After wandering cross country through these dry meadows of mule-ears and other flowers, you will come to a series of springs and creeks that flow off the ridge, giving rise to communities of thousands of wildflowers so densely packed that there will be no soil showing, only lush green foliage beneath a riot of color.

After the drought years of '87 and '88 little bloomed along these creekbeds, but in good years, after a heavy snow fall, they come alive with shoulder-high plants of the lavender Large-leaved Lupine (*Lupinus polyphyllus*) and dark-purple Monkshood (*Aconitum columbianum*). Monks in purple! What a delight!

Take a moment to look at each monkshood flower and you will see that it resembles a little monk's rounded hood. Clusters of reproductive parts peer out of the rounded hood. These flowers are interesting, because the inside shape of the flowers is just the size of the bumblebee that pollinates them. The flower evolved to match its pollinator and is so dependent upon the bumblebee that it does not reproduce in areas where the bees are absent.

Glaucous Larkspur (*Dephinium glaucum*) also blooms on stems that can grow up to 5 feet tall, with stalks of intense, blue-purple flowers. Look closely at the flowers that are still in bud, at the top of the stem, and you will see how this flower received its botanical name, *Delphinium*, which comes from the Latin word for "dolphin." Each little bud sits atop a tiny stem and seems to be floating through an ocean of air, like a tiny dolphin floating in the sea.

Monkshood

You will also find the large, white umbels of Cow Parsnip (*Heracleum lanatum*) that bloom above huge, maple-like leaves. Each stem carries hundreds of tiny

75

flowers that radiate outward in "umbel fashion," like the spokes of an umbrella.

The bright reds of Giant Paintbrush (*Castilleja miniata*) bring more color to this rainbow garden, as do the pinks and yellows of the lower-growing monkey flowers (*Mimulus lewisii, M. guttatus*) and Arrowleaf Senecios (*Senecio triangularis*). Nearby, the red and yellow flowers of Crimson Columbine (*Aquilegia formosa*) nod in gentle grace, and white and green orchids (*Habenaria dilatata, H. sparsiflora*) bring subtle, though exotic, form to this varied garden.

Sheltered at the feet of these taller plants, along the mossy stream banks, are hundreds of treasures that are worth getting down on your hands and knees to find. Little blue veronicas, pink willow herbs and tiny yellow primrose monkeyflowers bloom in profusion. This lush garden is a wonderful place to watch the various pollinators at work or to have fun with a macro lens.

Approaching the Summit
As you reach the jagged rocks below the summit, you will discover an unusual flower that blooms, at this elevation, from late-June through early-July. Though the oddly beautiful Steer's Head (*Dicentra uniflora*) is not rare at Tahoe, it is easily missed, because it blooms early in the season and is inconspicuous until it is spotted. Once you know what its leaves look like, and where it is most likely to bloom, you will find yourself coming upon it often. Its pink to white flower rises only a few inches off the ground above finely-divided, gray-green leaves. Once you locate one plant, as is so often true, your now increased level of awareness will suddenly open your eyes to the hundreds of little steer's heads that cover the soil beneath your feet.

As you bend down to meet this little flower at its own level, you will see that it truly looks like a miniature replica of a sun-bleached steer's head, like the kind that eerily rests on desert floors. Nature's mimicry is amazing; it seems inconceivable that such a form would be duplicated in a delicate little flower, or vise versa.

Its botanical name, *Dicentra uniflora,* refers to the 2-spurred flower form *(dicentra)* and the single flower *(uniflora)* that grows on each stem. Steer's Head is closely related to the Bleeding Heart, a popular nursery plant and one that grows wild beneath the dogwoods in the foothills by Nevada City.

Summit Rock Gardens

After finding the Steer's Head, you have only a short walk to the summit of Castle Peak, where you will find many flowers braving the weather, seeking shelter among the jagged rocks. The plants that grow in such harsh, mountain-top environments have evolved special forms to survive in the intense sunlight, the fierce desiccating winds and cold temperatures. Most grow close to the ground for protection and have developed silvery hairs, or a powdery coating, on their leaves and stems to protect delicate plant tissue from the intensity of the sun and the drying effects of the wind.

The Woolly Sunflower *(Eriophyllum lanatum)* has such a protective covering. This flower is easily identified by its drooping petals which are an intense golden-yellow. They brightly stand out against the sandy soil. Its genus name, *Eriophyllum,* comes from the Greek word *erion* for "wool" and *phyllon* for "leaf." *Lanatum* also means woolly. Whoever named this daisy was quite taken by its downy covering.

You will also find other warmly coated plants like those of Drummond's Anemone *(Anemone drummondii).* All parts of this anemone are hairy—its leaves, stems and even the sepals. After fertilization the sepals drop off, and its flowers become rounded, densely-haired, fruiting heads decorated with clusters of hairy, slender styles.

The Silver-leaf Raillardella *(Raillardella argentea)* with its narrow, shiny, silky-haired leaves brightly reflects the sun's rays. It is a member of the Composite Family with yellow blossoms made up entirely of disk flowers. (See the Sherwood Forest hike for a discussion of disk flowers and the Composite Family.)

Look too for another member of the Composite Family, the White-stem Goldenbush *(Haplopappus macronema)* which is a small shrub, about a foot tall, with yellow disk flowers and white, densely woolly stems. It is a treat to find these plants at such a low elevation. Later on we will find them again on 10,776 foot Mt. Rose, after considerably more hiking.

A Moonlight Picnic at the Summit

The top of Castle Peak is a wonderful spot to search for alpine plants and a beautiful place to watch the sun set and a full moon rise. I once did this with my husband, Phil, and a group of friends. We left late in the afternoon, hiking up the trail with packs filled with our favorite hors d'oeuvres, wine and other goodies.

As we approached the mountain top, we found a level area near one of the spectacular, spring-fed gardens. Here we spread out colorful table cloths, tiny vases with domestic flowers, and an array of hors d'oeuvres and wines. After enjoying each other's creations of marinated mushrooms, homemade pate and pasta and fresh fruit marinated in champagne, we hiked to the ridge to find a comfortable spot to enjoy the final glow of the setting sun and to await the arrival of the full moon.

As the moon rose, it sent moonbeams down upon us to light our way through the fields of mule-ears to the trail out. The hike through the dense woods was dark and exciting, but when the trail passed by granite slabs and open slopes, our way was clearly lit, as if soft floodlights had been turned on by the Gods.

Moonlight hiking is a wonderful experience — trees take on new personalities, coming into their own at night with a power and magic not found during the day. And then of course there are the stars that envelope one like a sparkling canopy, a reminder of the mystery of all life.

Warren Lake

Through Coon Canyon to Warren Lake

Highlighted Flowers
- Brook Saxifrage
  (Saxifraga punctata)
- Creeping Phlox
  (Phlox diffusa)
- Sierra Primrose
  (Primula suffrutescens)
- Davis' Knotweed
  (Polygonum davisiae)
- Western Aster
  (Aster occidentalis)
- Mountain Mule-ears
  (Wyethia mollis)
- Elephant Heads
  (Pedicularis groenlandica)
- Cassiope
  (Cassiope mertensiana)
- Corn Lily
  (Veratrum californicum)

Overnight
One way   7 1/2 miles
Trail begins at 7200', climbs to 8570' and drops to 7210'
Net gain/total gain 10'/2110'
Topo map USGS Donner Pass, Calif
Wildflower Season July through August

Warren Lake lies serene and protected at the base of a steep mountain. On hot summer days its waters mirror the clouds above, while white cassiope blooms on the exposed talus slopes that surround the lake. The long, arduous trail in, though tiring because of the many ups and downs, is exhilarating because of the luxuriant meadows, sweeping hillsides of flowers and peaceful sense of isolation.

Trailhead Directions
Follow the directions and trail description for the two previous hikes until you arrive at the mule-ear field. Instead of hiking cross-country toward the peak, you will continue along the trail.

Picking up the Trail
A few hundred yards beyond the mule-ear field, you will arrive at a wonderful seep garden, usually filled

Cassiope

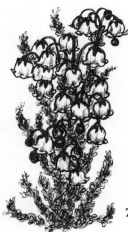

79

with color in early-July. A whole day could easily be spent photographing, botanizing or just plain enjoying in this one small area.

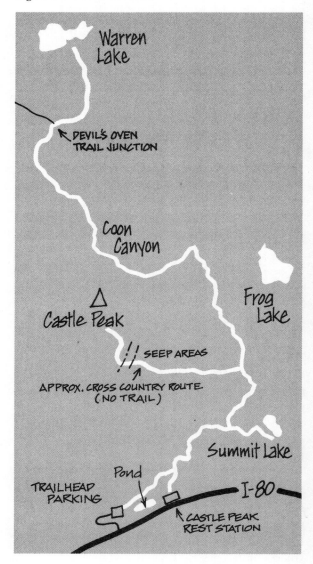

After this garden, you will cross a creek lined with flowers. If you take a moment to search among the flowers, you should find the lovely blossoms of the Brook Saxifrage (*Saxifraga punctata*). Its white flowers are only about 1/2 inch wide and bloom in loose clusters, on reddish stems that are about a foot tall. Since the flower is inconspicuous, you may more easily find it if you first look for its leaves. They are lush-green and rounded in form, and they create basal mats along the margins of the stream. Once you know the leaves, it will be easy to find the flower.

Be sure to pull out your hand lens to view this delicate flower. Each petal, which is marked with 2 yellow dots, narrows at the base to form a thin stalk before joining the glandular stem. Its bright red anthers are gorgeous against the white of the petals. Its sepals are also red and tightly reflexed against the stem. The ovary, as is typical of the saxifrages, is prominently 2-beaked and bright red after fertilization.

Spectacular Hillsides of Pink Primrose

After returning to the trail, you will soon cross another creek. At this point look far off toward the broad hillside at your left for clusters of bright pink flowers. The Sierra Primrose *(Primula suffrutescens)* usually blooms from early- to late-July by the thousands on the hillside in one of the largest and most spectacular primrose displays at Tahoe.

Its flowers are a gorgeous rose-pink with bright yellow throats. They bloom atop leafless stems that are about 6 inches tall. Its leathery leaves are basal, forming tight bunches beneath each stem. Be sure to head through the trees and up the slope for a closer look at its flowers.

The Sierra Primrose was one of John Muir's favorites and is found at high elevations from 8,000 to 13,500 feet. Because of its preference for such high, north facing slopes, it does not usually burst forth into bloom until summer. Of course what we call summer, or July, is really spring at these elevations.

The American botanist Asa Gray first identified and collected this primrose in 1872, while hiking to Clouds Rest in Yosemite with John Muir and Galen Clark. Gray may have given it its botanical name,

*Sierra
Primrose*

81

but I am sure it was named and loved by the Yosemite Indians long before Gray's discovery.

Lavender Phlox and Red Knotweed

If you find that you are too early for the primrose, you may still be treated in June to the lavender-to-white flowers of the Creeping Phlox *(Phlox diffusa)*. If you arrive in August or September, the mountainside may be a mass of red from the changing leaves of Davis' Knotweed *(Polygonum davisiae)*.

After returning to the trail and continuing on, look for the deep purple, daisy-like flowers of Western Aster *(Aster occidentalis)* that bloom in August. This aster can be identified by its leaves that clasp the stem. In the same area in July, look for the fragrant, low growing plants of Brewer's Lupine *(Lupinus breweri)*. Its bluish pea flowers carry a white spot on each banner. The flowers grow in clusters about 1 inch long on stems that are about 4 inches tall. Its hairy, palmate leaves form mats of gray-green on the sandy soil surface.

Entering the Red Fir Forest

After the creeks, you will enter a red fir forest. As you wander along the path, the White Hawkweed *(Hieracium albiflorum)* may catch your eye. The 1/2 inch wide blossoms grow near the top of loosely-branched stems, that may be anywhere from 1 to 3 feet tall. The vertical stems rise straight up from straggly-haired basal leaves. Its flowers, which look like small white dandelions, are made up of ray flowers only, that house both male and female reproductive parts. Thus each petal is actually a separate flower capable of producing a separate plant.

Its genus name, *Hieracium*, is from the Greek word *hieros* for "hawk." Long ago it was believed that hawks could spot these plants from afar and would land on the forest floor to eat them to further improve their vision. If they could spot this small flower in the woods in flight, I can't imagine that their vision needed improvement, but nevertheless it was used as an herbal remedy to enhance eyesight. The species' name, *albiflorum,* means "white flowered."

Another species of hawkweed, the Shaggy Hawkweed *(Hieracium horridum),* grows in scattered communities along the trail in rocky environments. Its flower is yellow and it leaves are incredibly hairy, which led to its name, *horridum,* which comes from Latin for "bristly" or "hairy."

Also along the trail in the trees, look for the fernlike leaves of the Pinewoods Lousewort *(Pedicularis semibarbata).* Its pinnate leaves are wavy-edged and lie flat on the ground, hiding its yellow, tubular flowers that grow at the base of the plant.

As you continue along the trail, you will be treated to panoramic views, especially near the summit above private Frog Lake. When you arrive at the headwaters of the south fork of Prosser Creek in upper Coon Canyon, you will be about half way to the lake; those who have had enough hiking may want to turn around after enjoying this area of lush seeps and little waterfalls, but for those who continue on, there is more beauty ahead.

In a year of abundant moisture, the slopes in this area of Coon Canyon will be covered with flowers. Glaucous Larkspur *(Delphinium glaucum),* Monkshood *(Aconitum columbianum)* and Large-leaved Lupine *(Lupinus polyphyllus)* bloom purple on stems about 5 feet tall. Alongside them, Elephant Heads *(Pedicularis groenlandica)* and Alpine Shooting Stars *(Dodecatheon alpinum)* bloom pink, among yellow Arrowleaf Senecios *(Senecio triangularis).*

The Devil's Oven Lake Junction
After continuing along the trail, past the east-facing slope between Castle and Basin Peaks, where the corn lilies often grow in white profusion, you will arrive at the trail junction with Devil's Oven Lake. (Be sure to carry a topo map, as the trail fades in places.) At this junction, take the trail to the right and head east through the chaparral, up to the saddle.

Pinewoods Lousewort

83

After hiking a short distance along the ridge, you will sight the lake to the north.

At this point you may continue along the trail, or drop directly down the mountain, until you arrive at the lake. I usually do the latter, since I have found the best displays of Cassiope in this way.

Nodding Bells of White Cassiope

The white Cassiope (*Cassiope mertensiana*) usually blooms here in late-July or early-August, on rocky shelves in small patches of soil. Its nodding, white flowers look like tiny bells with little, red sepal "caps." Its leaves are needle-like, growing on evergreen branches that carpet the ground in prickly, tight mats. John Muir loved Cassiope's delicate beauty and once exclaimed after finding it in Yosemite,

> "I met cassiope growing in fringes among the battered rocks. Her blossoms had faded long ago, but they were still clinging with happy memories to the evergreen sprays, and still so beautiful as to thrill every fiber of one's being . . ."

You will also find other little beauties among the rocks as you drop down to the south shore of the lake. Its waters are a lovely deep blue, and its tree-lined shore meanders beneath steep granitic walls. Its shoreline offers several good campsites, especially by the creek on the southern shore. The descent to the lake may be jarring, but once there you will most likely be assured several days of total privacy to enjoy skinny dipping, fishing or any other pleasures that might move your soul.

Donner Lake

Lakeside Gardens of Satiny Wintergreens

Highlighted Flowers

- Wild Strawberry
  (*Fragaria platypetala*)
- Pinedrops
  (*Pterospora andromedea*)
- Bog Wintergreen
  (*Pyrola asarifolia*)
- One-sided Wintergreen
  (*Pyrola secunda*)
- Prince's Pine
  (*Chimaphila menziesii*)
- Leichtlin's Camas Lily
  (*Camassia leichtlinii*)
- Porterella
  (*Porterella carnosula*)
- Least Navarretia
  (*Navarretia minima*)

𝕩𝕜𝕩 *(excellent wheelchair access)*

One day
2 1/2 mile level loop
Trail elevation   6,000'
Topo map USGS Donner Pass, Calif.
USGS Truckee, Calif.
Wildflower Season   Mid-May through July

The waters of Donner Lake lie blue and peaceful at the base of the granitic, boulder-strewn slopes of Donner Summit. The oval basin that holds its blue waters was carved by ancient glaciers that slowly ground their way down through the canyon thousands of years ago.

Along the shoreline of the lake, conifers form dense groves that shelter the satiny pink flowers of wintergreen. In June before the tourist season is underway, the park is a peaceful, gentle place. Sitting in one of its small meadows, amidst penstemons, porterellas and camas lilies, you'll feel as isolated and contented as if you were in a backcountry meadow, making it is a special place for those who cannot hike long distances.

In late-June through July, the forest duff gives rise to wild strawberries, sticky brown pinedrops and white thimbleberries. During the summer, its sandy beaches and cool waters offer a respite from the heat

Bog Winter-green

85

of an August afternoon, and by fall all of the people have "gone home" and once again it becomes a place of gentle solitude.

Trailhead Directions

Going west on Interstate 80, take the Donner Lake turnoff, just past the Department of Agriculture Produce Inspection Station. After exiting, go left at the stop sign and over the freeway, down to the second stop sign. At this point, head straight .3 miles past the stop sign, along Donner Pass Road, to the Donner Memorial State Park entrance. Going east on Interstate 80, take the first Donner Lake exit and circle down to Donner Pass Road. At the stop sign, turn left and go along the shore of the lake for about 3 miles until you arrive at the park entrance.

A Visit to the Donner Museum

Before exploring the park and its wildflowers on your own, you may want take a few minutes to visit the museum to learn about the Donner Party. They offer a self-guided, half-mile nature tour that will give you a perspective on the park and show you where members of the Donner Party camped during a tragic winter in the past.

The Donner Party was a group of early-emigrants to California, who had planned to cross Donner Summit on their way to reach the fertile Sacramento Valley. They arrived with their six wagons at the Alder Creek area, just north of Truckee, on October 28, 1846, after six months of exhausting travel from Illinois. They had only to cross Donner Summit to be safely on their way to new lives in the Central Valley, when a series of unfortunate events blocked their passage. A broken wagon axle, an early-season blinding snow storm, a lack of experience with the mountains and tremendous snow depths combined to make travel impossible.

The Donner Party experience is a grim reminder that Nature can be merciless if we are ignorant of her ways. But she can also be gentle, if we know how to operate within the rules. John Muir loved the experience of storms. He felt that this was "a time when Nature has something rare to show us." He took great delight in climbing a tree and swaying back and forth in the wind, while listening to the music of the pine needles. He felt that those who stayed at home during stormy weather, "dry and defrauded of all the glory" were "souls starved in the midst of abundance." If we are both respectful of and in tune with Nature, we can truly be as at home during a sudden storm, as we are on a sunny day.

The Trail Begins

After a visit to the museum, wander over to the guard house and check out the trail map on the wall so you can visualize the loop trail and decide where you want to go. I like to walk through the woods near the lake's edge. There in the sun-filtered light among the conifers, I usually find at least 3 different members of the Rose Family, all of whom share the traits of 5 petals and many reproductive parts. See if you can find them for yourself before I name them. One will have yellow flowers and two will be white. See if you can observe them and see what they share in common, as members of the same family. Then ask yourself how they differ, as each is placed in a separate genus.

The Wild Strawberry *(Fragaria platypetala)*, which has white flowers that bloom in carpets just above the leaves, may be familiar to those of you with vegetable gardens. Like the domestic plants, it has reddish runners that root at the nodes to form new plants, creating loose mats of green on the pine-needled floor. The leaves, which can be brewed into a tea, are slightly hairy and toothed at the upper edges. If you are in the park in August, you will find its tiny red berries — if the animals haven't gotten there first.

Look also for the Thimbleberry *(Rubus parviflorus)*, which has 2 inch wide flowers, with white crinkly petals and clusters of yellow stamens and pistils in the center. Its leaves are large, maple-like and slightly hairy. It grows in damp wooded areas in semi-shade, like the strawberry, and produces a sweet, red fruit that sits in a cup-like receptacle.

A third member of the Rose Family, the Sticky Cinquefoil *(Potentilla glandulosa)*, has yellow flowers that bloom in small clusters atop hairy, glandular stems, that are at least a foot tall. Its leaves are pinnately compound (arranged in parallel rows along the stems) and are serrate along the edges. The yellow petals become narrowed at the base, exposing the green sepals to form a lovely pattern. Look at the backside of the flower and you'll see tiny bracts, called sepalettes, between the sepals — a common trait of members of this genus. The cinquefoil generally grows in areas that are sunnier and drier than the strawberry.

Many of our favorite fruits come from the Rose Family, like the cherry, apple, plum and peach. Next time you have a chance to look at the flowers of these fruit trees, compare them with the wild rose structure and you will find a similar floral pattern. The Rose Family flower is unusual in that the petals and stamens do not reside either above or below the ovary, as in most flowers, but rather are positioned midway, in a bowl-shaped receptacle, and are attached in a whorl around the edge of the bowl.

The Sticky Plants of Pinedrops

As you wander among the trees, look also for the reddish brown plants of Pinedrops *(Pterospora andromedea)* that grow about 2 to 3 feet tall. If you look at the stems of these plants, you won't see green leaves but rather brownish scales that grow along the stalk. Since this plant lacks green leaves, it cannot produce its own food through photosynthesis. Therefore, like the snow plant and coral root, it lives off organic matter in the forest duff, through the help of soil fungi that coat its roots. This symbiotic relationship is discussed on the Prey Meadow hike.

At the top of the stalk, you'll find 40 or more urn-shaped flowers that are very sticky to the touch — in fact, all parts of this plant are sticky due to the thousands of glandular-tipped hairs that cover its surface. The sticky fluid is released from special cells that grow at the tip of each hair. Look through your hand lens and you'll see tiny drops of shiny liquid adhering to the hairs. Botanists feel that such stickiness along the stalk helps prevent ants and other poor pollinators from reaching the flowers, thus leaving the job to more effective pollinators, like bees and flies.

Take a moment to look closely at the reproductive parts. Notice the lovely and delicate structure of the stamen. Look too at the rounded stigma, with its tiny depression in the center that helps hold the pollen grains securely in place. As you look at the different flowers in the park, check out the stigma and stamens of each to see how they differ, and how they are similar. You might ask yourself how these differences and similarities help in the process of pollination.

Many of you may know Pinedrops best by its rounded seed pods and tall stalks that remain standing for several seasons. It is most noticeable contrasted against a winter's blanket of snow. The seeds produced in the rounded pods are microscopic and are released in the fall by the thousands, with each one carrying a little sail that allows it to catch the wind to be distributed far from the parent plant. This seed shape gave rise to its name, *pterospora*, which in Greek means "winged seed."

The Woodland Wintergreens

Donner Park's woods support several members of the Wintergreen Family. These are perennial, woody herbs that have leathery, basal, evergreen leaves. Even though the wintergreens have leaves which carry out photosynthesis, they also gain nutrients from decaying matter through a saprophytic relationship with soil fungi. This relationship is similar to that of the Pinedrops.

The wintergreen's 4 to 5 petals are separate at the

base and surround the 10 stamens. Typically, the single pistil angles outward, as it protrudes below the corolla. Wintergreen flowers are generally pink or white and grow along the top of a, usually, leafless stem. If you're one who loves detail, look at an anther with your hand lens and you'll find a small terminal pore from which the pollen is released.

One of the prettiest members of this family is the Bog Wintergreen *(Pyrola asarifolia)*. In mid-June through July, it blooms in satiny dark pink at the base of trees and willows, all along the trail near the edge of the lake. Its basal leaves are a leathery, deep green with slightly toothed, wavy edges. Notice how the pistil sweeps downward and outward, out of the way of the anthers. If this plant is new to you, be sure to come here to make its acquaintance, because it's a rare sight to see it growing in such profusion and to find it in so accessible an area.

Look also for the partly parasitic plants of the One-sided *(Pyrola secunda)* and the White-veined Wintergreens *(P. picta)*. They are well represented in the park so this is a good place to compare the different species.

You may also find a special form of the Pyrola picta, *(Pyrola picta, forma aphylla)* that is parasitic, for it lacks green leaves. It has gorgeous light pink flowers (or sometimes white) near the top of the stem, with purple, scale-like leaves along its stem. This plant is rare at this higher elevation, but it was found by Evelyn Bennett in her yard in the Donner Tract, only a few blocks away. So, though I have not found it in the park, you might still want to keep your eyes open for it. It commonly grows in woodland areas of the Coast Range, Montana and British Columbia.

When walking among the conifers, also look near the base of the trees for the small, nodding Wintergreen flowers of Prince's Pine *(Chimaphila menziesii)*. The plants grow only about 4 to 6 inches tall, with lance-like to oval-shaped leaves that are sharply toothed. Be sure to take the time to look closely at its unusual flower; the green, glistening ovary and stigma are surrounded by prominent anthers and are backdropped by satiny petals.

Its name, *chimaphila*, comes from Greek and means "lover of winter," for its leathery leaves stay green all winter long under the snow. This plant is also called Pipsissewa, which is Cree Indian for "its juice breaks it into small pieces." In the past, this plant was used to break up gallstones. The leaves of certain species of pipsissewa were also once added as an ingredient in root beer.

Meadows of Camas Lilies
In about 3/4 mile from the park entry booth, you will find two small meadows that link up, end to end. Where you'll find the gorgeous blue-purple flowers of Leichtlin's Camas Lily *(Camassia leichtlinii)* blooming in late-May through June.

As is typical of members of the Lily Family, it has parallel veined, grass-like leaves and flower parts in increments of 3. Several flowers bloom along each stalk, while the uppermost buds tightly bunch together at the top of the stem in gorgeous shades of iridescent blue.

As discussed on the Sagehen East hike, the camas lily was important to the Washos, for its beauty, as well as for its delicious bulb. This species is named in honor of Max Leichtlin who lived in the late-1800's to early-1900's, in Germany, and who introduced many new plant variations to horticulture.

Leichtlin's
Camas
Lily

The Flowers of Vernal Pools
As you walk through the meadows, look for small vernal pools that usually dry up by early-June, turning the bottoms into mud-cracked depressions. There you will find the minuscule, white flowers of the Least Navarretia *(Navarretia minima)* blooming above needle-like leaves. Near them will be the exquisite, lavender flowers of Porterella *(Porterella carnosula)*. Both of these plants are consistently found in Tahoe's vernal pools. These are shallow depressions that catch the early snow melt

91

in spring to form seasonal pools, which then dry up by early-summer. As soon as the water recedes, it is followed by these little belly plants that carpet the ground with fragrance and color.

After exploring the meadows, you may want to return to the lake's edge and continue on to the sandy beaches of China Cove, that look out across Donner's waters to the mountains of Donner Pass. The Cove is 1.2 miles from the entry booth along the level trail. The sunsets here are lovely, especially on a cloudy day, so be sure to linger until early-evening, if you have the time.

A Visitor to Nature?

Donner Park is lovely, but in going to a park, we usually feel like visitors, and so we often experience less Nature-connection than we would in the wild. Of course, it is we who set up this separation. The Donner Park's Nature Trail brochure welcomes us but then goes on to say, "Here, man is a visitor to Nature's home." Though this was done to remind us to be sensitive to the plants and animals in the park, it is upsetting to me, because man is never a visitor in Nature's home. Each of us is as much a child of Nature as are the plants and animals, and thus this park is our home too. (It is interesting to note that the word human comes from humus, which means earth. Our own name is a reminder of our earth-connection.)

I hope in time we will not need to label ourselves as visitors to remember to be gentle, for such gentleness will be natural when we return to our Nature-connection through re-education and immersion. Then an understanding and reverence for all life will flow naturally through our people, and we will begin to heal the damage we have done to the earth.

• Marsh Marigold
  (*Caltha howellii*)
• Sierra Rein Orchid
  (*Habenaria dilatata*)
• Great Polemonium
  (*Polemonium caeruleum*)
• Bog Saxifrage
  (*Saxifraga oregana*)
• Northern Bog Violet
  (*Viola nephrophylla*)
• Brewer's Bittercress
  (*Cardamine breweri*)
• Marchantia
  (*Marchantia polymorpha*)
• Low Phacelia
  (*Phacelia humilis*)
• Yellow Lupine
  (*Lupinus arbustus*,
  ssp. *calcaratus*)

Sagehen Creek West

A Boggy Meadow of Marsh Marigolds and Orchids

Level stroll 1/4 mile	
Trail elevation 6200'	
Topo map USGS Truckee, Calif.	
Wildflower Season May through July	

A long upper Sagehen Creek, one could easily spend an entire day leisurely exploring the rich variety of flowers that grow in its boggy seep gardens. Marsh marigolds and rein orchids bloom white in June, while polemonium, lupine and elephant heads rise purple and pink out of the grasses in July. This is a place to come to paint or photograph; its proximity to the road makes equipment carrying easy. It is also a magical place to enjoy with children to experience the cycles of a flower community from spring through fall.

Trailhead Directions

Heading east on Interstate 80 out of Truckee, take the Sierraville exit, which is just past the downtown Truckee exit, and head north over the freeway onto Highway 89 toward Quincy. (Just after crossing over the freeway, you'll spot the Truckee Ranger Station on your left, where you can pick up maps of the Tahoe National Forest.) After driving about 7.4 miles,

Marsh Marigold

93

you'll cross Sagehen Creek where, on your right, you'll see a dirt turnout. You may park there or along the shoulder. The mosquitos can be annoying, so be sure to bring an herbal repellent, like Green Ban.

The "Trail" Begins

After parking, cross to the west side of the highway. Since there is no trail, just make your own way to the gardens by walking along the south side of Sagehen Creek, through the lodgepole pines. Within a few

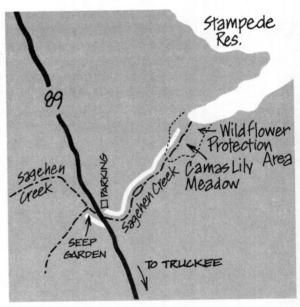

hundred feet, you will arrive at the gardens. At this point, wander uphill along the tiny tributaries. To minimize plant damage, try to stay out of the most boggy areas by walking along logs, or on rocks, when possible.

Exploring the Gardens in Spring

Spring is a time to rejoice in the annual renewal of life, and Sagehen Creek is a lovely place to begin the celebration. Its meadows become lush in late-May, and by early-June, hundreds of Marsh Marigolds (*Caltha howellii*) come into full bloom. The marigold is a gorgeous plant with large, 2 inch wide, shiny white blossoms, housing clusters of orange-yellow stamens and pistils. It grows 1 to 2 feet tall with glossy-green, basal leaves that are rounded and wavy-edged. You will sometimes find it standing in water, seemingly undaunted by the ice crystals that formed on the water's surface during the night.

If you look for the flower in bud, you'll see that it is enclosed in white. In most flowers, the sepals are green, but in the marigold, they are white. Many Buttercup Family members, like the marigold, lack true petals. Thus, instead of being green, the sepals are shaped and colored like petals to attract insects. Its genus name, *Caltha,* comes from the Greek word kalathos which means "a goblet" and refers to the flowers in bud.

Several weeks later, as the marigolds begin to fade, other patches of white appear in the gardens from the tiny, 1/2 inch long flowers of the Sierra Rein Orchid *(Habenaria dilatata).* They grow tightly clustered along the 1 to 3 foot tall stem. I know of no other meadow at Tahoe where this orchid grows so abundantly.

Look closely and you will see that each little flower is made up of 2 upper petals and 1 sepal, that combine to form a hood-like structure, typical of orchids. The lower petal, which is long and thin, acts as an insect landing pad, as it hangs downward between the 2 spreading sepals. An even longer, and thinner, nectar spur curves downward from the back of the lower petal, resembling a horse's rein. It is from this "rein" that its genus name, *Habenaria,* is derived — *habena* being Latin for "rein." *Dilatata* means "spread out" and refers to the widening of the lower petal near the flower's center.

The Exotic Orchids

Most people think of orchids as rare, exotic flowers found only in the tropics. Exotic they are, with complex shapes ranging in size from 30 inches to the tiniest of individuals, but rare they are not, for the

Sierra Rein Orchid

95

orchid belongs to one of the world's largest flower families with close to 35,000 species. While most orchids do live in the tropics, others live in various environments throughout the world, with at least 5 species found at Tahoe.

Orchids come in unusual shapes, most likely because of a closely evolving relationship with pollinators. Many orchids have come to rely on only a single insect for pollination, causing interesting adaptations in both flower and insect. The rein orchid may have a long nectar spur for its tiny size, but imagine the Angraecum Orchid in Madagascar which has a 12 inch long spur with the nectar residing in the tip. When Darwin first came upon this flower, he theorized that there must be an insect with a 12 inch proboscis that pollinates it. It seems logical, but botanists of the time laughed at him, until its pollinator was found — a moth with a proboscis of over 12 inches. Imagine the young moth trying to "learn" how to uncoil such a long "tongue" and getting confused about how to put it back! Just think of all the important events that we know nothing of, that occur on the world's stage each day.

Orchids have also evolved even more bizarre shapes. As the German botanist Breyneirs wrote in the 17th Century, "If nature ever showed her playfulness in the formation of plants, this is visible in the most striking way among orchids...They take on the form of little birds, lizards...of man and woman, of a melancholy toad, or a chattering monkey." One orchid has evolved to where its flower looks and smells like a female fly. The orchid is pollinated by the male fly, apparently in a mistaken attempt to mate with a female. In some cases, botanists have even found that the flower is preferred by the male fly!

Other orchids create an amazing array of scents. There are at least 50 aromatic compounds found among members of the Orchid Family. Out of these compounds, hundreds of variations are created, with each species concocting its own scent. Some orchids duplicate certain scents or change their fragrance during different times of the day. Some may smell like rotting meat to attract flies, while others change their daytime fragrance to a new one in the evening to attract the pollinators that are out. Sometimes the scents are original, and in other cases, they may duplicate those of the rose or other flowers. Some scents last but a short time, others longer. Some orchids will wait as long as 3 months in full flower to be pollinated, after which time the scent disappears and the plant's energy turns toward seed production.

Other Members of the Meadow

In early-July, the Great Polemonium *(Polemonium caeruleum)* comes into bloom with blue-purple flowers on stems that are about 3 feet tall. Alongside it, look for the equally tall stems and tight, white clusters of Bog Saxifrage *(Saxifraga oregana)*. You'll also find the pink flowers of Alpine Shooting Stars *(Dodecatheon alpinum)* and Elephant Heads *(Pedicularis groenlandica)*. These flowers are discussed on other hikes but grow in colorful abundance here.

As you search the meadow for other treasures, be sure to look down low among the grasses, especially between the large Marsh Marigold patch and the Elephant Heads. There, in July, you will find the parasitic plants of the Naked Broomrape *(Orobanche uniflora)*, hidden in the grass. A single, tubular flower sits upon each stem, that is about an inch tall. Its short stem seems too small for the size of the lavender-to-creamy yellow flower that blooms upon it.

Look too, in the same area in June, for a little, blue-purple violet. This is the only place that I've found it at Tahoe. It is called the Northern Bog Violet *(Viola nephrophylla)* and blooms with kidney-shaped leaves that are scalloped along the edges. Its petals are densely covered with hairs at the base, and its 3 lower petals are marked in dark veins. It may be distinguished from the Western Long-spurred Violet *(Violet adunca)*, that we saw on the Loch Leven hike by its small nectar spur and by its

Naked Broomrape

97

lack of leaf-bearing stems. (Its leaves come directly out of the root stalks.)

Not far from the violet, in July, you'll find another purple flower, the Large-leaved Lupine (*Lupinus polyphyllus*). Its 30 or more small flowers grow densely along the stalk and rise on stems that can be 3 to 4 feet tall. Each little flower is made up of a shape distinctive of pea flowers. The broad upper petal is called the banner, the 2 small side petals are called wings, and the 2 bottom petals are fused together at the tip forming a shape like a canoe, called the keel. The keel houses the reproductive parts, the stamens and the pistil.

If you spend a few minutes sitting by a group of lupines, several will probably be visited by their main pollinator, the bee. As the bee busily searches a flower for nectar, it lands on the keel. Its weight pushes the keel down, allowing the long, stiff, curved sheath of stamens and pistil to pop out, jabbing its belly with pollen. See if you can observe this for yourself and then do what the bee does. Push down the keel so the reproductive parts pop out and see if you can determine which are the stamens and which is the pistil.

After pollination, the flowers form fuzzy pea pods that are over an inch long. The seeds are poisonous to us, but Native Americans knew how to process them to safely brew them into a medicinal tea. It has also been reported that chipmunks, squirrels and deer enjoy them with no apparent side affects. According to an amazing report, scientists several years ago found 10,000 year old lupine seeds frozen in the Arctic ice. They planted the seeds, and they germinated and grew!

The large, palmate leaves of the lupine fan out gracefully beneath the flower stalks — all lupines carry this palmate leaf-form. The species' name, *polyphyllus*, comes from the Greek words *phyllon* for "leaf" and *poly* for "many" which aptly describes its growth. Native Americans also gathered and ate the leaves and stems of this plant, which are reported to

pea
flower
close-up

be safe before flowering but poisonous afterward.

The genus name, *Lupinus*, comes from the Latin *lupus* for "wolf." The Romans named this group of plants lupus because they often found lupines growing in depleted soils. Because of this, they believed that the lupine devoured soil nutrients from the soil, like a wolf devours its food. But rather than depleting the soil, the reverse is true. Lupines are nitrogen-fixing plants. Through bacteria in small swellings on the lupine's roots, nitrogen in the air in the soil is converted into a form of nitrogen that the plant can assimilate. Through this process, lupines and other members of the Pea Family actually enrich the soil with nitrogen. (Experienced gardeners use these plants to naturally enrich their soils, instead of using damaging, chemical fertilizers.)

After leaving the lupines, hike along the edges of the various small creeks that flow through the boggy area. While you do so, look for the blue flowers of Brooklime (*Veronica americana*) growing along the soggy banks. The plants grow up to about 2 feet tall and have large, lance-like leaves. Its 4 petals form a small, 1/4 inch wide saucer and its throat is bright yellow. It has only 2 stamens and a prominent, though tiny, ovary out of which rises the single pistil.

If you look alongside the Brooklime, right in the creek, you'll find the 4-petaled, white flowers of Brewer's Bittercress (*Cardamine breweri*). It's easy to identify by its pinnate leaves that end in a large, oval-to-rounded, terminal leaflet.

The Intriguing Marchantia

Perhaps the most interesting plant you'll come upon in the small creeks in the meadow is one that doesn't flower. It is a member of a primitive group of plants, called Bryophytes, that appeared on the earth long before the flowering plants. To find this plant, which is named Marchantia (*Marchantia polymorpha*), search the banks of the creeks for a leathery leaf that grows flat against the ground in mats among the mosses.

In late-June through July, you will find that some

of the leaves support a small structure about 1/2 inch tall that looks like a tiny palm tree. Others support a flat disk that sits atop a short stem. You'll also find tiny, bowl-shaped objects sitting on the surface of some of the leaves.

These structures are the means by which the Marchantia reproduces itself, in an interesting two part process. The little "palm tree" rising out of the leaf is the female part that produces female germ cells, while the disk structure produces male germ cells. After it is released from the disk, the male germ cell swims through the water, driven by tiny cilia, to reach a female cell within the "palm tree." It must reach the female within about an hour or all is lost, for after an hour it is no longer viable. When the female cell is receptive, part of the palm tree droops close to the leaf surface and releases a mucilaginous substance that is very attractive to the male cell. Because this process depends upon the male swimming to the female, these plants are found only in wet areas. After the male and female cells fuse, the cells divide to form a new little structure that produces spore. The spores then form the leaf-shaped plants that gave rise to the "palm tree" and disk, and the cycle is repeated anew.

The Marchantia also reproduces itself asexually in two ways: leaf tissue may break off to form new plants, or a little bowl-shaped structure on the leaf surface, called a gemmae cup, may produce small disks of green tissue at the base of the cup. A raindrop hitting the tissue, knocks it out of the cup, and it begins a new life separate from the parent plant. These little cups usually appear several weeks after the palm tree and disk structures, in late-July or August.

Leaving the Meadow to Visit Drier Areas

As you wander out of the wet meadow into the drier areas past the lodgepole pines, look for wild strawberries, yellow cinquefoils and the brownish, nodding flowers of

Marchantia

Spotted Mountain Bells *(Fritillaria atropurpurea)*. These flowers can be best appreciated if you take the time to look closely at them. This is also true of the purple Low Phacelia *(Phacelia humilis)* that grows in sandy, open flats just beyond the trees. It only rises about 1/2 to a few inches about the ground. Its little, coiled flower heads make a mass of color on the sandy soils.

If you wander uphill beyond the phacelias, you may find a plant that is rare at Tahoe. It is a subspecies of the Crest Lupine and is called *Lupinus arbustus, ssp. calcaratus*. It is distinct because, unlike the other lavender to blue lupines at Tahoe, its flowers are yellow. It grows beneath the lodgepoles in dry soil and is striking against the tan of the bark.

As you stand among the flowers at Sagehen Creek, you may want to make a note to return to this area frequently during the season to follow the changes in the plant community. If you do so, you'll find that the display changes about every two weeks as new plants come into the height of their glory, while others fade from bloom as they busily begin making seed.

The Sagehen Field Station

After leaving the meadow, you may wish to follow Sagehen Creek upstream, before returning to your car. If you were to follow the creek for several miles, you would eventually reach the University of California Research Station. It was begun by Starker Leopold, who was the son of Aldo Leopold, the author of *A Sand County Almanac*. Aldo, who observed Nature from his farm in Sand County, once wrote,

> "Like winds and sunsets, wild things were taken for granted until progress began to do away with them. Now we face the question whether a still higher standard of living is worth its cost in things natural, wild, and free. For us of the minority, the opportunity to see geese is more important than television, and the chance to find a pasque-flower is a right as inalienable as free speech."

"Progress" that destroys our right to see wild geese in free flight or to marvel at a pasque-flower in spring is not true progress. It is, in reality, a tragedy for it is a taking away of those things in life that bring us the greatest peace and opportunity for reflection. It is through such quiet moments that man regains his perspective and returns to the right path.

Each of us must decide what is most important, what kind of life we want to live and what costs we are no longer willing to incur. If we set our minds to it, we can have a healthy environment and true progress, for the universe is abundant. The important thing is that we must make a choice in our own lives to live more simply and gently on the land. It is a law of Nature that we cannot do as we have been doing; we cannot take more than we give. When we live in balance, we live far happier lives.

At the research station students and instructors live in gentle balance with the land, conducting studies on the flora and fauna of the Northern Sierra. Students, and other scientists, come from all over the world to gather here in the summer to conduct research and exchange ideas.

On your way back to Truckee you might want to visit the Donner Camp Historical Site. We discussed the story of the Donner Party on the previous hike. The blackened tree, where the Donners built their lean-to and campfire the first night, still stands in silent witness to their struggle to survive. The site is 4 1/2 miles south of Sagehen Creek on the east side of Highway 89.

- Mountain Rose
  (Rosa woodsii)
- Water Buttercup
  (Ranunculus aquatilis)
- Rocky Mountain Butterweed
  (Senecio cymbalarioides)
- Sand Corn
  (Zigadenus paniculatus)
- Plumas Ivesia
  (Ivesia sericoleuca)
- Quamash Camas Lily
  (Camassia quamash)
- Blue-eyed Grass
  (Sisyrinchium idahoense)
- Alpine Shooting Star
  (Dodecatheon alpinum)
- Self Heal
  (Prunella vulgaris)
- Hairy Paintbrush
  (Castilleja pilosa)

Sagehen Creek East

A Sea of Blue Camas Lilies

𝕏𝕏

One day	
One way 2 miles	
Trail begins/ends 6200'/5900'	
Net loss/total loss 300'/300'	
Topo map USGS Truckee, Calif.	
Wildflower Season May through July	

The Sagehen Creek East hike begins among fragrant wild roses, that bloom in July, and ends in a solid sea of blue from the camas lilies that come into flower in June. In a reservoir beyond the lilies in early-summer, Canada Geese raise their young, while nearby in the meadow, bluebirds dart about catching insects on the wing. The trail passes ponds, created by beaver dams and leads to a small, flower-filled meadow that will be protected forever from the grazing of sheep. In the fall, Sagehen Creek is a place to come to enjoy the yellows, browns and reds of changing leaves and to daydream in thick, grassy meadows.

Trailhead Directions

See directions for previous hike. Park on the shoulder, on the east side of the road, or in the dirt turnout. From there, the trail follows the north shore of the creek.

Mountain Rose

103

The Trail Begins

The trail begins on the north, wooded side of the river by shrubs of fragrant Mountain Roses *(Rosa woodsii)*. These exquisitely simple flowers usually

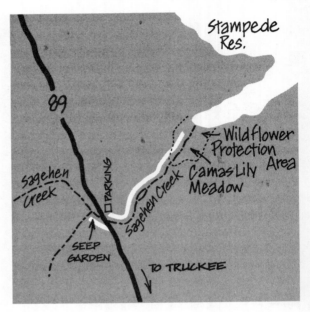

come into bloom in July with pink, feminine blossoms that seem to float among the leaves. Each flower is decorated with over 60 stamens, with golden anthers that cluster around the many pistils in the flower's center.

The thorny branches of these 3 to 4 foot tall shrubs discourage animals and people from gathering the flowers. The Warm Springs Indians in Oregon called the wild rose, "Ska pash-wee" which meant "Mean old lady she sticks you!"

If you come here in the fall, you will find the roses replaced by fleshy, red fruits called rose hips. These fruits house the ripening seeds and, because they are high in Vitamin C, they were an important part of the diet of native peoples. The coastal indians combined the hips with dried salmon to add nutrition and interest to their daily diet of fish. The Washos, who came to Tahoe's meadows each summer, gathered them for tea or ate them raw. Rose hip tea is readily available in grocery stores, while dried rose hips can be purchased at many health food stores and combined with apples to make a delightful jam.

A Representative of an Old Family
The Rose Family is a large and diverse family with over 100 genera and 3,000 species worldwide. The 22 genera in the Sierra include both strawberries and thimbleberries which have sweet, edible fruit. Peaches, cherries, blackberries and apples are also members of the Rose Family. The common characteristics of this family are 5 petals with many stamens and pistils.

Such large numbers of stamens and pistils usually mean a plant is very old on the evolutionary scale. (See the Pole Creek hike for a discussion of this.) In looking at a rose, we can appreciate its simple, but lovely, structure and honor its longevity, for it was blooming on this earth hundreds of thousands of years before grasses, lilies, orchids or most other flowers and still is successfully doing so.

If you rush out to count the petals of the roses that you come across, don't be confused by the commercial ones for their petal number has been increased by horticulturalists. Somewhere along the line these specialists figured out how to stimulate the plant, causing it to create petals from plant tissue that normally would have gone into the production of stamens. These new species of multi-petaled flowers were bred to make a "more beautiful" and saleable product. Beauty is subjective, but I feel there is no rose, more beautiful, with its simplicity and honest purity, than a wild one. Before you walk on, close your eyes and bury your nose in the sweet fragrance of a blossom — your spirits will soar.

After enjoying the roses, wander over to the creek and search its banks for the white, floating blossoms of the Water Buttercup (*Ranunculus aquatilis*). Its flowers bloom on a plant that is as primitive as the rose. Its brown, linear leaves lie beneath the surface of the water, undulating in the current. They can be found several hundred feet east of the cement culvert that runs under Highway 89. This creek is home to the largest colonies of these flowers that I have ever seen.

The Intricate Flowers of Squaw Carpet

As you continue along the trail close to the creek, you will pass through wooded areas blanketed with the tiny, bluish flowers of Squaw Carpet *(Ceanothus prostratus)*. This plant grows on pine-needled, forested floors and roots at the branches, forming dense mats that are sometimes as much as 50 feet across.

These mats are so dense, and the little holly-like leaves so prickly, that squirrels and other animals have trouble penetrating them to search for seeds. Because of this, the plant acts as a nursery for conifer seeds, protecting them from animals and keeping them cool and moist until they germinate. Look closely and you will usually find 20 or 30 little seedlings rising above the leaves.

The Squaw Carpet's blue flowers, which bloom in May or June, are lovely when viewed through a hand lens. Their unusual, spoon-shaped petals radiate outward from a bowl-shaped center, as is typical of members of the Ceanothus or Wild Lilac Family.

Flowers among the Grasses

After returning to the trail, follow the stream as it winds its way past grassy banks and small meadows. As you wander through the grass, look for the bright-yellow, daisy-like flowers of the Rocky Mountain Butterweed *(Senecio cymbalarioides)*. We have seen two other members of this genus on our other hikes (the Arrowleaf Senecio and the Single-stemmed Senecio), and although this flower has the senecio look, its blossoms tend to be more tidy than the other two species, and it only grows up to about 8 to 12 inches tall. Its basal leaves are toothed, with smaller leaves growing along the stem.

Other flowers also bloom in the grasses from June

Squaw Carpet

through early-August, among them penstemons, paintbrushes and lupines. Look too for the yellow mustard flowers of a plant called Wintercress *(Barbarea orthoceras)*. Its 1/2 inch wide flowers bloom in small clusters at the top of a stem that is about 2 feet tall and are soon followed by linear seed pods, that spread outward and upward. Its leaves are helpful in identifying the plant. They are pinnate (arranged in parallel rows along the stem) with a larger, rounded terminal leaflet. To key in on this particular species, look closely at the sepals. They are a greenish yellow, and two of them are swollen at the base.

Look also for the Water Cress *(Rorippa nasturtium-aquaticum)* that can be found in a small tributary in this first meadow, several hundred yards beyond the parking turnout. Its 1/4 inch wide flowers have 4 petals and grow in a compact cluster at the tips of the stems. Since the stems root at the nodes, the plant grows thickly, almost choking the creek in some areas. It rises about a foot to 18 inches above the muddy bottom. Its pinnate leaves have rounded leaflets that grow densely along the stem.

Flowers among the Sagebrush

Soon the willows become so dense in the meadow that you will probably want to return to the trail. As you pass into dryish areas, look for the small, lavender flowers of Low Phacelia *(Phacelia humilis)*. They grow in tight coils that look like caterpillars. They bloom above tiny, oval- to lance-shaped leaves and in some areas carpet the sandy floor in masses of purple.

An even tinier purple flower, the Violet Allophyllum *(Allophyllum violaceum)*, grows in the same area with the phacelia. Its color is an exquisite, deep violet-blue. If you spot this, you have excellent eyes. Its flower is only about 1/4 to 1/8 inch wide and grows on plants usually only a few inches tall. The herbage is covered with short hairs, and the leaves are narrow and often have 2 lobes at the base — a helpful way to identify members of this genus.

Another plant that grows in similar dry areas, that is larger and easier to locate, is the Sand Corn (*Zigadenus paniculatus*). It grows about 18 inches tall, with grass-like leaves. Its flowers are yellowish white and grow in clusters near the top of the stems. Look for it scattered among the sagebrush. If you examine one of the flowers, you will find a tiny, green nectar gland at the base of each petal and sepal. this plant is closely related to the Death Camas (*Zigadenus venenosus*) that grows in Shirley Canyon.

Trailside Beaver Ponds

As you continue along the trail, you will soon arrive at downed aspens, knawed willows and flooded areas — all indicators that Mountain Beaver (*Castor canadensis*) are nearby. These animals are not native to the high, eastern Sierra. They were introduced from the Central Valley by trappers in the 1800's and can drastically alter the environment, when concentrated in small areas. To consume the inner bark and to gather branches for their dens, they chop down large quantities of cottonwoods, aspens and willows. In the building of their dens, beavers dam up creeks, forming ponds that flood out and kill the surrounding vegetation.

The dens are located near the top of the large pile of sticks and branches that form the dam. There they raise their young and find protection from predators and the winter's cold. The living space may be up to 5 feet in diameter and is entered through one or more hidden, underwater entrances.

Beavers mate in late-winter and usually pair for life. They bear an average litter of 4 to 5 kits three months later in early-spring. The young are only about 5 to 6 inches long at birth, but they are born with their eyes wide open, fully covered with fur and are ready to take to the water inside the lodge within 24 hours. Within two days they have learned to dive and within a week are confident swimmers ready to leave the protection of the lodge. With their webbed feet and powerful bodies, beavers are strong swimmers. After six weeks the young are weaned and begin taking part in the family's activities. They usually stay with the parents until their second year, after which they wander off to start lives of their own.

Beavers are not often seen during the day because they are primarily nocturnal, coming out at dusk or in the early evening. This would be a wonderful place to visit on a warm summer evening, under a full moon, to quietly watch the beavers at work and play.

After passing the dams, the trail leaves the creek and then crosses an old fence that was once used to contain cattle. When the trail becomes faint, confusing or just disappears altogether, continue walking parallel to the creek and within about two miles you will arrive at the big meadow near Stampede Reservoir.

Camas Lilies as Far as the Eye Can See

This huge, open meadow gives rise to thousands of blue-purple Quamash Camas Lilies (*Camassia quamash*) that usually bloom from late-May through mid-June. It is the largest solid field of camas lilies that I know of in all of Tahoe. In the past before grazing was allowed, such flowers must have been a common sight in meadows throughout Tahoe. I feel we've lost something very precious by turning these fragile, wet areas into grazing land.

For 4,000 years native peoples came to such meadows at Tahoe each spring after the snows had melted. The Washos, of western Nevada, continued their annual migration up until as recently as 1920. Whenever I stand in this meadow, I recall with nostalgia that it was not long ago that the Washos still came together here to gather the camas lily's bulbs. Then the meadow was alive with the laughter of women and children digging up the bulbs with long pointed sticks.

After the bulbs were gathered, they were roasted. Often a festival followed the gathering with everyone taking part in the celebration. The men were in charge of collecting the wood and green branches, and the women brought in mounds of washed bulbs. Large pits 20 feet in diameter were dug, and the wood was placed inside and burned until it formed hot coals. Green branches of alder were then placed in the pit and topped with the bulbs, ashes and hot coals. After several layers, the entire mixture was covered with branches, leaves and grass and left to bake for over a day. After pulling the bulbs out of the earthen oven and while they were still warm, the black bark was stripped off, and the bulbs were hand pressed into sweet cakes, with the fragrant aroma of vanilla and the consistency of maple sugar.

I don't suggest that anyone try to roast and eat camas lilies because of their growing scarcity and because there is another flower, the Death Camas (*Zigadenas venenosus*), that has a poisonous bulb closely resembling that of the camas lily. It grows at Tahoe in similar wet environments.

The camas lily is common throughout the west; it once covered thousands of acres in Idaho with its sea of blue flowers. Meriwether Lewis wrote in his journal on June 12, 1806, "...the quawmash is now in blume and from the colour of its bloom at a short distance it resembles lakes of fine clear water, so complete in this deseption that on first sight I could have swoarn it was water."

The Nez Perce of Idaho gathered the lily and gave it its name, quamash, which is their word for "sweet." The lily was a main staple in their diet and vital to their survival. Chief Joseph went to war in the late 1870's against the early settlers, when their pigs began to uproot and eat the bulbs threatening to destroy what, for thousands of years, had been a mainstay of the Nez Perces' diet.

A Colorful Lesson in Basic Botany
This meadow is a wonderful place to bring children to introduce them to the beauty of wildflowers and to basic botany, for the flowers of the camas lily are lovely and large, and their parts are "color-coded."

The star-shaped flowers grow along stems up to about 3 feet tall, with 20 to 30 flowers on each stem. If you are new to botany, stop and look closely at the flowers; it will help you to understand the process of fertilization.

Most flowers are composed of three basic structures: the sepals, which are normally green and enclose the flower in bud, the petals, which attract insects, and the male and female reproductive parts, which sit in the flower's center.

This plant deviates a bit from the normal pattern in that its sepals are not green but rather are the same shape and color as the petals, so the flower appears to have 6 petals. This is typical of the Lily Family which helps it to put on a greater show of color to attract insects. Look at the flowers in bud and you will see that, instead of being green, the sepals are a gorgeous iridescent blue-purple.

The reproductive parts are housed in the flower's center. The female reproductive part is called a pistil and is composed of a stigma, style and ovary. The ovary is the lime-green, oval object nestled in the flower's center. The ovary produces the ovules (unfertilized eggs) which, after fertilization, become seeds. The light-lavender style rises out of the ovary and is topped with the 3-lobed, lavender stigma. It is the stigma that receives the pollen for fertilization.

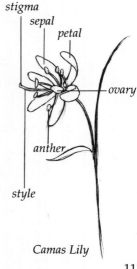

Camas Lily

The stamen, or male part, is composed of the anther and filament. As in humans, the male is simpler but just as important! The anthers are easy to locate, because they are bright yellow and sit delicately hinged on the end of each filament. Anthers are little sacs that produce pollen and then burst when ripe to release the pollen grains.

Pollen is distributed from flower to flower by birds, insects or the wind. After finding its way to the stigma, the pollen germinates in a sticky fluid on the end of the stigma. It then sends a tube-like structure down the style to the ovary, with the style nurturing the tube as it grows downward. After penetrating the ovary, a sperm cell is released from the tip of the tube to unite with an ovule to form a fertilized egg or seed. As the ovary swells with ripening seeds, the petals and sepals twist around the ovary and finally drop off. Eventually the ovary bursts to release the seeds onto the soil to produce next year's plants.

It is amazing to me to realize, that although life on this planet takes on an incredible variety of complex shapes, colors and sizes, as it responds to its environmental and other survival needs, most life shares a similar method of reproduction. Why is it that plants and animals have taken on so many varied and intricate forms, while the process of reproduction in all life remains essentially the same? (Perhaps a good thing needn't be changed!)

Other Flowers of the Meadow

The camas lily is only one of a number of lovely life forms that lives in the meadow. The Water Plantain Buttercup *(Ranunculus alismaefolius)* flowers in late-May and early-June, sometimes forming fragrant carpets of solid yellow.

In late-June through July, many other plants bloom in the meadow. The belly flowers of navarretia, phlox and gilia bring tiny bits of color to the drying soil, while Meadow Penstemon *(Penstemon rydbergii)* creates large splotches of purple among the drying camas lilies.

A flower that I have found nowhere else at Tahoe, but in this meadow, is called the Plumas Ivesia *(Ivesia sericoleuca)*. It usually blooms in July in drying areas among the camas lilies. Its flowers vary from white to yellow and have 5 petals with numerous reproductive parts, but what is most noticeable about the plant are its pinnate leaves. The leaves are about 8 inches long and are divided into so many tiny leaflets, growing so compactly along the stem, that there is little space between them. The leaves spread out along the ground, while the flowers rise above them at the ends of the stems in loose clusters.

The Birds of Sagehen

After enjoying the meadow, wander toward Stampede Reservoir where you may hear the deep resonating honking of Canada Geese *(Branta canadensis)*. These extraordinary birds are one of the few animals that mate for life. They return to the lake to raise their young in June and July and to graze on the abundant grasses and seeds in the meadow. While most of the geese are feeding, several sentries will stand guard ready to sound a warning if they are approached too closely. When danger threatens, they all head for the water, with the goslings protected between each set of parents.

They are beautiful, intelligent birds. When I lived on Lake Tahoe, I often watched them play on a neighbor's boat house. One would sit in the water while its mate flapped to the pitched roof of the house. After sitting for a moment on the top of the roof, it would joyfully slide down into the water. I sat entranced, watching them take turns one sunny morning.

Canada Geese are the largest birds you'll see in the meadow, but be sure to keep your eyes open for Mountain Bluebirds *(Sialia currucoides)* flitting and darting as they catch insects in flight. The female is a nondescript brown and builds her nest in the holes of trees, while the male is a gorgeous vivid blue, with a soft blue chest.

If you are lucky, you will also hear the exquisitely beautiful song of a Red-winged Blackbird *(Agelaius phoeniceus)*. It is easy to identify by its liquid, gurgling notes that end with a trill and by the red mark on the upper part of its black wings. It breeds in marshes and along streams, where it forms a nest by weaving a cup out of the reeds and grasses, which it lashes to cat-tails, tules or other firm upright stems. The female is dark brown and spotted. She is rarely seen because she hides in the reeds, camouflaged to escape predators.

Sheep Grazing in the Sierra

As you approach the lake, you will spot a fenced-off area to the right that was put up by the Tahoe Chapter of the California Native Plant Society (with support from the statewide Native Plant Society). It is a wildflower protection and enjoyment area. Many people don't realize that cattle and sheep still graze in the Tahoe Sierra on private and Forest Service land. I had thought such grazing was a thing of the past until one day I came upon a devastated garden and a day later ran into the sheepherder near Pole Creek with a thousand head of sheep. The following year Sagehen was trampled by such a herd. After seeing the devastation, my friend and colleague, Laird Blackwell, and I decided to approach the Forest Service to work with them to try to set up protected areas to preserve these special gardens.

It began with a dream, but was finally realized after several years when the Truckee Ranger Station, under District Ranger Joanne Roubique, issued us a permit to set aside three protected areas — this one in Sagehen Meadow, one on a seep garden on Castle Peak and one in a lovely stream zone of Pole Creek.

John Muir Comes to Tahoe

Our dream was given shape by the generous donation of time by Lee Stetson, a talented and sensitive man, who came to Tahoe to give three benefit showings of his two plays "Conversations with a Tramp" and "Stickeen." After two years of steeping himself in John Muir's letters, books and journals and seven months of living in Yosemite Valley, Mr. Stetson wrote his first play, "Conversations with a Tramp." This one-man performance, portraying John Muir, his life and values has been described as a "riveting one-man theatrical tour de force" and indeed it is; don't miss it. He offers both plays in Yosemite Valley every year during the summer, neither of which should be missed.

Sheep grazing was an issue that greatly concerned John Muir, who saw its damage after he spent one summer in the Sierra as a contract sheep herder. It wrought such destruction in Yosemite in the 1860's that Muir spearheaded a drive to outlaw these "hoofed locusts," as he called them, from the valley. Hopefully, some day grazing will no longer be allowed on public lands in the Sierra; when that day comes, the fence will be torn down with great celebration!

A Garden Protected from Sheep

The wildflower protection area is a wonderful spot to spend a day relaxing and learning to key out flowers. (Norman F. Weeden's, *A Sierra Nevada Flora*, is the best Tahoe key.) To help you do this, I will run through a list of a few of the many plants that bloom here. Since I will only mention each flower briefly, be sure to pull out your botany reference book to identify the flower, if it is new to you. Then once you know what it is, you can practice using the key. This will help you to understand and learn the terminology, by comparing the book descriptions with the flowers right in front of you. There is a gate on the south-west corner. Late-June through mid-July is normally the height of the bloom.

After entering through the gate, (be sure to close it when you leave) look for the tiny, white flowers of Mountain Chickweed *(Stellaria longipes)* snuggled in the grass. This small perennial blooms with 5 petals that are so cleft to the base that it looks as if there were 10 linear petals beneath the bright red anthers.

Other "grass snugglers" are the delicately marked, violet flowers of Self Heal *(Prunella vulgaris)*. They bloom inside brownish purple bracts, on spikes that grow up to about 6 inches tall. Each little, tubular flower has 2 lips — one that is vertical and one that is 3-lobed, in a shape that looks like a little girl with 2 arms bent downward above her ragged skirt.

Just after entering the protection area, you may find the flowers of the Western Buttercup *(Ranunculus occidentalis)* with shiny, yellow petals on plants that grow up to about 3 feet tall. The rounded leaves,

Self Heal

115

which grow upright out of the stems, are 3-lobed and then lobed again along the edges. It is a smaller flower than the Water Plantain Buttercup, and its petals usually number 5. Look beneath the petals and you will find pointed, reflexed sepals.

Flowers in Wet Areas of the Meadow

As you approach the creek, look for the wet environment flowers of the Bog Mallow *(Sidalcea oregana)* that bloom pink, tightly clustered along the stalk. The mallows carry fused reproductive parts and bowl-shaped flowers, with white nectar lines on the petals.

Look also for the white flowers of the Sierra Rein Orchid *(Habenaria dilatata)* that grow densely along the stem. Near the orchids, you may find the lovely flowers of the Blue-eyed Grass *(Sisyrinchium idahoense)*. Each of its 6 blue-purple petals, which are actually 3 sepals and 3 petals, is marked with deep purple nectar lines, while the flower's center is bright yellow and surrounded by a purple ring.

The Swamp Onion *(Allium validum)* grows in the same wet environment. Its cluster of rose-red flowers sits atop solitary stems, that rise about 1 to 3 feet out of the soggy soil. Inhale its fragrance and you will know it is an onion.

At its side, you'll usually find both species of elephant heads *(Pedicularis groenlandica and P. attollens)*. The larger of the two is called Elephant Heads. Its pink flowers form a definite elephant shape, while the Little Elephant Heads are smaller, with flowers that look less like its name. This is a great place to compare the two species, as they are not usually found blooming together.

Alpine Shooting Stars *(Dodecatheon alpinum)* can be found lining the creek in a curving band of pink, while Seep-spring Monkeyflowers *(Mimulus guttatus)* grow in yellow profusion by the upper part of the creek.

If you kneel close to the creek, look for the delicate, blue flowers (and some in pink) of Brooklime

(Veronica americana). Its 4 petals form flowers that grow in loose, terminal clusters above lance-to-oval leaves that have serrated edges. Its 2 stamens and single style (which rises out of the yellow ovary) gracefully droop out of the center of the flower. Little nectar lines mark each petal.

A flower that is common in wet meadows at Tahoe is the Western Bistort *(Polygonum bistortoides)*. You can find it by looking for a round-to-oval head of small white flowers. Its fuzzy reproductive parts protrude beyond the petals and are topped by yellow anthers. The blossoms sit on sturdy stems that are about 2 feet tall, which support basal, lance-like leaves.

More color is brought into the meadow with the flowers of Giant Red Paintbrush *(Castilleja miniata)* that contrast intensely with the lush green grasses and leaves of other plants. Great Polemonium *(Polemonium caeruleum)* also grows among the grasses, with flowers that are a gorgeous blue-purple. The flower tube is yellow and gives rise to a protruding pistil surrounded by stamens with yellow anthers. Both plants are easy to spot, as they grow about 2 to 3 feet tall.

The tiniest flower you may find is the Least Navarretia *(Navarretia minima)*. Its white flower is only about 4 millimeters wide. Its leaf lobes are linear and spine tipped. These little annuals have flowers that sit in spiny, densely-bracted heads.

Flowers at the Meadow's Edge

In drier areas, look for the red-pink flowers of Copeland's Owl's Clover *(Orthocarpus copelandii)*. Each tubular flower is almost hidden in the colored bracts that sit upon stems with lance-like leaves. You will also find the early-June blooming, brown, primitive flowers of the Peony *(Paeonia brownii)*. In the same area look for the pink, star-shaped flowers of the Sierra Onion *(Allium campanulatum)* that form a loose umbel of 15 to 40 beautifully marked flowers in June and July.

My favorite dry environment flower in the enclosure is the Hairy Paintbrush *(Castilleja pilosa)*. I prefer to call it the Pink Sagehen Paintbrush, because it is such a lovely pastel shade of pink and "hairy" seems too harsh a word for a flower that is so soft and velvety. This plant used to be classified as an Orthocarpus or Owl's Clover, a genus very closely related to the Paintbrushes or Castillejas.

If you decide to practice keying out the flowers, I recommend that you carry a notebook to write down your own descriptions and that you sketch the flowers as you see them. This is the most thorough and enjoyable way to remember the flowers and the best way to appreciate their individuality as well as your own!

Mt. Rose

Exploring a True Alpine Garden

🚶🏕♿ (first 2 1/2 miles)

One day/overnight	
One way 6 miles	
Trail begins/ends 8840'/10,776'	
Net gain/total gain 1936'/2136'	
Topo map USGS Mt. Rose, Nv.	
Wildflower Season Late-June to September	

M t. Rose, at 10,776 feet, is the third highest peak at Tahoe and one of the few places in the Basin where one can experience a true alpine environment. The steep climb to the alpine community is preceded by a gentle trail, which meanders through dry hillsides of lupines, mule-ears and penstemon, and along creekside gardens of shoulder-high larkspur and ground-carpeting monkey flowers. Here the sunsets turn distant peaks golden and then rosy, while at your feet, green meadows lie moist and fragrant, as the late-afternoon shadows lengthen.

Trailhead Directions

Pick up the Mt. Rose Highway (#431) just outside of Incline Village and drive about 8 miles toward Reno (and just past Tahoe Meadows) to the chained-off dirt road and cinder block building, that sits up on the left hand side of the highway. There is plenty of parking on the shoulder alongside the road. If you

Highlighted Flowers

- Brewer's Lupine
  (*Lupinus breweri*)
- Woody-fruited
  Evening Primrose
  (*Oenothera xylocarpa*)
- Lewis' Monkeyflower
  (*Mimulus lewisii*)
- Alpine Gentian
  (*Gentiana newberryi*)
- Seep-spring Monkeyflower
  (*Mimulus guttatus*)
- Large-leaved Lupine
  (*Lupinus polyphyllus*)
- Alpine Buttercup
  (*Ranunculus eschscholtzii*)
- Alpine Gold
  (*Hulsea algida*)
- Showy Polemonium
  (*Polemonium pulcherrimum*)
- Cut-leaved Daisy
  (*Erigeron compositus*)

*Great
Polemonium*

119

can work your way past the gate, the logging road will accommodate wheel chairs. Although I recommend it only for those with strong arms and nubby tires, who are in good shape.

The Trail Begins

The trail begins on an old jeep road that passes beneath dusty, open, volcanic slopes of golden Mountain Mule-ears *(Wyethia mollis)* and Arrow-leaved Balsam Root *(Balsamorhiza sagittata),* red Wavy-leaved Paintbrush *(Castilleja applegatei)* and white and lav-

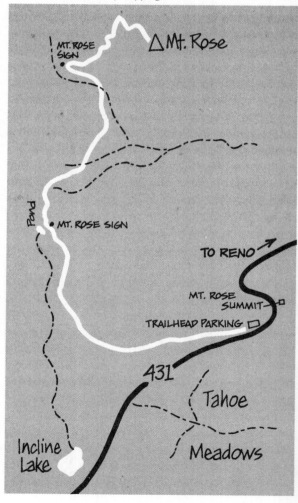

ender Anderson's Lupine *(Lupinus andersonii)*.

Several species of lupine grow along the trail, but Anderson's Lupine is one of the first you'll find. Its small, white-to-lavender flowers grow on stalks on shrub-like plants that line the trail. If you stay late on the mountain, and find yourself hiking out at dusk, you will have the pleasure of seeing its light-colored flowers softly glowing in the dark, as if to bid you a gentle farewell.

In this first mile of trail there are lovely views of Lake Tahoe, backdropped by Desolation Wilderness and other distant ranges, while down below in the trees rests small Incline Lake. If you hike this trail on a warm day in July or August, you will be treated to the minty fragrance of Sagebrush *(Artemisia tridentata)* and Mountain Pennyroyal *(Monardella odoratissima)*.

In late-July through August, the beautiful flowers of Fireweed *(Epilobium angustifolium)* bloom rose-pink on leafy stems that are about 3 feet tall. Its flower design is gorgeous: green, triangular sepals rise between each satiny pink petal. Its graceful, downy-white stigma, which protrudes prominently out of the flower's center, becomes 4-clefted when mature, with each cleft curling at the end. Check out the stigmas on several of the flowers and you will see that they are in different stages of receptiveness, and some (when the anthers are ripe) are even bent out of the way.

This graceful stigma is the conduit for fertilization of the ovules in the ovary. The ovary is inferior and easily located as a swelling in the stem below the petals. The term "inferior ovary" indicates where the ovary sits in relationship to the petals. An inferior ovary rests below where the petals join the stem, a superior one above the petal juncture. Knowing the ovary position will help you in keying out flowers.

Penstemons Decorate the Slopes

Also lining the trail in this area will be wonderful patches of the Showy Penstemon *(Penstemon speciosus)*. It blooms in July, or even into August, with tubular flowers that are yellow in bud and a deep blue-purple in bloom. A second species of penstemon blooms in the same area, at the same time, and is named Azure Penstemon *(P. azureus)*. Its blue-violet flowers are similar and also yellow in bud.

These two penstemons can be distinguished from one another by their growth pattern and leaf shape. The Showy Penstemon has linear leaves all along the stem and its flowers usually bloom on plants that send up only a few stems per plant cluster. If you stand back to compare them, you will see that the stems and leaves of the Showy Penstemon have a coarse, leathery look.

The Azure Penstemon has lance-like, lower leaves while its upper leaves are broadly oval and clasp the stem. Its flowers also have a different "feel." The Azure Penstemon has a more graceful look and each plant sends up many stems of flowers.

A Flower with the Fragrance of Coconut

After walking for about a mile, begin looking for a 4 inch wide, showy, yellow flower that casually rests on the dry slopes along the trail. Mt. Rose is the only known location at Tahoe for this eastern Sierran plant, the Woody-fruited Evening Primrose *(Oenothera xylocarpa)*.

When looking closely at the flower, which usually blooms throughout the month of July, be sure to inhale its coconut fragrance. This lovely blossom looks as if it belongs in Hawaii, rather than on a dry mountain slope, covered with snow for half the year. Several showy species of primroses, ranging in color from pink to yellow, are sold in local nurseries at Tahoe; they will add wonderful color and fragrance to dry areas of your garden, or heart!

As the name suggests, most evening primroses open in the evening. Their opening is short-lived for regardless of whether they are fertilized or not, by late afternoon of the next day they close forever, as a kind of "now or never flower." After closing, the 4 petals tightly twist around themselves and turn a

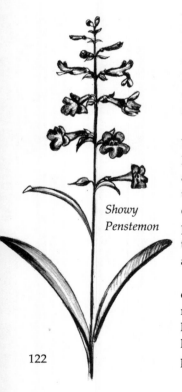

Showy Penstemon

deep red.

As with the Fireweed, its 4 petals and inferior ovary place it in the Evening Primrose Family. Its ovary can be located by the swelling in the stem just below the petals, close to the ground. Some evening primroses have ovaries so inferior that they are actually below ground. When the fertilized ovary swells and bursts, the seeds are immediately deposited into the soil. This may not be an effective dispersal mechanism, but it certainly guarantees that the seeds will find a supportive and immediate bed within which to germinate.

Carpets of Fragrant Lupine

As you leave the evening primroses behind, you will enter an environment of dense Lodgepole Pines *(Pinus contorta, var. murrayana)*. And carpeting the forest floor in July will be fragrant mats of Brewer's Lupine *(Lupinus breweri)*. This low-growing, blue-flowered lupine has a yellow or white spot on its banner. Its palmate leaves are silky-silver and form velvety mats among the pine needles. These carpets are the densest and most beautiful I have seen of this species at Tahoe and are a teasing suggestion of the beauty that lies ahead.

The Songs of Mountain Chickadees

As you wander through the forest for another 1/2 mile, there will be few flowers, other than the lupines, but you may be treated to the lilting songs of Mountain Chickadees *(Parus gambeli)*. In my early days of hiking, its sweet song welcomed me to the mountains; it was only later that I learned who sang with such joy.

The chickadee is a small, gray bird with black on the top of its head, chin and throat. A black stripe decorates the eyes. It flits from tree to tree searching for insects and splitting open lodgepole pine needles to eat the tiny larvae of needle-miner moths. You will often spot it hanging upside-down as it forages, seemingly just as comfortable in that position as it is right-side-up.

In April or May, chickadees form pairs, select their territory and begin building little nests in tree cavities made by woodpeckers. They line the bottom of their nests with feathers and animal hair, and as the female incubates the eggs, she is faithfully fed by the male. They are one of the few birds that remain in the woods throughout the winter, seeming to enjoy stormy days as happily as they do sunny ones.

Tom Brown, one of the most experienced survivalists in the country, once asked his Apache teacher, Stalking Wolf, to name his favorite animal. Instead of choosing a soaring eagle or a powerful bear, Stalking Wolf chose the chickadee, for as he said, the chickadee is cheerful and enthusiastic even on the dreariest of days. Because of its inner strength, he said, the chickadee is like a ray of sunshine in the darkest of storms and can be a symbol to us to radiate our strengths, even when the moment may seem bleak.

Gardens of Pink Lewis' Monkeyflowers
Within 1/2 mile, the trail again opens up to lovely views of Lake Tahoe and to a lush creek garden on the downhill side of the trail, where you will find 5 foot tall Glaucous Larkspur (*Delphinium glaucum*), interspersed with the largest monkey flower at Tahoe, the Lewis' Monkey Flower (*Mimulus lewisii*).

Lewis' Monkey Flower usually blooms in pink profusion from mid-July through August. Its tubular flowers have 5 flaring petals and bloom on shrublike plants which grow up to about 4 feet tall. If you climb down the slope and sit quietly among its flowers, you may discover an intriguing visitor that darts about and hovers like a hummingbird as it feeds. This strange, little brown creature, with its lovely markings, is a Sphinx Moth (*Celerio lineata*), and it will delight you and your children, if you take the time to enjoy it as it sips nectar through its long proboscis. It doesn't seem to notice curious onlookers and may remain pollinating hundreds of flowers for over an hour or more. The books say that it feeds at dusk, and while that may be its preferred time, I have found it out pollinating throughout the day.

A Flowery Meadow

After resuming the trail, an easy 1/4 mile hike along the old logging road will take you to a pond which sits off to the left of the trail. Near its shores in early-July, look for Alpine Shooting Stars *(Dodecatheon alpinum)*, Elephant Heads *(Pedicularis groenlandica)* and Water Plantain Buttercups *(Ranunculus alismaefolius)*. Just beyond the pond in late-July and August, hundreds of Soft Arnica *(Arnica mollis)* turn the meadow yellow. The daisy-like flowers of Soft Arnica usually grow in masses on stems that are about 2 feet tall. Their leaves are lance-shaped and downy soft and emit an earthy fragrance when squeezed.

During the months of July and August, many other wet environment flowers can be found blooming by the lake. Among them will be the Bog Saxifrage *(Saxifraga oregana)*, the yellow Arrowleaf Senecio *(Senecio triangularis)*, the white Sierra Rein Orchid *(Habenaria dilatata)* and the purple Whorled Penstemon *(Penstemon heterodoxus)*. The meadow usually remains wet and lush throughout the summer, offering a wide variety of flowers all season long.

The meadow and pond are accessible by wheel chair — a little dirt road leaves the main trail and leads to the pond. The main trail to this point can be rutty in parts but should be manageable, though the distance and slight uphill climb will require powerful arms and lots of enthusiasm. It is important to stay out of the wet areas of the meadow with a wheelchair, as the tires could cause great damage to the fragile environment.

A Shallow Pond of Noisy Tree Frogs

As you approach the pond, you may hear an almost deafening chorus of Pacific Tree Frogs *(Hyla regilla)*, but as you approach, they will abruptly stop.

The singing is performed by the male who inflates

125

a throat pouch in romantic display to the female. These little creatures are only 1 to 2 inches long. A black stripe marks the side of the head and often a T- or Y-shaped mark lines the top of its head. Its body coloring varies from tan, gray or black to green or brownish red. The name is confusing since these frogs don't live in trees but in the mud of Sierran ponds up to 11,000 feet!

They spawn in early-summer, with the female laying eggs in a mass of soft, sticky jelly that adheres to the blades and stems of plants at the pond's edge. In late-summer, the tadpoles emerge and slither into the pond to grow and then begin their amazing transformation into frogs.

The Rarely Seen Alpine Gentian

A few hundred yards after the pond, you will arrive at a fork in the trail and a sign that directs you to head to the right toward Mt. Rose. Just a few hundred feet after this juncture (on the slope above and to the left of the trail), look carefully in wet areas among the rocks in August or early-September and you may find the tubular flowers of the Alpine Gentian (Gentiana newberryi). This is the only place I have ever found this gentian growing at Tahoe, although it is reported to grow elsewhere, at similar high elevations of from 7,000 to 12,000 feet.

Its large, tubular flowers come in whitish tones of pale blue or lavender and are speckled with green spots. The tube is over an inch long and about 1/2 inch wide and supports 4 to 5 flaring petals. Its flowers bloom on top of single stems only a few inches off the ground. Since it does not appear every year, this is one flower you may have to be persistent about to find.

Panicles of White Corn Lilies

After passing a wet area, which in June gives rise to fragrant gardens of buttercups and marsh marigolds, the trail continues along an old jeep road past the tall, coarse-leaved plants of the Corn Lily (Veratrum *californicum).* As is typical of the Lily Family, the Corn Lily has parallel-veined leaves, which are prominently apparent on this plant.

When they first come up in spring, the leaves sheath the large, sturdy stem, giving the plant the appearance of a corn stalk. Later in the season, the wide leaves spread out, looking like coarsely-veined boat hulls. If snow has been abundant during the winter, they will be about 3 to 5 feet tall with terminal panicles of hundreds of 6-petaled white flowers. As John Muir once said, "It is a plant determined to be seen."

It is also determined not to be eaten, for the entire plant is toxic. It can slow down a person's heart beat until death occurs. There are even occasional reports of it having poisoned pollinating bees! Because of this poison, the cured roots were made into a tea by Washo women and taken for birth control, while the dried roots can be used as a natural insecticide.

Corn Lilies are sensitive to the proper amount of moisture. If they don't get enough, they struggle unhappily putting out only a few blooms. If they are not robustly growing and blooming when you hike the trail, be sure to revisit the area after a winter of plenty of snow, for then they will put on one of the best corn lily displays at Tahoe.

A Creekside Ribbon of Yellow

After these gardens, the trail descends to cross a small creek which is usually dry by late-July. At this point, you will head to the right and pass more wet areas of shooting stars, buttercups, elephant heads and the blue flowers of the Great Polemonium *(Polemonium caeruleum).* Its flowers bloom along stems that are about 3 feet tall. A curved stigma and 5 stamens, topped with bright yellow anthers, protrude out of the flower's center.

Just beyond this garden, you will find a creek exquisitely lined in solid yellow with thousands of Seep-spring Monkey Flowers *(Mimulus guttatus).* This cheery flower grows up to about 2 feet tall. As is typical of members of the Figwort Family, its flower is tubular with 5 flaring petal lobes. Red dots decorate the lower petals and fuzzy yellow hairs, in the throat, gather pollen from visiting insects. Since there is always plenty of water here, this is a wonderful place to enjoy lunch, to photograph and to relax, while others in the group continue on to the top of Mt. Rose. From here the trail continues to descend until it crosses another creek with more lush flower gardens where you will see downed lodgepole pines from a powerful avalanche that occurred in the winter of 1985. The destruction caused by the avalanche is an awe-inspiring sight. It is astounding to contemplate, but a resort, complete with casinos, has been proposed in an avalanche zone not far from this spot! Let us hope that the battle now being fought in the courts will prevent such folly and stop the desecration of this beautiful area.

A Jungle of Purple Lupine

But for a moment let's consider a happier thought. Have you ever wanted to lose yourself in a wild garden, to let down and immerse yourself in a purple sea of sensual fragrance — in plants so dense with shoulder-high flowers that you must push hundreds of blossoms aside to pass through? This was my experience on my first visit to Mt. Rose, in an area of larkspur and lupine along the trail, where it levels out just before the steady climb to the summit. Unfortunately, the next year someone had pruned them back to widen the trail. I hope that this enthusiastic soul has chosen other areas to hike, so that the flowers will be left to their own, so that some day soon this jungle of lavender blossoms can again be experienced.

If you stop there for a moment, you will be able to watch bees as they pollinate the lupines. Notice the orange or yellow pollen balls that cling to the bee's hind legs. After the bee collects the pollen, she grooms her body to redistribute the pollen, storing it on her hind legs until she returns to the hive. It is the fe-

Seep-spring
Monkeyflower

128

males that do the gathering, working from sun up to sun down, without rest to support the hive. Their wings move at about 200 beats per minute, and after 4 to 6 weeks the wings are often so ragged and worn out that the bees cannot fly, and thus they die. The next time I put honey on a muffin, I'll give thanks to these wonderful little creatures.

Beginning the Ascent

After this area the trail climbs more steeply as it traverses dry hillsides that are abundantly covered with flowers in July. Then you will head north to begin the ascent up a steep gully. Soon after this point, if you look carefully, you will spot the shiny yellow, wavy-edged petals of the Alpine Buttercup (*Ranunculus eschscholtzii*). It snuggles in among the roots of an old, weathered tree along the trail. You will also see it up on the top of Mt. Rose, its blossoms innocently peeking out from rock shelters to present just what is necessary for pollination.

Soon the trail crosses a creek that flows through a gully, giving rise to carpets of pink Rock Fringe (*Epilobium obcordatum*) in late-July. After crossing an open, sparsely-flowered slope, you will arrive at the saddle where the trail forks, by a sign that points the way to Mt. Rose's summit.

Arriving at the Alpine Community

After hiking along a series of switchbacks on the flanks of Mt. Rose, you will leave the canopy of pines and break out into the open, windswept environment of the alpine community. At this point the Whitebark Pines (*Pinus albicaulis*), the typical timberline tree, change from a moderate size of 20 to 30 feet to low, sprawling shrubs — clear evidence of the struggle they must go through to survive at such barren and windy elevations.

If you are lucky, you will find its gorgeous cones clinging to the branches. They are a deep, reddish brown and are up to 3 inches long. Its needles cluster in groups of 5, although you will occasionally find clusters of 4. You can easily differentiate Lodgepole Pines, which also grow abundantly up here, from Whitebark Pines because the lodgepole needles come in clusters of 2.

As you leave the shelter of the trees, you may need to pull out your jacket and gloves, for even on warm summer days it can turn painfully cold as you approach the top of the mountain. At other times you may find a day that is warm and inviting, with little or no wind on the top.

As you emerge into this exhilarating alpine world of brightly colored cushion plants, you can appreciate what a plant must go through to adapt to the intense sunlight, frigid temperatures, unrelenting wind and low moisture. To find shelter from the winds, they grow close to the earth, spreading horizontally rather than vertically. They often nestle beneath the shelter of a rock outcropping, enjoying the heat released by the rocks after the sun goes down. If you sit for a moment, you will see that even the bees adapt to the high elevation, just as the flowers do, by flying low to the ground to keep out of the wind.

The leaves of plants reflect the environment in which they live. Intense ultraviolet light can damage delicate plant tissue and, along with the wind, rob plants of vital moisture. As a reaction, the stems and leaves of alpine plants are usually covered with dense white hairs or a powdery substance for insulation and reflection. To reduce evaporation, the leaves are tiny, often leathery and usually very compact.

The leaves and growth pattern of alpine plants differ from plants of the same species at lower elevations. Spreading Phlox (*Phlox diffusa*) has an amazing range of 3,000 to 11,500 feet. At lake level its thin, needle-like leaves grow loosely along the stems, but at high elevations, these same leaves are so compact, it is impossible to penetrate them, even with a finger. This form helps the plant to resist winds that can tear or desiccate the leaves and helps it retain heat during cold nights. Studies have shown that night-time temperatures inside these dense masses can be as much as 20 degrees warmer than the outside air.

Alpine plants have only a few months, or in some cases only a few weeks, each year to spread, bloom and reproduce. Therefore most alpine plants are perennials. This gives them a head start, enabling them to devote energy during their short growing season to producing flowers, instead of using precious energy and resources to grow new root systems and stems as annuals must do.

Since the growing season is short, very little growth is put on in a year. When you find a thick, bonsai-like stem, it is a pretty good guess that the plant has been growing for a long time, perhaps for over a 100 years. The struggle they must go through is a reminder to us to respect alpine plants by not picking or damaging them in any way. Staying on the trail will help to protect them. A rock accidentally kicked and dislodged can destroy a whole habitat for plants, that may have been struggling to survive for 50 years or more.

The Showy Blooms of Alpine Flowers

Leaves may reflect this wild, exposed home by being tiny and compact, but flowers generally bloom just as large and brightly, regardless of the elevation. Since the flowers appear during the most hospitable time of the year and are not responsible for conserving moisture, their size and shape is not influenced, as leaves are, by the environmental factors of water, sunlight and exposure. Thus the flowers of many alpine plants, in contrast to their compact leaves, appear showier than their lower elevation cousins.

One of my favorite plants in this alpine community is the Showy Polemonium *(Polemonium pulcherrimum)*. Its purple, bowl-shaped flowers bloom above tiny, oval leaves, with lovely blossoms that look much too fragile to survive at such a high elevation. The first time I came upon it, I felt it needed to be carried down lower to a more gentle home. Yet it is here by choice for it grows mainly above 8,000 feet.

Alpine Gold *(Hulsea algida)*, with its large, bright,

daisy-like flowers and green, hairy leaves, also brightens the alpine ridges. Amazingly, it prefers to live above 9,500 up to 14,000 feet. The large size of its flower (2 inches in diameter) and the intense fragrance of its leaves (gently squeeze them between your fingers) make this flower easy to identify.

Look also for the white flowers of the Alpine Cryptantha *(Cryptantha humilis)*. It has the typical Borage Family structure of 5 petals and a central, raised ring. It is a showy flower at this elevation with pure white flowers that stand out in bright contrast against the gray-brown rocks and sandy soil.

Comparing the Cushion Plants

As you approach the summit of Mt. Rose, you will find many of the same cushion plants that we came upon on earlier hikes. Among them will be several little daisy plants that may confuse you when you first try to identify them. (Botanically speaking, daisy is a term used for members of the Erigeron genus.) The Cut-leaved Daisy *(Erigeron compositus)* has a single flower upon each stem with yellow disk flowers and white, numerous rays that are often inconspicuous or even lacking. If you are unfamiliar with ray and disk flowers, check out the Sherwood Forest hike, where they are discussed in detail. If you look closely at the compact basal leaves, you will see that they are long-stemmed and divided into little leaves that are shaped somewhat like a mitten.

Dwarf Alpine Daisy *(Erigeron pygmaeus)* has vivid-purple to violet colored rays and yellow disk flowers. Its grayish, linear to lance-like, smoothed-edged leaves grow at the base of the plant in dense rosettes, while each bare stem supports a single flower. This daisy has been found only on Freel Peak and Mt. Rose in the Tahoe area, preferring elevations above 10,000 feet.

Whenever I sit on the summit of Mt. Rose, looking at the various clusters of alpine flowers snuggled in the rocks, I love to recall John Muir's words. To him, the alpine plants were, "...gentle mountaineers face to face with the sky, kept safe and warm by a thousand miracles, seeming always the finer and purer the wilder and stormier their homes."

A Reversal in Plant Succession

The flowers along the trail to Mt. Rose, and those at the summit, bloom successively over a several month period but in a manner that reverses the normal order of things. Typically, spring arrives by May at lake-level at Tahoe. Finally by late-July or even August it arrives at the higher elevations, as the snow recedes and the ground thaws out. Mt. Rose is unusual in that it reverses this normal pattern because of its above timberline peak. At the top of the mountain, shallow snow covers its ridges. This shallow snow depth is caused by the lack of protective tree cover. Without trees, snow is blown off by high winds or evaporated by the intense solar radiation. As a result, snow buildup is minimal, compared to lower elevations with their sheltered gullies and dense tree cover.

So when the warmth of spring arrives, the ridge tops, with their minimal snow cover, melt early to expose the alpine community by late-June or early-July. Several thousand feet below, the snow may still be very deep and will remain until early- to mid-July. So when you hike Mt. Rose to see the alpine plants, be prepared to walk on a trail of snow on the lower mountain (which will still be easy to follow) and then plan to return several weeks later to enjoy the lower elevation flowers.

The first to bloom down lower in early- to mid-July are marsh marigolds, violets, buttercups, shooting stars and elephant heads. In mid-July through August, the lupines, evening primroses, monkeyflowers and other plants come into full, fragrant bloom.

A Mountaintop Gift

It is an amazing world up here, one which seems wilder and more pure than any other mountain environment, one in which you will be glad to be alive as

133

you stand on the top, surveying the 360 degree views from Mt. Rose's summit. To the south you will see the expansive blue waters of Lake Tahoe and the snow covered ridges of Desolation Wilderness. To the southeast the brown hills of Carson City in Nevada roll away from you, and to the west the irregular shorelines of Stampede and Boca Reservoirs can be seen lying just north of Truckee. On a very clear day, you will even be able to see Lassen Peak, over one hundred miles to the north. As Henry David Thoreau once said, "Simply to see a distant horizon through clean air — the fine outline of a distant hill or a blue mountain-top through some new vista is wealth enough for one afternoon." And so it is!

At night the views are brought closer with the lights of Reno and Carson Valley, sparkling in exquisite yellows, reds and whites. And sunrise is worth the cold night spent nestled down in the open, rocky "shelter" at the summit. The shelter is nothing more than a small windbreak, but it is a god-send on a cold day or evening.

It can be very cold at the top at night, even in the middle of summer. I once awakened at dawn with a sleeping bag full of hundreds of little moths that had been brought to the summit by a wind current. After being deposited by the wind, they sought shelter in my warm, downy sleeping bag, which was a new experience for me, but a pretty luxurious way-station for these small, wind-drifted adventurers.

After enjoying the summit of Mt. Rose, you will begin the long downhill hike out, which is a delight after the long uphill trudging, but I must warn you that the last two miles along the old logging road are the toughest part of the whole trip. It seems to go on forever, just at the time when you feel most tired and think you are almost off the mountain. So if your spirits falter at this point, just know that I am with you, because I've been there too!

The Tahoe Meadows

An Exercise in Seeing

Highlighted Flowers
- Water Plantain Buttercup
  (Ranunculus alismaefolius)
- Marsh Marigold
  (Caltha howellii)
- Elephant Heads
  (Pedicularis groenlandica)
- Little Elephant Heads
  (Pedicularis attollens)
- Alpine Shooting Star
  (Dodecatheon alpinum)
- Meadow Penstemon
  (Penstemon rydbergii)
- Giant Red Paintbrush
  (Castilleja miniata)
- Large-leaved Avens
  (Geum macrophyllum)

๙ĸ

One day/overnight
A roadside meadow @ 8600'
(Take a pencil and paper)
Topo Map Mt. Rose, Nv.
Wildflower Season   Late-June through August

"If my soul could get away from this so called prison, ... I should hover over the beauty of our own good star. I should study Nature's laws in all their crossings and unions...But my first journey would be into the inner substance of flowers."

John Muir

In Tahoe Meadows we will journey into the inner substance of flowers and perhaps even into the inner substance of ourselves. The Tahoe Meadows are made up of wet expanses of green, resting in a small draw between two rounded peaks. In a good year, the main meadow becomes a carpet of gold from the buttercups that bloom in late-June. As the days become warmer, the golden expanse gradually changes to a sea of purple and then to a scattering of reds, yellows, pinks and lavenders, among the green grasses.

135

Trailhead Directions

Driving toward Incline Village on Highway 28 from North Tahoe, turn left onto the Mt. Rose Highway (#431). Drive 7 miles until you arrive at the large, open meadow on the right. (See map on previous hike for meadow's location.)

The "Trail" Begins

After arriving at the zigzaggy poles that create a loose fence to protect the meadow from off-road vehicles, park anywhere off the road and wander into the meadow. There is no trail through the meadow, but as soon as you enter its gardens, you will be immersed in another world and unaware of the proximity of the road.

The meadow is interlaced with small streams so it is quite wet all summer long, which means it is wonderfully flower-filled but too wet for hiking boots. Tennis shoes are fine, if you don't mind slogging through the mud in them, though on a cool day this can be uncomfortable; I suggest that you wear rubber boots.

I hope that you visit the meadow several times during the season to experience its changing moods. In a good year, in mid-June, a golden expanse of Water Plantain Buttercups *(Ranunculus alismaefolius)* will envelop you in their sweet fragrance as soon as you enter the meadow. About two weeks after the height of this yellow display, the buttercups begin going to seed and Meadow Penstemons *(Penstemon rydbergii)* come into full purple bloom. In a good year, thousands of little tubular flowers create such a mass of pink-purple that it will take your breath away.

Contrasting with this purple, will be the shiny white petals of the Marsh Marigold *(Caltha howellii)* that usually blooms in early-July. The marigold has wavy edged, kidney-shaped leaves which are a rich, succulent-green as they grow in luxuriant profusion. Like the Water Plantain Buttercup, the Marsh Marigold is a member of the Buttercup Family — notice its large number of reproductive parts, which is

Marsh Marigold seeds

Buttercup seeds

typical of this primitive family.

After the flower is fertilized, the stamens and sepals (it has no true petals) drop off, and the ovaries swell to form a cluster of vertical, hook-tipped seeds. If you find both buttercups and marigolds in seed at the same time, compare their seeds and you will be able to see why they are grouped into the same family.

Elephants Abound in Tahoe's Meadows

By the time July is in full swing, Alpine Shooting Stars (*Dodecatheon alpinum*) will be nodding pink along the grassy banks of the meadow's slowly meandering creeks. Also blooming pink alongside the shooting stars will be communities of elephants. Not the type that would crush a meadow of flowers, but ones that fit right into the community — little flowers that look just like elephant heads with tiny, rounded foreheads, outstretched trunks and floppy ears.

You will find two species of elephant heads growing in the meadow which will give you an opportunity to compare them. The larger of the two species is called Elephant Heads (*Pedicularis groenlandica*) and grows about 1 to 2 feet high with many pink flowers along its stem. The individual flowers on this species clearly resemble little pachyderm heads. Each stem rises above lovely, basal, fern-like leaves that are green and tinged in purple.

Little Elephant Head flower

The other species called Little Elephant Heads (*Pedicularis attollens*) is smaller, growing only about 6 inches to a foot tall with fewer pink flowers along the stem. The oddly-shaped, upturned trunk of this species makes each flower look less like an elephant's head than the other, larger species.

Elephant Head flower

From a Flower's Point of View

As you explore the creeks that flow through the meadow, you will gradually be led toward the groves of willows on the north side, where you will find a profusion of color. Giant Red Paintbrush (*Castilleja*

137

miniata), yellow Arrowhead Senecio *(Senecio triangularis)* and Large-leaved Lupine *(Lupinus polyphyllus)* bloom tall amidst the ground-carpeting, white flowers of the Toad Lily *(Claytonia chamissoi)* and the blues of Alpine Veronica *(Veronica alpina).*

Look closely among the veronicas until you find a plant in seed. Its capsules are cute; they grow in the shape of a tiny heart out of which rises the thread-like style. Compare the style and ovary before and after fertilization, through your hand lens, to see the change it goes through in its cycle from bloom to fruit.

As you look out across the meadow, the fuzzy white flower heads of Bistort *(Polygonum bistortoides)* can be seen in July blooming atop stems that are about 2 feet tall. As is typical of the Buckwheat Family, it lacks petals. The white blossom is really just a tuft of colored sepals.

After checking out these and other plants that grow in the meadow, take a few minutes to sit back and look out at all the flowers surrounding you. Look at their shapes, sizes, colors; inhale their fragrances. Allow yourself to be pulled into them, to feel their essence.

Can you sense what it might be like to be a flower — to have your "feet" in the cold, oozing mud and your "face" turned upward toward raindrops, blue skies or the leaves of other plants? How would it feel to be jiggle-jangled by bees as they search your polleny parts?!

When you are ready, take your pencil and paper out of your pack and go sit by one of your favorite flowers. As you observe it, carefully draw all you see: its leaves, stems, blossoms. No one is looking over your shoulder so don't worry about your artistry. It is not important here — this is not a drawing exercise!

When you have finished, put your pencil and paper down and look at your flower again for about five minutes. Do as you did earlier and feel what it would be like to be that flower by putting yourself inside it. Look out at the world from its perspective. How would it feel to have leaves, a nodding head, to be exposed to rain, snow and days of glorious sunshine. How would it be to live among a community of fragrant, colorful corollas and buzzing insects.

After about five minutes or so turn your back on your flower and sit for a minute or two thinking about it. Then pick up your pencil and paper and draw the essence of your flower, not the details, but what it is about the flower that moves you.

After you have finished, compare both drawings. What does each drawing say about how you approached the flower? In the first, you drew from your head in an analytical mode. In the second, from your heart. Each are "valid" expressions of the flower, but what does your second drawing tell you about yourself? (I don't mean that you can't draw!) What characteristics of the flower were important to you and how did you express them? Do the characteristics you chose to emphasize relate to you and to how you view the world?

This exercise is fun to do with another person or with a group. It's amazing what you can learn about yourself, and it will help you to look more closely at the detail of plants to appreciate the miracle of each flower.

A New Experience

Freeing ourselves from set ways of looking out at the world can bring spontaneity and great richness into our lives. Come back to this meadow another day but choose a different type of day. If today was sunny, come back in a wild rainstorm or on a gentle foggy morning. Or come back at night under a full moon. It is so close to the road that you needn't fear becoming lost in the dark or in a storm, though do bring a compass, as you could become disoriented from the road.

It is so easy to stay home when the weather looks rainy or cold and yet these are actually the most exciting times to be out; these are the times when we feel most alive, most connected with Nature and most in tune with the vital forces flowing through us. And it is the time when Nature also seems most open.

On a sunny day the trees, flowers and animals, as we do, bask lazily in the sun's warmth or busily go about their business of food gathering. But in a storm, the trees dance in wild abandon, and the animals join in, celebrating their joy in being alive. I first experienced this celebration in a wet, windy snowstorm one spring in Shirley Canyon. Birds were wildly flying up and down the canyon, taking no notice of me in their delight. After fading into the background to watch the birds, animals and plant life, I decided to enjoy it too. I stretched out on a big, flat, exposed rock and let the rain and snow fall upon me — I never felt the cold, only an exuberance at feeling so free and alive.

I hadn't realized it before, but until that moment I had always been a guest, a welcomed and loved one perhaps, but still a guest among the trees and flowers. But on that day, I became a part of the family because I came stripped of my normal convention, ready to join in their celebration, ready to see them in all their glory on their terms. It created an opening in me that helped me to feel more deeply connected to the universe, leaving behind a self-consciousness that in a subtle way had kept me separated without my realizing it.

- Lewis' Monkeyflower
  (*Mimulus lewisii*)
- Alpine Lily
  (*Lilium parvum*)
- Azure Penstemon
  (*Penstemon azureus*)
- Lobb's Buckwheat
  (*Eriogonum lobbii*)
- Mountain Mule-ears
  (*Wyethia mollis*)
- Spotted Mountain Bells
  (*Fritillaria atropurpurea*)
- Sierra Primrose
  (*Primula suffrutescens*)
- Clustered Broomrape
  (*Orobanche fasciculata*)
- California Fuchsia
  (*Zauschneria californica*)
- Explorer's Gentian
  (*Gentiana calycosa*)

The Ridge Route

From Donner Pass to Squaw Valley

One day/overnight
Total trip   15 miles
Trip profile: A trail with fabulous views that begins at 7100', climbs in 7 miles to about 8600' by Tinker Knob, then gradually descends over the next 8 miles to 6200' in Squaw Valley. You will need two cars, or a drop-off, since the trip ends 15 miles south of where it began.
Topo maps USGS Donner Pass, Calif.
USGS Granite Chief, Calif.
USGS Tahoe, Calif.
Wildflower Season   July through September

Meadow Penstemon

The Ridge Route travels the crest of the Sierra along the ridges and saddles of four major peaks from Donner Summit to Squaw Valley. Breathtaking views of distant mountain ranges extend for miles in every direction. Hawks soar on the warm updrafts, and lush green meadows nestle in small valleys far below. Open slopes of yellows, pinks and purples form swaths of undulating color on windy days, while pink primroses, and fall-blooming fuchsias and gentians, rise like small jewels out of the talus slopes.

Trailhead Directions

Heading west on Interstate 80 out of Truckee, take the Donner Lake exit .1 mile past the U. S. Depart-

141

ment of Agriculture Produce Inspection Station (known locally as the Bug Station). At the exit-ramp stop sign, turn left and head over the freeway to the next stop sign. Continue through the intersection on Donner Pass Road, past the Donner Memorial State Park.

At the west end of Donner Lake, you will begin the climb up old Highway 40. On this drier, steep side of the crest, the vegetation is sparse, compared to the western side, because it is in the rain shadow of the Sierra. Storms usually begin over the Pacific Ocean. As the clouds rise to pass over the Sierra Crest, they release their moisture, so that by the time the clouds reach the eastern Sierra little moisture is left.

As you climb, you will spot train tracks off to the left that were built in the 1860's as part of the first transcontinental railway. Thousands of Chinese emigrants, and others, spent dangerous, grueling hours blasting and excavating tunnels out of the steep mountainside to create a bed for the tracks. The wooden sheds that cover the tracks, were built for protection from the avalanches that frequently occur on the steep mountainsides.

Near the crest of the summit, and just before the bridge, there is a turnout with lovely views of Donner Lake. One-half mile past the turnout, you will arrive at the Alpine Skills Institute and the first road to the left. Take this road and continue for about .1 of a mile to a road on the left, with a Pacific Crest Trail sign a couple hundred feet in that reads, "Mt. Judah 1 1/2, Mt. Lincoln 2 1/2." From this point, the trail is well marked and easy to follow all the way to Squaw Valley.

As the route is generally above timberline, and travels the crest with little or no water available, good camping is limited. If you choose to camp, carry your own water and be adventuresome about site selection! The most level, sheltered areas are past Tinker Knob. If you are a Sierra Club member, you may reserve space and spend the night in the Benson Hut, which is about mid-way along the trail. Contact the

Sierra Club at the Clair Tappaan Lodge on Donner Summit for information. Be sure to carry water for a day hike, as well as for an overnight — the springs along the trail, though wonderful for flowers, are generally too small and muddy to be a dependable source of water.

After a winter of heavy snow, the ridges may be snow-bound until mid-July; in other years the trail may be free of snow several weeks earlier, so be sure to check conditions before you begin your hike. (The crest line of the route can be seen from Interstate 80, and the Truckee Ranger station should have updated information on the route.)

The Trail Begins

From the Pacific Crest Trail sign you will head south traveling uphill through wooded seep gardens of yellow and pink monkeyflowers *(Mimulus lewisii, M. guttatus)*, orange lilies *(Lilium parvum)* and yellow senecios *(Senecio triangularis)*, that bloom in July. You will also pass large stands of pink fireweed *(Epilobium angustifolium)*, that generally come into bloom by early-August. These gardens are magical, as the early morning sunlight filters through the trees to highlight the flowers and ferns.

Within a few minutes, you will leave the woods behind and begin a steep climb up a switchbacked trail, that looks down upon Lake Mary to the west. The open, granitic slopes that line the trail give rise to pink and purple penstemons, yellow sedums and other rock garden treasures. If you hit it right, you will find the best penstemon displays in all of Tahoe on this trail. The display begins in early-July, as pink cascades of Mountain Pride *(Penstemon newberryi)* flow over the rocks, and it lasts into August, as purple clusters of the Showy and Azure Penstemons *(P. speciosus, azureus)* come into full bloom to form gorgeous patches of color all along the trail.

Few trails at Tahoe offer so many species of penstemon, so this is your opportunity to key in on the characteristics of this genus. As you climb above the

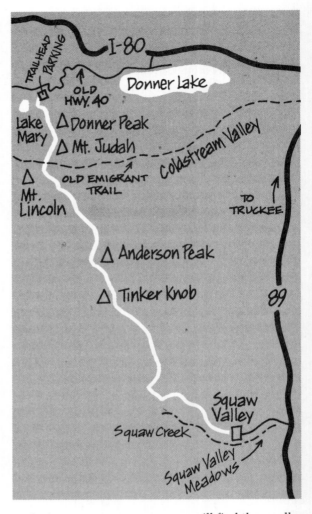

rocks into more open areas, you will find the smaller, bluish-purple, tubular flowers of the Meadow Penstemon *(P. rydbergii)*. Though it is usually found in damp meadows, you will come upon it blooming in sparse groups alongside the trail. Its flowers form tight whorls around a stem that is about 12 inches tall, and they are similar to the Whorled Penstemon *(P. heterodoxus)* of higher elevations. These two species are difficult to tell apart, unless you look closely. The Meadow Penstemon lacks the glandular hairs that grow on the flowers of the whorled one.

If you leave the trail to search the rocks, look for Tahoe's only white species. The Hot Rock Penstemon *(P. deustus)* grows about a foot tall, with small, tubular flowers in whorls along its upper stem. It can be found in scattered colonies blooming above leathery leaves. The tough coating on the leaves helps the plant to conserve moisture in its dry environment.

Look too for the graceful Gay Penstemon *(P. laetus);* you will find it within a mile of the trailhead, near a small creek that crosses the path. It blooms with loose, open clusters of bluish-purple flowers, that are tubular and more narrow than the other penstemons. Its glandular-hairy stems are about 2 feet tall and are often reddish tinged. Check the staminoid (the stamen without the anther) and you will see that it is bald. This is an important characteristic in keying out species of penstemon, as was discussed on the Loch Leven hike.

As you wander along the trail, you will also find a flower that you may not at first recognize as a penstemon. Lemmon's Penstemon, *(P. lemmonii)* appears as a happy little flower, that blooms in brownish yellow on open, shrub-like plants. It grows all along the trail on the Shirley Canyon hike.

Six Foot Tall Buckwheats

After hiking the first mile of the trail, you will arrive at large communities of Tahoe's tallest buckwheat, the Alpine Knotweed. Its botanical name, *Polygonum phytolacceafolium,* is one example of why Latin names have a frightful reputation! But if we break down the name, I think you'll find it less intimidating. *Phyto* is Greek for "plant," and *laccea* is derived from Italian for "waxy." *Folium* is Latin for "leaf." So it is just a plant with waxy leaves.

It is easy to identify by its cluster of tiny white flowers at the top of the 4 to 6 foot tall stems. Lance-like leaves grow all along the main stem, and if you look at the base of each leaf stem, you will find a brown, papery sheathing, called the ocrea. It is the ocrea that helps identify this plant as a member of

Gay
Penstemon

145

the *Polygonum* genus. The name *polygonum* means "many kneed" or "many jointed" and refers to the jointed, knee-like swellings along the nodes of the stem.

In this same area, you should find whole slopes covered with the flowers of pink mallow *(Sidalcea glaucescens)* and fragrant pennyroyal *(Monardella odoratissima)* that bloom in profusion, in a good year, from July into September. After hiking another 1/2 mile through these gardens toward the western flank of Mt. Judah, the trail crosses a logging road by a sign that reads "Donner Pass 1 1/2 Mile."

Soon after this point the trail will level out as you traverse the slope beneath Mt. Judah. This will give you a break before you begin to climb Mt. Lincoln and will allow you to get into your own hiking rhythm as you wind your way through open fields of flowers and past seep gardens usually rich with color. One of the brightest flowers along this part of the trail will be the California Helianthella *(Helianthella californica)*. Its yellow, daisy-like flowers can be identified by two characteristics: a single flower head that blooms atop an approximately 2 foot tall stem and 2 lance-like leaves that usually radiate outward just beneath each flower head.

A Metaphor of the Clouds

The trail builders on this hike gave us a great gift. Usually, in order to explore high peaks, one must huff and puff up steep trails and then lose all that was gained as the trail drops down into a canyon before climbing again to the next peak. With a heavy pack (or even without one!) such exertion can be demoralizing. The joy of the Ridge Route is that it starts high and generally remains high as it follows the contour of the ridgeline, taking you to peak after peak. Thus you can enjoy the rhythm of a relatively level trail while still experiencing the exhilaration of being free and on top of the world.

I have many fond memories of my walks along the Ridge Route, when my mind was cleansed of all thoughts or concerns, of the thrill of looking down upon the soaring flight of a sparrow hawk or up at the exciting build-up of cumulus clouds on a hot afternoon.

If there are clouds before you today as you hike the trail, you might want to take a few minutes to stretch out and enjoy the scene and some thoughts from John Muir.

"One may fancy the clouds themselves are plants, springing up in the sky-fields at the call of the sun, growing in beauty until they reach their prime, scattering rain and hail like berries and seeds, then wilting and dying."

It constantly amazes me to see how similar the patterns are that unite us all, for the life of a cloud is a metaphor, not only for the flowers, but for each one of us.

After enjoying the clouds, or perhaps just the distant views if your day is a cloudless one, you will travel through more seep gardens of lupines, yampahs and cow parsnips. The Cow Parsnip (*Heracleum lanatum*) can be identified by its huge, maple-like leaves that are often 2 feet wide. Large, flat-topped clusters of tiny, white flowers bloom in umbel form — with flower stems that radiate outward from a central point.

Cow Parsnip

Crossing the Old Emigrant Trail

Soon you will arrive at a trail-fork, which is within 2 miles of the trailhead. Though you'll want to head straight at the fork, take a few moments first to walk along the left branch, on the old Overland Emigrant Trail. Here in 1846, the first wagon crossed the Sierran Crest before dropping down into the rich Sacramento Valley. It is hard to believe that thousands of pioneers once passed along this simple dirt road in search of a new life. The Tahoe National Forest map marks the route in red. You can follow it on the map as it leaves Alder Creek just north of Truckee, climbs to the south of Mt. Judah and then generally parallels Interstate 80. After crossing Bear Valley and lovely Bear Creek, the trail passed near Dutch Flat.

If you walk along the left trail for a few hundred yards, you will arrive at a sign that marks the spot where the emigrants dragged their wagons 1600 feet up and over the summit, out of Coldstream Valley and Emigrant Canyon. Looking down at their bouldered route below, one can't help but be overwhelmed by the sheer determination and courage of these early travelers.

It is also beautiful to stop for a moment at this spot to contemplate a more recent historical event. A ski resort was proposed several years ago for Coldstream Valley and the surrounding area. When the developers were unable to continue with the project, Walter Hewlett came in and purchased the land to stop any other plans for its development. Under his ownership, the valley, and the emigrant's route that passes through it, will be preserved forever in their natural state. Because of his generosity and sensitivity to the land, Tahoe has gained a bit more ground in its fight against unchecked development.

Following the Crest Past Mt. Lincoln

After returning to the main trail, within 1/4 mile you will arrive at a small saddle on the flanks of Mt. Lincoln and a sign that reads "Anderson Peak 4, Tinker Knob 6." At this point the trail will take you uphill, across the ski runs, along the eastern side of Mt. Lincoln. You will crest the saddle and travel along a contour line, where you will catch glimpses of Donner Lake with Anderson Peak dominating the view to the south.

As the trail descends, you will pass through wet gardens of columbines, saxifrages and elephant heads and across hillsides of lupines, that turn the slopes purple, beneath graceful stands of Mountain Hemlock (*Tsuga mertensiana*). The hemlock is one of the most beautiful of all our conifers. Its gray-green needles

148

take on the form of a star as you look down the axis of the branch, and the topmost tip droops as if to declare that it has expended all its energy on the magnificent growth below.

Like a true alpine mountaineer, this tree prefers a rugged, northern exposure. In many places on the steep mountainsides, trunks can be found leaning down the slopes, from the heavy snows that forced them, as saplings, to the ground each winter. Even trees 40 feet or taller will bend under the weight of heavy, icy snows and may remain buried all winter until the sun's warmth frees them in spring.

On these windswept ridges, hemlocks only 7 inches in diameter may have weathered the winters for 80 years or more. Perhaps because of the rugged environment and short growing season of its alpine home, the cones of the hemlock mature within one year as opposed to the normal two years for most conifers. The cones are only about 2 inches long. They shed their seeds in the fall and soon thereafter the cones are released to return precious nutrients to the ground.

Climbing the Saddle to Anderson Peak

Within 1/2 mile, the trail climbs out of the trees toward the broad, open saddle that leads to Anderson Peak. Here you will wander through large fields of golden mule-ears, red gilias and pink onions and past small groups of lavender loco weed and dagger pod. If you hike the trail in mid-July, you should find these flowers at the height of their bloom and can expect flower color through the end of August. Come September, blue gentians bloom in small groups along the trail, and bright red fuchsias, in some of the most lavish displays in all of Tahoe, can be found near the trail's end in Shirley Canyon.

You will also find one of Tahoe's most easily identifiable buckwheats. Flat on the ground, Lobb's Buckwheat (*Eriogonum lobbii*) blooms with clusters of creamy flowers that form a compact, 2 inch ball at the end of bare, sprawling stems. If you follow the

149

stem to its "other end," you will find silvery-white leaves forming a velvety, basal rosette upon the sandy soil. Though it is not a showy plant, I feel a fondness for it, because as the flower heads age, they turn a wonderful rosy color — a gentle reminder perhaps that we too can become rosier with age.

A Fritillary that Defines Itself

As you begin to traverse the treeless, wind-swept ridge to Mt. Anderson, look for the gorgeous, but inconspicuous, flowers of Spotted Mountain Bells (*Fritillaria atropurpurea*). They bloom alongside the trail in late-June through mid-July.

As with most members of the Lily Family, its petals and sepals are identical, making the flower look as if it has 6 petals. The nodding, inch-wide blossoms are a spotted, brownish purple. Large, creamy yellow anthers attach themselves, at various angles, to the filaments and surround the sticky stigma. Be sure to get down on your hands and knees to look up into its lovely face.

The Lily Family is one of my favorites. It fills our wild mountain gardens with beauty and variety and often with a few surprises. Nature's surprises are one of my greatest joys. Just when I think I have defined a tiny part of the flower world and am tempted to categorize that knowledge into a little authoritative box and put the lid on, out jumps something new to both humble and delight me.

I thought I knew this species of fritillary well, until I hiked the Ridge Route and found it growing in a new and stocky form on Anderson Peak. Several years ago Sherman Chickering, in an article in the California Native Plant Society's Fremontia magazine, commented that he too had come upon two forms of this fritillary that were different from its descriptions in most botanical references. He had found one that grows in wooded areas, that is slender and graceful, and this one that grows stouter on these exposed, gravelly slopes.

Since most botanical references do not identify

these two different forms, it would be confusing for you to key them out in the field. As described by Sherman, both types in this area vary from the text specifications of such classical botanical references as Munz, Abrams and Jepson. He found the petals and sepals to be oblong rather than rhombic; some of the flowers were brownish purple with green spots, rather than with white spots, as defined in the references; and others were green with brownish purple spots. Most of the flowers were flattened, as opposed to bell-shaped, and, "None bore any resemblance to the drawing in Abrams."

The more I botanize, the more I find such field variations, which for me just makes the whole experience more fun. Botanists claim that both types are the same species and merely represent adaptions to two different environments. But, perhaps with time, more detailed study will show them to be separate species. In any event, I hope you hike the trail at a time when, as Sherman said, he found as many as 1,000 in an area of only 1/4 square mile.

If you hike the trail in late-July or early-August, the fritillary will have gone to seed with upright, rounded pods replacing the nodding flowers. As with most members of the Lily Family, its seed pods are lovely and easy to identify after the flowers have faded. (See page 331.)

Fields of Golden Mule-ears and Blue Flax

As you continue along the trail, you will soon come across more fields of golden Mule-ears (*Wyethia mollis*) and Balsam Roots (*Balsamorhiza sagittata*) that bloom from July through early-August. These spectacular, golden fields also give rise to hundreds of Blue Flax (*Linum perenne*) that seem to mirror the sky with their petals of blue. And beneath it all, Copeland's Owl's Clover (*Orthocarpus copelandii*), short and modest, blooms in tufts of vivid pink.

After passing wild, conglomerate formations of volcanic rock, you will come upon cushions of muted color from compact, sub-alpine plants that lift their blossoms to the sun's rays. This volcanic rock is left over from an ancient eruption that occurred before the Sierran Crest began its uplift. The vent was located just east of the forested knoll that stands before you on the north side of the peak. It is a dramatic sight to stand on the edge of the old volcanic flow on this knoll and look down the cliffs into the old vent that now houses serene meadows below.

A Night in the Benson Hut

As you approach the flanks of Anderson Peak, you will find a cabin hidden in the trees, above and to the left of the trail. The Benson Hut is one of four backcountry, Sierra Club huts at Tahoe, which is available for member use on a reservation basis. I once came upon the cabin in winter when I was skiing the Ridge Route with my son, Mike, and found it so deeply buried in snow, that we had to shovel down several feet to enter through the second story.

The Sierra has the heaviest snowfall of any range in the continental United States, but its winters are warmed by days of sunshine, where tiny rainbows dance in the sparkling snow and skies radiate the most intense blue I have ever seen. The Ridge Route offers excellent cross-country skiing, and Mike and I had planned two days to do the route so we could enjoy being out at day's end. Sunset that night blazed deep pink, then orange and finally a peaceful gray as the light slowly faded beyond the distant Coast Range. We spent the night in the hut, beneath 20 feet of snow, our only contact with the outside world, a little tunnel from the attic.

Hiking the route in summer will help you to determine its feasibility in winter, although it should be attempted only by experienced, backcountry travelers, since most of the terrain is steep and avalanche danger extreme. What might appear easy in the summer is not necessarily so in winter because of sudden weather changes and heavy snow drifts.

After leaving the Benson Hut, the trail will take you, in late-July, past fabulous gardens of the pink

Sierra Primrose *(Primula suffrutescens)*. You will find them blooming above leathery leaves, carpeting the rocks along the north slopes of the Peak. As you begin to circle around to the south side, you will find great shrubby patches of the Bush Cinquefoil *(Potentilla fruiticosa)* that blooms with bright yellow flowers in July. This plant is available at local nurseries and does well in Tahoe's home gardens.

Tinker Knob Backdropped by Lake Views

As the trail begins to climb to the saddle leading to Tinker Knob, you will come to glorious patches of Azure Penstemon cascading in joyful abandon over the rocks, above and below the trail, in late-July.

As you leave the switchbacks behind and approach the knob, the surrounding landscape will lie before you like a lifeless moonscape. But with close inspection, you will discover small alpine plants tenaciously clinging to the sparse soil. If you look among the alpine community, you may find the small, purplish flowers of the Clustered Broomrape *(Orobanche fasciculata)* that usually come into bloom in late-July or August. The tubular flowers sit atop compact stems that are often fused together to form one thick base, that rises only a few inches off the ground. The plants are hairy and glandular (look for the little shiny drops of liquid on the ends of the hairs), and they lack green leaves.

The broomrape lives by consuming nutrients from the roots of neighboring plants, like those of the buckwheats, phacelias and sagebrushes. In fact, some species of broomrapes are so host-specific that they can be identified by the plant they parasitize. The genus name, *Orobanche,* comes from the Greek word *orobos* which means "clinging plant" and *ancho* which means "to strangle." The name Broomrape is said to be derived from a species of this genus that parasitizes the Broom or Cytisus shrub (whose branches were used for broomhandles in Europe). Rape refers to the name of the rooty vegetable of the Broom tuber.

As you leave this little plant with the formidable

name, you will be able to look beyond the expanse of brown to the blues of Lake Tahoe, and within a short distance you will come to a sign directing you to Squaw Valley, 6 miles away. From this point on, the trail is a steady downhill, except for a slight climb over a saddle before the descent into Shirley Canyon.

Before dropping down through the canyon into the valley, you will come to one final trail junction with a sign that reads, "Squaw Valley 4, Granite Chief Mt. 1 1/2." At this point it is all downhill through gardens of Fireweed, in July and August, and past granitic walls that house deep-blue gentians and hundreds of bright red fuchsias in August and September. This final part of the hike is described in detail on the Shirley Canyon hike.

Though July is the best time to enjoy the greatest display of flower color along the trail, fall is also wonderful. Then the days are windy and brisk, and the fuchsia and gentian brightly grace the slopes, as if to say good-by to the flower season with one final exuberant blaze of color, as a sort of prelude to snowy winter days of homemade bread, tureens of soups and evenings spent by the fire.

Pole Creek

A Hike for Little Children and Other Zen Souls

One day	
One way From 1/2 to 3 miles	
Trail begins/ends 6000'/7200	
Net gain/total gain 1200'/1200'	
Topo map USGS Tahoe, Calif.	
Wildflower Season June through August	

Rachael Carson once said, "If a child is to keep alive his inborn sense of wonder, he needs the companionship of at least one adult who can share it, rediscovering with him, the joy, excitement and mystery of the world we live in."

Pole Creek is a wonderful place to share this joy and mystery. Near the trail is a small vernal pool that supports hundreds of little frogs that hide among carpets of flowers at the pool's edge. There are sphinx moths that hover like hummingbirds as they pollinate bright pink thistles, mushrooms that dissolve in pools of ink and tiny fern gardens hidden in small caverns in rocky ledges. And there is Basque Meadow, where bored sheep herders from the past carved their fantasies and frustrations into the white bark of quaking aspens in a form of art not very appropriate for young children!

Anderson's Thistle

155

Trailhead Directions

The trailhead is near the Big Chief Lodge on Highway 89. Out of Truckee, drive 6.3 miles south on Highway 89, until you arrive at the paved Forest Service road on the right, about 100 yards past the Lodge. Out of Tahoe City, head toward Truckee on Highway 89. After driving past the entrance to Squaw Valley, drive another 2.4 miles to the Forest Service road. There is ample parking along the road after you turn off the highway.

This hike gives young children, the elderly and those in wheel chairs the opportunity to see backcountry gardens with little or no hiking, because the different meadows may be reached along a logging road that is usually passable in a passenger car. It is also an enjoyable hike for those who want the exercise of the entire 11 mile round trip. It is 1/2 mile to the first meadow and vernal pool with the little frogs, 3 miles to Basque Meadow and 4.7 miles to the road's end. From there, you can hike another 1/2 mile along a generally level but rutted road and then cross-country to a creek that flows through wonderful rock gardens.

The Trail Begins

To find the first meadow, head up the Forest Service road through the opened gate. Soon the road turns to gravel and within about 1/4 mile makes a big bend to the right. At this point, off to the left, you'll find the first small meadow of fragrant buttercups and great little belly flowers, that begin blooming in early-June.

Several species of buttercups bloom at Tahoe, but the first to appear in spring is the Water Plantain Buttercup (*Ranunculus alismaefolius*). By June, in a good year, it covers this first meadow with yellow blossoms that appear above narrow, lance-like leaves.

Its flowers are about an inch wide and while most books say this species has only 5 petals, I have found the number varies. I once discovered one exuberant little flower with 22 petals. Buttercups are easy to

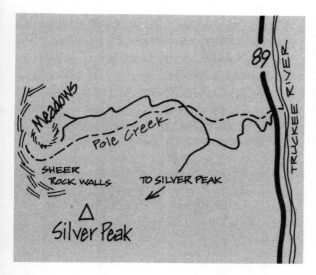

identify by their shiny yellow petals. This shininess is caused by light that is reflected off a layer of white starch grains, that reside just beneath the layer of pigment cells.

Buttercups have been appreciated for thousands of years. The name, *Ranunculus,* was given to them by Pliny, a Roman naturalist, who lived from 79 to 29 A. D. It means "little frog" and was a name given to buttercups, because they share the same wet environment as these water-loving amphibians. *Alismaefolius* is in reference to the leaves (foliage) which look like those of the Alisma Water Plantain in the Alismatacea Family.

The Evolution of Flowers

Buttercups are primitive flowers that appeared millions of years before man began to occupy the earth. They represent a place on the evolutionary scale that is between the more ancient ferns or pines and the more recent lilies, orchids and violets.

For over 450 million years, plants have been evolving and adapting to slow climatic changes and to the wide variety of pollinators that they depend upon for survival. Based on fossil remains, botanists have begun to piece together a record of this evolution.

157

What they have found is that over time flowers have developed fewer, more complex and more efficient reproductive structures.

Look closely at a buttercup and you will see that it lacks nectar lines or other elaborate petal markings. Its petals are simple and uniform in shape, and its flowers house large numbers of stamens and pistils. A buttercup attracts whatever pollinators may be out and about, the efficient along with the inefficient, and produces large amounts of pollen in a hit or miss method.

Compare a buttercup's flower to the more recently evolved flowers of the violet or lily. Notice that these flowers carry nectar lines or other elaborate petal markings. They also come in a wide variety of shapes and contrasting colors. These different forms evolved because they were more effective in attracting the more efficient pollinators like bees and moths.

With more effective parts, the parts could be fewer in number. As a result, a more advanced flower will tend to have fewer pistils and stamens, but these parts will be flashier. Compare a buttercup's 30 pistils and 80 stamens to a lily's 1 pistil and 3 or 6 stamens. Notice too how these parts vary in shape and color between the more ancient and more recent flowers.

With these details in mind, you can look at a flower and generally determine where it might sit on the evolutionary scale. Of course, more recently evolved flowers are not necessarily superior to the more primitive ones. I am sure that a buttercup would consider itself to be as successful as a lily. It has been around longer and grows quite happily in many different environments throughout the world, for its very primitiveness or simplicity has allowed it to adapt to change, to spread throughout the world and to continue to thrive. In any event, the variety of both evolutionary trends adds great richness to our lives.

Seeds that Taste Like Popcorn

Somewhere, far back in time, flowers developed nectar to discourage insects and birds from eating the pollen. It must have been an ancient development because even the buttercup carries this feature. If you look at the base of each petal, you will see little nectar pockets.

When pollinators visit a flower, attracted by its color, design or nectar, fertilization can take place. In the buttercup, pollination is followed by clusters of seeds that appear on the flower head. Each round and flattened seed is called an akene and has a tiny beak that points outward. The shape of the various akenes is a helpful guide in keying out different species of buttercups.

Buttercup seeds were an important part of the diet of Native Americans. After being gathered by the women and children, they were tossed in tightly woven, flat baskets with hot coals to parch out their bitter taste and to remove the husks. The seeds, which tasted like popcorn, were then ground on a stone mortar, or they were stored in little baskets to be passed out to family and guests as a delicacy.

Belly Flowers among the Grasses

As you wander around the edge of the buttercup meadow, you'll find many flowers that can best be seen down on your belly. The light blue flowers of the Alpine Veronica *(Veronica alpina)* bloom with 4 petals on stems only a few inches tall. The shiny white flowers of the Toad Lily *(Claytonia chamissoi)* carpet wet areas by sending out red runners that root in the soggy soil.

You will also find the yellow Primrose Monkey Flower *(Mimulus primuloides)* blooming at the top of an upright, thread-like stem. The lower petals are usually spotted with red dots and the throat covered with yellow hairs. Near it will be tiny, pink willow herbs and velvety green mosses that are like dense forests to traveling insects.

It is fun, with a young child, to lay out a 10 foot string in a circle to see how many species of flowers and insects you both can observe. Together, you can imagine what the world must be like to the small creatures that live within it. Introducing a child to wildflowers will also introduce him or her to the insects, birds and other members of the natural community, for as John Muir once said, "When we try to pick out anything by itself, we find it hitched to everything else in the Universe." An understanding of this interrelationship is one of the greatest gifts we can give to our children, for it will help them to see the richness and connection of all life.

Late-May through early-June is the best time to introduce young children to the adventures of wild gardens, because at this time of year the flowers are blooming at the lower elevations, making them easily accessible to little legs. Later in the season, most of the flowers will be found at higher elevations and will involve longer and more tiring hikes.

Porterellas Shelter Little Frogs
After enjoying the buttercup meadow, walk in a westerly direction across the dirt road that branches off from the logging road. Within about 100 yards, you will come to a vernal pool that begins to dry up in early- to mid-June. As it dries, it becomes completely carpeted with the small, exquisite flowers of Porterella (*Porterella carnosula*). Their blue corollas have yellow and white spots at the base and are tubular, with 5 flaring petals. This small annual is infrequently found at Tahoe, and this is the only place where I have found it inundated with little frogs.

South of this pond you'll find a grassy meadow that leads to a creek that is partially obscured by alders and willows. This is a lovely place to spend the day, or you may continue along the logging road for another 2 1/2 miles to Basque Meadow to see the carvings on the aspens.

A Mushroom that Dissolves into Ink
Before arriving at Basque Meadow, you will begin a gradual uphill climb which will take you past roadside gardens of monkeyflowers, senecios and paint-

Porterella

brushes. Along the way you may pass an intriguing mushroom sitting in a pool of black ink. It appears alongside the road in July and August and is called Inky Caps *(Coprinus comatus).*

This ink pool is the result of a process that the mushroom goes through in order to release its spores. As the spores at the edge of the cap mature, an enzyme is released that dissolves the surrounding tissue, turning it into a black liquid. With the dissolving of the tissue, the edge of the cap curls back and spreads outward, pulling the gills apart and releasing the spores into the air. All that is left at the end is the mushroom stalk surrounded by a pool of ink.

Mushrooms, which are primitive plants, release tremendous amounts of spores. Botanists have calculated that if every one of the seven trillion spores that develop from just one Giant Puffball mushroom were to reach maturity, these plants would encircle the earth five times. If each of these mushrooms produced spores that all germinated into mature plants, we would find the earth covered with a puffball mass that would be eight hundred times that of the earth's weight. As it is, only a minuscule fraction of the spores produced ever form new plants, so for the time being we are quite safe!

Home of the Endangered Cutthroat Trout
After a short downhill walk, you will arrive at the bridge that crosses Pole Creek which is now a protected area for Tahoe's Federally and State listed Lahontan Cutthroat Trout. These native trout used to be abundant in Lake Tahoe and the surrounding streams. Then when the white man moved into Tahoe, commercial and sport fishing interests brought new species of trout into the Lake. The cutthroat were unable to compete and were gradually eliminated. The last cutthroad was caught in the lake in 1940. The Department of Fish and Game is now trying to help them make a comeback in some of the streams at Tahoe by killing off other species and reintroducing the cutthroat.

Arriving at Basque Meadow

After crossing the creek, turn left and continue for .6 mile until you come to Basque Meadow, which will be on the left. If you get there before the sheep arrive in late-June through early-July, you will find a wonderful array of wet environment plants, like the white Sierra Rein Orchid *(Habenaria dilatata)* and the green Sparsley Flowered Bog Orchid *(H. sparsiflora)*.

You'll also find the Giant Red Paintbrush *(Castilleja miniata)* interspersed with other flowers throughout the meadow. The paintbrush is an interesting flower to examine closely. When you look at the "flower" and see red, you are not looking at petals but at red bracts that hide the true flower. If you gently push the brightly colored bracts aside, you will expose the greenish yellow flower in the center. You will know it is the true flower because the reproductive parts rise out of it.

Like other members of the Figwort Family, the paintbrush is a tubular, 2-lipped flower. The upper lip is divided into 2 lobes and the lower lip into 3. The problem is that no matter how closely you check out the flower, you'll have difficulty finding these lobes. That is unless you know that the 2 upper petal lobes are fused and appear as 1, while botanically speaking, the lower petals are the green nubbins that rest midway along the flower.

It is such confusions as these that can best be cleared up by a botany field class or by hiking with an experienced botanist. By receiving some basic help in the beginning, you'll reduce much of the frustration that comes with self-taught botany.

Aspens Record the Past

After walking through this small meadow, head toward the grove of aspens that grows at its fringe. There you will find sheepherders' doodlings carved into the white bark of these lovely trees. The sheepherders spent weeks alone in the Sierra watching over their sheep. I suppose they needed an outlet for their frustrations and fantasies and thus left us this unique

*Paintbrush
flower*

and personal art form. Sheep were also grazed in the meadows around Northstar, but when Northstar was developed into a family resort, the management scraped the carvings off the trees, because they felt they were unsuitable for a family-oriented resort!

A Trembling Leaf Dance

Quaking Aspens *(Populus tremuloides)* are one of Tahoe's loveliest deciduous trees and are easily identified by the wonderful fluttering of their leaves. No other leaves quake with such abandon, not even those of their close relative, the cottonwood, which also grows along the creeks and in meadows at Tahoe. This unique quaking dance occurs, because the long, flattened leaf stalks are attached 90 degrees to the leaf blade's surface. These opposite surfaces catch and release the tiniest breeze to set up the dance that so delights our senses.

Aspens are not only beautiful to look at, but they are interesting trees as well, for they photosynthesize in their bark before the leaves have formed in the spring. If you gently scratch the white bark, you'll see the green of the chlorophyll. This gives them a head start on food production after the long period of winter dormancy.

Aspens come into flower in early-spring with catkins of separate male and female flowers. The pollen is spread by the wind, and the seeds that form float away as tiny balls of white fluff. But the life of an aspen seed is difficult. A high percentage are infertile and because those that are viable are so vulnerable to climatic conditions, they must sprout soon after contacting the soil or they will die. Since the seeds are released early in spring, when conditions are often still too cold for successful germination, most seeds do die. Therefore, reproduction of aspens is more often accomplished vegetatively from root sproutings, which pop up like weeds to create large groves of trees.

Destructive Grazing in the Sierra

After checking out the carvings on the aspens, return to the logging road. Soon you will pass open fields of mule-ears and balsam roots, that are lovely if you get there before a thousand head of sheep have moved through the area. They don't eat the leaves, but they devour most of the flower heads, so there will be little color left.

Many people don't realize that sheep and cattle are still allowed to graze on public land in the Tahoe National Forest, within the fragile Tahoe Basin and on lands outside of it. The granting of such grazing permits was the source of strong debate in Congress in 1988, a debate which continues in Congress and elsewhere. The General Accounting Office, an auditing and fact-finding arm of Congress, reported in June of 1988, that in the 16 western states public lands have been seriously eroded by largely unsupervised commercial livestock grazing.

The agency was particularly critical of the Bureau of Land Management, and somewhat less so of the U. S. Forest Service, for their lack of proper management of the program. Issues important at Tahoe are the damage done to fragile stream zones, to wet meadows and to erosion-prone hillsides; the destruction done to wild gardens in areas of high recreational value; the lack of funds to hire the manpower necessary to monitor the program; and the inadequacy of fees collected from the permitees, which account for only about 30 to 37 per cent of the program's cost.

Too often I have come upon wet meadows, creekside gardens and fragile hillsides that have been trampled by sheep and that reek of urine and feces. No animal, native to its environment, moves with such destructiveness over the land. Such damage to a high Sierran meadow may take a lifetime to heal. It is time that we respect the vulnerability of the Sierra and become realistic about its capacity to serve all of our needs. An excellent book dealing with the history and abuse from grazing is *Sacred Cows at the*

Continuing along the Logging Road

As you hike past the fields of mule-ears, you will find the shrubs of the Sierra Gooseberry *(Ribes roezlii)*. They grow about 4 feet tall, alongside the logging road, and bloom in July with reddish purple, tubular flowers that hang downward from the ends of the branches. The flowers are followed in August and September by rounded, red fruits that are covered with prickles. The fruit makes a delicious jelly after the prickles are strained out. In the fall, the leaves turn a vibrant red, heralding the beginning of winter.

Also along the road will be the approximately 4 foot tall plants of Anderson's Thistle *(Cirsium andersonii)*. This rose-red thistle is a member of the Composite Family and is made up of disk flowers only. (See the Sherwood Forest hike for a discussion of disk flowers.) If you pull one of the flowers out of the head, you will see that it is made up of a tubular, 5-petaled flower. The petal lobes are thread-like and radiate outward. In the center sits the pink, thread-like pistil. These flowers are a favorite with the sphinx moth. You'll find them on summery afternoons hovering over the flowers like hummingbirds.

The genus name, *Cirsium*, is from the Greek word *kirsos* which means "a swollen vein." According to the herbal traditions of the past, thistles were used to treat this ailment. Its roots and stems were also eaten by native peoples in an emergency, and the thistledown was used as tinder.

After hiking about 1.7 miles past the Basque meadow, you'll arrive at a small pond where the road ends. At this point, another road to the left heads across the pond's outlet creek up to a large meadow. Beyond the meadow, craggy ridges rise majestically. The Ridge Route follows this ridgeline — from that hike you look down into this meadow. Those who have 4-wheel drive, or high clearance, can drive the 1/4 mile to the meadow, although the walk is very pleasant and generally level.

The Flowers of the Upper Meadows

After arriving at the meadow, leave the road and head toward the mountain walls that backdrop it to explore the creeks that flow off Silver Peak and the ridgeline. At this point all your hiking will be cross-country, but it is easy to keep your orientation. Along the creeks in late-June through early-August, you'll find many flowers in bloom, although the abundance of the display will depend upon the previous winter's snowpack.

The spring-blooming Drummond's Anemone (*Anemone drummondii*) usually comes into flower by early-June, although in some years, after a winter of heavy snow, it doesn't make an appearance until early-July. By mid-July elephant heads, paintbrushes, orchids and lupines bloom alongside the creek and are soon followed by the large, deep blue flowers of the Explorer's Gentian (*Gentiana calycosa*).

As you climb up to the rocks that backdrop these gardens, you will find more treasures, like the graceful, red columbines (*Aquilegia formosa*) that grow in moist gardens and the tubular red flowers of the fuchsia (*Zauschneria californica*) that cascade over and off the rocks.

Exploring the rocky ledges is especially fun because of the miniature gardens that grow here. Some gardens house little mossy areas with tiny ferns, saxifrages and monkeyflowers. They grow lushly in little sheltered spots, fed by the slowly dripping water that flows out of the cracks in the wall.

It was in these rocks that I first came upon the Peak Saxifrage (*Saxifraga nidifica*) one day in late-June. It has tiny white flowers that grow on 6 to 12 inch tall, glandular-hairy stems. The smoothly edged-to-barely toothed leaves are roughly egg-shaped and grow in a basal tuft. This is the only place at Tahoe where I've found this flower.

Another Special Find

On the same day in late-June, I made another new discovery on a sunny, sandy ledge not far from the saxifrage. It was the profusion of bright pink flowers that first attracted me. I knew it was a member of the Mustard Family because of its 4 petals and superior ovary. As I looked closer, I saw dagger-like seed-pods growing in a loose cluster above the grayish green, lance-like, basal leaves. By the seed pods, it was obvious that I had found the Dagger Pod *(Phoenoicaulis cheiranthoides)*, a common flower of the Great Basin that has migrated up the eastern slopes of the Sierra Nevada.

Another pink flower that flows among the rocks and along the ground near the creek is the Rock Fringe *(Epilobium obcordatum)*. It is discussed on the Sherwood Forest hike, but it is also gorgeous here and usually is in full bloom by early-July.

As you wander near the creeks, look for a bright yellow flower in full sun that sits like a cup close to the ground. The Northern Sun Cup *(Oenothera heterantha)* blooms right on top of a basal cluster of leaves, and it too is an eastern Sierran plant. If you look closely at the flower, you will see that it has 4 petals and an inferior ovary — an indication that it is in the Evening Primrose Family.

If you wander in among the trees and along the creeks near Silver Peak, you may also find the bright pink flowers of the Sierra Primrose *(Primula suffrutescens)*. Although they don't bloom profusely here, they are lovely as they grow nestled beneath the trees. Their usual environment is a north facing slope among exposed rocks, so it is a treat to find them here.

The Lovely Grass of Parnassus

Another flower that is not commonly found at Tahoe also grows here at Pole Creek. You will find it right along the creek's edge, among the rocks in July and August. It blooms with creamy white flowers atop naked stems, that are about a foot tall. Its greenish

167

veined petals taper at the base where they are decorated with fringe.

It was this petal fringe that lead to its name, Fringed Grass of Parnassus *(Parnassia fimbriata)*. It is a gorgeous, intricate flower, that is not really a grass, as evidenced by its heart-shaped leaves. The name grass comes from the past when the terms grass and plant were used interchangeably. Its common name is in remembrance of Mt. Parnassus in Greece.

The Grass of Parnassus is a sneaky little flower because it entices insects by what look like sugary nectar glands. These glands are really just sterile stamens located at the base of each petal that mimic glistening, greenish yellow nectar glands. (The true stamens radiate outward between the petals.) Insects are thus drawn to the center of the flower to gather the "nectar," and in the process they pollinate the flower. The greenish yellow ovary also beckons insects with its glistening, lobed stigma.

Some of the land in this area of the hike is privately held, while the public land is managed by the Forest Service. A Forest Service map will show you these areas; I encourage you to hike on the public lands.

Pole Creek is a wonderful spot to go to be peaceful. I hope that those of you who visit the area will have many hours of solitude and serenity in its wild gardens, and that on some special day you will share the "joy, excitement and mystery" of this magical place with someone dear to you.

Shirley Canyon

A Gateway to the Pacific Crest Trail

🚶🚶

One day	
One way	*3 miles*
Trail begins/ends	*6200'/8400'*
Net gain/total gain	*2400'/2600'*
Topo maps	*USGS Granite Chief, Calif.*
	USGS Tahoe, Calif.
Wildflower Season	*Late-May through September*

In Shirley Canyon during springtime an exuberant creek rushes, splashes and sings in torrents of great delight dropping over granite walls and rushing through narrow gorges — a jubilant journey, that is subdued to a gentle wandering only when its waters travel across broad granitic slabs or linger momentarily in quiet pools. In the canyon's icy waters, a powerful, little bird swims upstream gathering delicious morsels, while along its banks, wooded glens give rise to orange lilies and red columbines that bloom with gentle grace.

Trailhead Directions

The entrance to Squaw Valley is located midway between Truckee and Tahoe City on Highway 89. From the entrance, take the road to where it turns left at the Village at Squaw Valley clock tower, toward the Squaw Valley Ski area and

Crimson
Columbine

169

the large, cement, tram building. Turn right just before the tram and drive to the end of the road. Then turn right again and drive through the Tram Condominiums until you arrive at a parking area near the base of the large granite wall. Pick up the sandy trail at this point and head northeast toward the trees and Squaw Creek. Trails lead up the canyon on both sides of the creek; later in the season when the creek is lower, you can easily boulder hop along its edge.

The Trail Begins

There are many ways to hike the canyon and weeks could be spent exploring all its special areas, but my favorite approach is to hike straight to the main creek and then follow it uphill, so that I don't miss the first gorgeous waterfall and pool that are several hundred

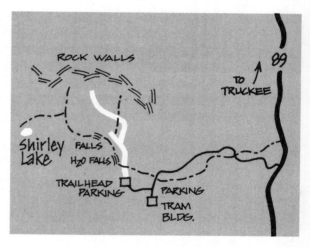

yards up the trail. In late-May through early-June, fragrant Creeping Phlox *(Phlox diffusa)* decorates the rocks on both sides of the creek, while from mid-June through early-July the tubular flowers of Mountain Pride *(Penstemon newberryi)* add splashes of vibrant pink. Also from late-June through July, hundreds of the star-shaped flowers of Scarlet Gilia *(Ipomopsis aggregata)* bloom among yellow tufts of Sulphur flower *(Eriogonum umbellatum)*, creating wonderful rock gardens on both sides of the creek.

Look also among the rocks, in dryish areas in June and July, for the creamy-yellow flowers of Pretty Face (*Brodiaea lutea*). They carry a dark mid-vein on each sepal and petal. This veining makes the flower look as pretty in bud as in bloom. Each flower stem rises from a central point on the main stem, in umbel fashion, like the spokes of an umbrella. If you look closely at the flower's center, you will see the broadly-shaped, light-blue filament which is forked at the apex.

In the same environment, you'll also find the pink, star-shaped flowers of the Sierra Onion (*Allium campanulatum*). Many flowers bloom on a single main stem, with each flower radiating outward in umbel fashion. Its 2-to-3 grasslike leaves often have dried up by the time the flowers come into bloom. Be sure to look at these exquisite flowers through your hand lens. Their 3 sepals and 3 petals have a satiny sheen and are elaborately decorated.

Brodiaeas and *Alliums* are two genera of the *Amaryllis* Family and may be distinguished from one another by the odor or lack of odor of their leaves and by the shape of the flowers. In the onion, or *Allium* genus, the petals and sepals are colored alike and are cleft to the base and its leaves have a strong onion odor. In the *Brodiaeas*, these flower parts are united into a basal tube below the flaring petals, and the plants are odorless.

Both *Brodiaeas* and *Alliums* were an important food source to Native Americans and were gathered by the Washos who came to Shirley Canyon each summer from Western Nevada. The leaves of onions flavored their foods, and the bulbs of both *Brodiaeas* and onions were dug up in the fall and roasted in earthen ovens. The seeds were also gathered and, after being roasted in willow baskets with hot rocks, were eaten as is or were ground into a flour.

Sierra
Onion

Wooded Gardens on the Creek's East Side
If you hike the canyon in late-May, be sure to explore this area on the east side of the creek among

the trees before you begin climbing toward the first waterfall. This early in the season few flowers will be in bloom, but you might just find the pinkish flowers of Steer's Head *(Dicentra uniflora)*. This is one of the most accessible places to find this strange little flower, which was discussed in the Moonlight on Castle Peak hike.

If you are exploring this same area among the trees later in the season, in August through September, look for the gorgeous, deep-blue flowers of Explorer's Gentian *(Gentiana calycosa)*. Its flower buds are a midnight blue and are as lovely in bud as they are in flower. It usually stays in bud for several weeks before finally bursting into glorious bloom. If you peer into the flower's center, you will see that it is sprinkled with green to yellow spots and that the petals are joined by a fringed, bluish membrane. There are only a few plants in this area, but those that are here are large and covered with many blossoms.

The Primitive Peony

In the same wooded area in June, look for the strange, nodding flowers of Brown's Peony *(Paeonia brownii)*. They bloom below fleshy, gray-green, deeply divided leaves. In order to see this flower, you must bend down and lift its face toward yours. Its green sepals are rounded and cup-shaped and its reddish brown petals are edged in yellow. Many stamens gather in the center around the 3 to 5 pistils. The green ovaries swell to a prominent 2 to 3 inches after fertilization. They are particularly noticeable, because the petals fall off as the ovaries ripen, although this is an ovary that would be difficult to miss, even with the petals intact!

Finding a Year-Round Resident

As you walk along the creek, keep your eyes open for one of the few birds that remains at Tahoe all winter. Look for a dark-gray bird, with a short tail, that is about the size of a robin. It is easy to identify as it bobs up and down on the rocks at the creek's edge. It is this bobbing behavior that led to its common name, Dipper *(Cinclus mexicanus)*. It bobs to declare its territory and to announce itself to a mate.

Dippers are solitary, except for when they pair to mate and raise their young. The nest is globular, about 1 foot in diameter and is made out of mossy materials. It is placed near rushing water or behind waterfalls where the spray of the moving water will keep the ball of moss moist. The female lays 3 to 6 white eggs in the spring. The young hatch within about 2 weeks and remain in the nest almost a month before leaving to begin their solitary, year-round lives on the stream.

The Dipper is one of the few birds that remains at Tahoe during the winter. Its thick, downy undercoat insulates it from the cold. It is the only songbird that feeds entirely in mountain waters. You will often spot it flying rapidly up the creek only a few inches above the surface in search of food. When it spots an insect, it plunges into the water without hesitation. Afterwards, it may continue to swim submerged through the rapids, propelled by its short but powerful wings. On other occasions, it casually walks along the sandy bottom of streams, as if taking an afternoon walk, while it forages for tasty bits of larvae. The Dipper lacks the webbed feet of most water birds, but perhaps this is to his advantage because it allows him to effectively grip the floor of the stream as he walks along it.

Woodland Gardens of Lilies

As you wander up the creek, look for gentle, sunlit glens that give rise to columbines, lilies and violets. The lovely Alpine Lily *(Lilium parvum)* blooms on stems up to about 4 feet tall. Its orange, tubular flowers are 1 to 2 inches long with slightly flaring, maroon-spotted petals that curve back at the tips. Instead of drooping like a flowery bell, it proudly raises its petaled face to the golden shafts of light that penetrate its woodland garden.

Its botanical name, *Lilium,* is derived from *leirion*

Alpine
Lily

173

which is the classical Greek word for "lily" and their word for "purity." The lily became the Greek symbol for purity because of the pure white color of certain lilies. *Parvum* means "small" and although the Alpine Lily is not a small flower, it is one of the smaller lilies.

In these wet gardens, look too for the large plants of Corn Lily *(Veratrum californicum),* with its stalks of white, star-shaped flowers. It is often found blooming alongside the even larger Cow Parsnip *(Heracleum lanatum)* — a plant with tiny flowers that grow in large umbels above huge, maple-shaped leaves.

In these shaded, wooded gardens, to the left of the creek, there is a tiny, green orchid that rises out of the pine-needled floor on stems up to about a foot tall. The Alaska Rein Orchid *(Habenaria unalascensis)* was discussed on the Benwood Meadow hike, but this is one of the few spots at the northshore where I have found it.

Gardens by the Waterfall

As you continue several hundred yards up the creek, you will come to the first waterfall and the lovely pools beneath. Near the pools in the shade of conifers, look for the crinkly petaled, white flowers of the Thimbleberry *(Rubus parviflorus).* They're particularly lovely in this area. By August, the flowers are replaced by a red fruit in a cup-like receptacle. In the 1791 diary of a voyage made from China to the northwest coast of America, the ship's naturalist, John Meares, wrote of this plant,

Thimbleberry seeds

> "On the rocky islands, and in the woods . . . is a species of raspberry of the most delicious flavour, and far superior to any fruit of that kind we had ever before tasted. It grows on a larger bush than our European raspberry, and is free of thorns; but the fruit itself is so delicate, that a shower of rain washes it entirely away."

The berry is so delicate that it will collapse in your

fingers as you try to pick it, but if you don't mind red fingers, you'll find the sweet berry to be a treat along the trail.

As you explore around the falls for flowers, look to the right edge, where in July you should find the yellow flowers of St. John's Wort (*Hypericum formosum*). They bloom in terminal clusters on stems that can be a foot or more tall. Its flower is easy to identify, because fuzzy looking stamens grow out of its center. The leaves usually have dark spots along the lower margin and grow opposite one another along the stem.

A Food-laden Chaparral Slope
After crossing the creek to find the St. John's Wort, you can continue up the slope along the small trail that passes through the Greenleaf Manzanita (*Arctostaphylos patula*). The manzanita blooms pink with nectar-laden, urn flowers in June. Look at these flowers closely and you will see that, like the columbines discussed on the Loch Leven hike, they have tiny holes made by nectar-stealing insects.

You will also pass the Pinemat Manzanita (*A. nevadensis*). It has similar-looking, white flowers and small leaves that grow on dense, ground-hugging shrubs. The small, red berries of both manzanitas were gathered by the Washos and made into a refreshing drink. They were also dried and added to hot dishes or to pinole, a mixture of seeds, dried fruit and meat.

Huckleberry Oak (*Quercus vaccinifolia*) blooms here with inconspicuous, yellow, male and female flowers. The acorns that followed the flowers in fall were gathered by the Washos who, after leaching out the tannic acid, cooked them into a nutritious, high protein mush or baked them into bread patties.

The Naming of Shirley Canyon
Shirley Canyon was named for Shirley Houghton who, along with his father C. S. Houghton, Joe Stanford, E. J. Okell, C. C. Bone and Senator Belshaw,

used to take annual trips into this once remote area to enjoy the isolation, beauty and great fishing. Their trips began in the late 1800's and continued through several generations. Shirley Lake and the canyon was named in honor of Shirley Houghton because he was usually the first to reach the lake and would be in the water by the time the others arrived.

This tradition was continued by C. S. Houghton's grandson, Winslow Hall, who related the story to me. One of the pools that lies at the base of one of the major falls was called "Joe's Frog Pool" because Joe Stanford always found a few frogs swimming there. After hiking up to Shirley Lake and taking a swim, they headed down into the Five Lakes Basin to Hell Hole. Here the fishing was reported to be so good that they would awaken each morning and, standing up in their sleeping bags, cast a line and catch a trout on each cast for breakfast!

Lacy Pink Flowers Bloom on Rock Ledges

Just after the manzanitas, you will pick up the dusty, main trail and continue up the mountain for a few hundred yards until you come to rounded, granite slabs. These slabs line the top of the gorge that channels Squaw Creek down over the rocks. As you look down into the swirling water below in June and July, keep your eyes open for the lacy blooms of the Pink Alum Root *(Heuchera rubescens)* that grow on rocky ledges and in vertical cracks above the creek. Its tiny flowers bloom on slender stems that may appear fragile, but its rootstocks are tough enough to penetrate cracks in rock walls. They tenaciously hold on through the years, until in some cases the expanding roots split open the rock.

Alum Root is a member of the Saxifrage Family, a name that means "rock breaker." This ability to split rocks led some herbalists in the 16th and 17th Centuries to conclude that this plant was given to man by the Gods to break up kidney stones. There was a belief then, called the Doctrine of Signatures, that plant forms or habits of growth were messages from the Gods of the plant's healing powers.

Native Americans apparently didn't receive the same message, but they did pound the roots to make a poultice which they then applied to sores and swellings. Herbalists have known for centuries that these plants are soothing on burns or cuts in nerve sensitive areas of the skin. This is because of an oil that enters the nerve endings to relieve pain. In Russia, St. John's Wort is grown for this oil, which is put into a pain-relieving skin cream.

The Glorious Washington Lily

If you head due north, for several hundred yards from the creek, at this point toward a wooded area near the base of a rock wall, you may find the spectacular, white flowers of the Washington Lily (*Lilium washingtonianum*). It usually blooms in mid-July and is one of the most beautiful wildflowers at Tahoe.

Its trumpet-shaped blossoms are as large as an Easter Lily and are often dotted red at the base and tinged with yellow. They are intensely fragrant and are often covered with hundreds of ants that come to enjoy the nectar. Since they are relished by deer, you must be lucky enough to get there first. If the deer arrive before you do, you can still identify the plants by their large, whorled leaves that grow along stems that are about 4 feet tall.

This lily, which was named in honor of Martha Washington, was a favorite of John Muir. When he came across it one July morning in 1869 in Yosemite, he wrote, "Found the white fragrant Washington lily, the finest of all the Sierra lilies...A lovely flower, worth going hungry and footsore endless miles to see. The whole world seems richer now that I have found this plant in so noble a landscape."

Continuing along the Trail

After retracing your steps to return to the main trail, you can continue up the mountain, along the east side of the creek, for about 1/4 mile, until you cross a feeder creek that, in July, is lush with orange lilies, blue-purple larkspurs and yellow senecios. After crossing the creek, look on the left side of the trail for the 3 to 4 foot tall stalks of pink Fireweed *(Epilobium angustifolium)*, which can be found blooming in July through early-August.

In another 1/4 mile, you will arrive at a split in the trail. The left fork will take you to wonderful waterfalls and pools with great granite slabs, perfect for sunbathing and picnicking. Eventually the trail leads to privately-owned Shirley Lake, a lake which was once beautiful, but which is now desecrated because of the ski lift and service road so near its shoreline.

I suggest that you enjoy the waterfalls and pools and then retrace your steps back to the fork in the trail. At this junction in July, the ground is usually carpeted in pink with Bridge's Gilia *(Gilia leptalea)* and Whisker Brush *(Linanthus ciliatus)*. These little flowers are true belly flowers, rising only a few inches off the ground and can best be appreciated down on your belly with a hand lens.

Bridge's Gilia is pink to violet with a yellow, pink or violet tube. If conditions are right the gilia may rise 6 inches or more out of the ground. Its leaves are narrow, and its flowers usually bloom in pairs on thread-like flower stems that can be several inches long.

The Whisker Brush is a pink, tubular flower with flaring petal lobes. Its lower petals are yellow, with red spots, and the throat is yellow. Each little solitary flower is surrounded by a dense cluster of hairy, needle-like leaves, which is the source of its common name.

After dusting off your belly and picking the rocks out of your knees, continue up the right fork which will take you through lush, shady groves of bracken fern, alpine lilies and columbines. In crossing the small creeks along the way, look for the white, star-shaped flowers of the Death Camas *(Zigadenus venenosus)*. The flowers cluster near the top of stems, that are about a foot tall, while grass-like leaves grow out of the base. This camas is poisonous and is one that could be confused with the bulb of the edible camas lily. It is important to never eat plants in the wild, unless you are certain of what you are eating.

After passing another creek with dense vegetation, you will climb through open, sunny slopes of Jessica's Stickseed *(Hackelia jessicae)* with its little, blue, forget-me-not flowers. Then you will cross open, volcanic slopes of the yellow, daisy-like flowers of Mountain Mule-ear *(Wyethia mollis)* and Balsam Root *(Balsamorhiza sagittata)*.

Next to the trail by the mule-ears there should be an old, weathered Pacific Crest Trail sign, if it is still standing. The sign will direct you straight ahead through a wooded area, and then across more open slopes of mule-ears and balsam roots and across seep gardens, bright with flower color.

Finding Two Rare Flowers

As you hike in these sunny open areas, be on the look out for two flowers that are infrequently found at Tahoe. They bloom right along the trail in mid- to late-July. The Slender Bird's Beak *(Cordylanthus tenuis)* looks just like its name and blooms on loosely growing plants that are about 2 feet tall. Its inconspicuous, greenish yellow blossoms are purple along the upper lip of the corolla and bloom in small clusters along the stems, above linear leaves.

The other flower, Lemmon's Penstemon *(Penstemon lemmonii)*, blooms yellow on bright green shrubby plants, that grow about 3 to 4 feet tall. The upper petal of this small, 1/2 inch long flower is a brownish purple, while purple nectar lines mark the lower petals. The flowers bloom in pairs at the ends of stems that also branch out in pairs. Its oval-shaped leaves are toothed and grow opposite one another.

Soon the trail becomes faint and would be difficult to follow across the open, granitic slabs if it were not for the ducks, or man made piles of 2 or 3 rocks, that mark the trail. You will often see these markers along the trails, put there by the Forest Service and other helpful souls to mark the way.

179

Red Fuchsia Decorate the Rocks

Looking down from this point, you'll have wonderful views into Squaw Valley's meadow. When white explorers first entered the large meadow, they found it inhabited mainly by Washo women and children (the men were out hunting) and so they named it Squaw Valley. For centuries the meadow and canyon was a popular summer retreat for the Washos. Trout were abundant in the creeks and the canyon housed plenty of game and herbs. It must have been a place of many happy memories, just as it is for many of us today.

If you hike along this area in late-July, look up at the steep walls for wonderful clusters of the scarlet California Fuchsia *(Zauchneria californica)*. Its vibrant flowers bloom at the end of leafy stems. Bright red reproductive parts flow enticingly out of the flaring petals. The fuchsia clings to rocky ledges, held there by penetrating roots that allow it to search deep for moisture.

Its soft, grey-green leaves form a gentle backdrop for the scarlet flowers. The leaves' hairy covering helps conserve moisture, by reducing the evaporative airflow over the leaf surface and by reflecting the sun's rays. Its leaves were important to native peoples who gathered them for a tea to help relieve kidney problems.

California Fuchsia

The genus name, *Zauschneria,* is after Johann Zauschner who was a Bohemian botanist in the 1700's. Its species name, *californica*, refers to its range throughout California.

Its gorgeous, tubular flowers bloom from late-July to September, in a good year, and provide vital nourishment for south migrating hummingbirds at a time when most wildflowers have withered and gone to seed.

Another late-bloomer, that grows in cracks and on ledges in these granite walls, is the Western Eupatorium *(Eupatorium occidentale)*. This member of the Composite Family has pink disk flowers with fuzzy-looking reproductive parts, that are longer than the flower tube. The flowers densely cluster at the end of stems that are about a foot tall. Along the stems grow gray-green, oval- to triangular-shaped leaves that are toothed and opposite.

As you look among the flowers on the rock ledges in July, you may find the white, tubular flowers of California Skullcap *(Scutellaria californica)*. These flowers, which are members of the Mint Family, have square stems and 2-lipped flowers, with a flower tube that is swollen in the middle. The flowers bloom in pairs out of the axils of the opposite, oblong leaves.

Cresting the Ridge
As you continue following the trail, it will climb to the rim of the canyon. From there it crosses a saddle and merges with the Pacific Crest Trail. At the top of the ridge will be wonderful views of distant mountain ranges and nearby Anderson Peak. At this point you can continue for miles through the back-country, or you may return to the valley floor.

A Visit to the Inn
On your return to the valley, you may want to visit The Olympic Village Inn at The Village at Squaw Valley to enjoy a cool drink or a meal. The Inn was the dining room for athletes during the 1960 Winter Olympic Games, and the recently restored buildings behind the restaurant were their dormitories.

During the twenty years following the Olympics, the buildings and grounds were allowed to deteriorate to the point where they became a disgrace to the valley. The Inn previously was a linoleum-floored cafeteria, while the buildings behind the Inn were ugly, dilapidated rectangles painted blue, red, green and purple. The lovely water garden, that now blooms with monkeyflowers and other natives, was a flat, dusty field with a few lonely lodgepole pines, and the small clock-tower building by the entrance was a run-down gas station.

Then Philip Carville, a resident of the valley and

the former President of Northstar, came in with a plan to renovate and rejuvenate the area, so that man-made development within the valley would be worthy of the natural beauty of the mountain. He formed an investment partnership with a savings and loan association and gave purpose and vision to the re-building of the man-destroyed portions of the valley, while leaving the natural areas intact. He began with the renovation of the Olympic Village Inn, which became the first phase in the beginning of Squaw Valley's turnaround.

Soon, county planners, valley residents and a few enlightened business leaders rallied together to revise the County General Plan. They lowered the planned-density in Squaw Valley and developed a program of long-range planning to include protection of environmentally sensitive areas, such as the meadow and the canyon. The Ski Corporation witnessed the improvement and then set out to upgrade and modernize its outdated facilities.

It was an exciting time in the valley, but then the economic crunch of the early-1980's hit the savings and loan industry. The financial partners of the Village at Squaw Valley did not have the strength or experience to develop a long-term project and so, the long term objective of a complete village at Squaw Valley was placed on hold. The renovated Olympic Village Inn still stands as a symbol of the beginning of Squaw Valley's turnaround.

Visiting Squaw Valley's Meadow

After visiting the Inn, you may want to take a few minutes on your way out to enjoy the meadow. It is usually at the height of its bloom in mid-July, but begins blooming in late-May or early-June. When in full bloom, it can be intense with the pinks of Bog Mallow *(Sidalcea oregana)*, the yellows of Arrow leaf Senecio and the reds of Giant Paintbrush *(Castilleja miniata)*, all glowing in backlit brilliance against a lacy sea of white Yampah *(Perideridia bolanderi)*.

While standing near the meadow, take a moment

to imagine what it must have been like one hundred years ago when the Washos summered here to fish its streams and gather berries and herbs. Not only was the creek full of native trout, but bears, cougars and coyotes freely wandered.

After the white man took the land from the Washos, the area lost its once revered status. In the early-1900's the meadow was used to graze cattle for a small dairy operation. In the 1950's, the mountain was developed for skiing. This led to erosion from the denuded slopes, which silted the creek and, in time, destroyed the native trout population. In the 1960's, the meadow was filled and plant communities destroyed to level the meadow for the parking lot, ice arena and other facilities for the Winter Olympic Games.

In this process of using and abusing the land, something very precious has been lost. As Gladys Smith wrote in her book, *A Flora of the Tahoe Basin and Neighboring Areas,*

"Years ago, sundew grew at the margins of a large swampy meadow which occupied the site where the Squaw Valley community now stands. The habitat was destroyed when the meadow was drained to make room for the 1960 Winter Olympics. In 12 short years Squaw Valley was to experience a meteoric rise and fall — from a quiet little alpine valley to the glamorous heights of the Winter Olympics, to the burdensome acquisition as a California state park, and at last to the heedless exploitation of private ownership which has to date shown no concern for environmental quality.

It saddens one to recall the picturesque little valley of yesterday, complete with its drosera bog, and to contemplate man's talent for destruction and his stubborn refusal to consider or even to look for alternate plans which might protect the unique features of the natural scene. For a drosera bog is unique — in its unusual assemblage of plants and in it rare occurrence in California. The price the people of California paid for the destruction of the Squaw Valley drosera bog was too costly for the merchandise they got in return."

Unfortunately we are still paying the price. Though the intent of the General Plan was to preserve the meadow and the canyon, the elected Supervisors of Placer County recently voted to allow the development of a golf course in the meadow and the cutting of trees in Shirley Canyon for the development of downhill skiing. (Two responsible members of the Board, Alex Ferreira and Mike Lee, are to be commended for voting against the amendment to the General Plan to allow tree cutting.)

Concerned residents and property owners in Squaw Valley have taken both issues to the courts to decide which interests will be honored, the right of present and future generations to enjoy and protect the wild beauty of the canyon and meadow or the narrow interests of the few who to date have shown a disregard for the environmental integrity of Squaw Valley.

A note on the positive side is that there are plans being proposed to clean up the creek and re-vegetate the ski hill (required by law) so that the creek can once again support native trout. Hopefully this will be implemented, as one step in a valley-wide effort to bring back some of the beauty that once reined in Squaw Valley. There is no way man could have created what Nature so generously gave to us in Squaw Valley. I just wish the white man could have entered this sacred temple, and lived and played within it, while still respecting the integrity of the land.

Antone Meadows

A Creek Garden of Rare Corydalis

One day	
One way	*2 miles*
Level trail begins	*6700'*
Topo map USGS Tahoe, Calif.	
Wildflower Season	*June through July*

Highlighted Flowers
- Water Buttercup
  (Ranunculus aquatilis)
- Alpine Shooting Star
  (Dodecatheon alpinum)
- Great Polemonium
  (Polemonium caeruleum)
- Bog Wintergreen
  (Pyrola asarifolia)
- Few-flowered Meadow Rue
  (Thalictrum sparsiflorum)
- Sierra Rein Orchid
  (Habenaria dilatata)
- Sierra Corydalis
  (Corydalis caseana)
- Heartleaf Arnica
  (Arnica cordifolia)

White-veined Mallow

The Antone Meadows lie nestled in a gentle slope above the blue waters of Lake Tahoe. From June through July, in a year of ample moisture, the meadows bloom in a swath of color like a rich tapestry. At the meadows' edge, pink shooting stars bloom in the sun-filtered light of lodgepoles, and wintergreens nod their satiny, pink blossoms in shaded willow gardens. Nearby, the rare corydalis blooms in profusion amidst white orchids, purple lupines and yellow monkeyflowers, along a rocky, meandering creek.

On warm summer afternoons, red-wing blackbirds trill their lyrical songs as they sweep through the meadows, while insects busily search the flowers for sweet nectar. For those who love to weave, photograph or paint, this is the place to come, for in the late afternoon light the grasses take on as beautiful an array of color as do the backlit flowers.

185

Trailhead Directions

Turn onto Old Mill Road (north of Tahoe City) off of North Lake Blvd and head uphill toward North Tahoe High School. Turn left on Polaris Road and drive past the high school to where a sign reads, "End of County Maintained Road." Park in the turnout and head in on the logging road. This road is ideal for mountain bikes. Those who cannot or do not wish to hike may drive to the first meadow, but high clearance is necessary as the road is usually rutted. Be sure to bring an herbal bug repellent in the spring or the mosquitos will relentlessly pursue you.

The Trail Begins

The trail begins at the old logging road by the sign and then soon forks. At the split, take the left or

Pine bough

Fir bough

lower fork and continue on through the dry forest of conifers and shrubs, which gives rise in June and July to red gilias and paintbrushes, blue-purple squaw carpet and yellow mule-ears.

As you hike through this sunlit, forested commu-

186

nity, take a moment to look closely at the White Firs (*Abies concolor*) that grow along the edge of the road. You can identify them by their short needles, that rise directly out of the branches. Compare these with the needles of the pines growing nearby. Pine needles grow in clusters, with a brown, papery fascicle surrounding the base of the needles.

Once you can distinguish between a fir and a pine by their needles, look up toward the tops of the various trees and you'll notice another difference — fir cones stand upright on the branches like Christmas tree lights, while pine cones hang downward from the branch tips.

Pink Flowers of the Mallow Family

As you wander along the trail, look for the pink, bowl-shaped flowers of the White-veined Mallow (*Sidalcea glaucescens*). They grow in sunny, dry openings along the trail's edge and bloom from late-June through August.

If you look closely at this flower, it will give you a key to identifying members of the Mallow Family, throughout the world. Look at the flower's center and you will see that the stamens and pistils are not separate, as in most flowers. Instead, the stamens are fused to form a single column. I'm sure many of you are familiar with the hibiscus and hollyhock, which, as members of this family, share the same characteristic.

If you look at several mallows, you will notice that something interesting is going on in the center of the anthers. In some, the anthers look like a white powdery cluster, in others, there is a red dot in the middle, while in other flowers, you will find a red, lobed structure rising out of the anther cluster. Can you tell what is happening? If so, do you know which ripens first, the anthers or the pistil?

If you compare several flowers, you'll see that the white anthers ripen before the red stigma appears. Then the red pistil begins to rise up and out of the anthers, looking at first like a tiny red dot. As it elongates, the "dot" becomes a red "thread" which later opens into a ripened, 5-parted stigma, eager and ready to receive pollen from another flower of the same species.

Try to observe this whole process for yourself. This difference in the maturing of the male and female reproductive parts is the flower's way of reducing the chance of self-fertilization and is one of the most common protective devices that plants employ. Look at other flowers along the trail to see if you can observe this process and try to determine at what stage the flower is in. This will sensitize you to the wonderful detail and constant change within a flower.

The leaves of the mallow are deeply divided into linear to oblong lobes on the upper stem, while the lower leaves are rounded and maple-like. Later on, in the meadow, you will see another species of mallow with a similar leaf pattern.

As you continue along the trail, you'll arrive at two more forks. If you head right at each junction, you will be on course. Don't forget to look up and around you, to take in the larger picture, especially the gorgeous views of Lake Tahoe that appear intermittently along the trial. After about 1 mile you will come to wet, creekside gardens and begin paralleling the creek. These gardens are only a suggestion of what lies ahead.

Soon the trail divides again and there you will take the middle fork and continue along the logging road or you may choose to walk by the creek's edge to enjoy the flowers along the way. After crossing a creek bed with dogwood and thimbleberries on its banks, you will come to another fork. At this fork, head left across the bridge, and if you are driving or riding a bike, leave your vehicle at this point.

White Floating Buttercups

After you cross the bridge, you will be close to the first meadow which is part of a series of meadows that create the large, meandering area called Antone Meadows. After leaving any vehicles behind, head to the right through the nursery of lodgepoles, along-side the man-made pond. At one time, the pond supported a small dairy operation that provided milk for Tahoe City. I hate to think of cattle in these meadows, but the fresh milk must have been wonderful.

If you come here in June, look for the white blossoms of the Water Buttercup *(Ranunculus aquatilis)* floating on the pond's surface. The flowers have 5 petals with small, yellow nectar glands at the base of each petal. Its submerged, floating stems grow about 5 feet long and carry masses of thread-like, brownish leaves that undulate in the currents beneath the water's surface. You will find these flowers in ponds and slowly moving streams in only a few areas at Tahoe.

At the pond's edge along the faint trail, look for the white Macloskey's Violet *(Viola macloskeyi),* with purple nectar lines on the petals, and the Carpet Clover *(Trifolium monanthum),* that blooms with small, white flowers above its 3 leaflets.

Arriving at the Meadow

Within a couple hundred yards of the bridge, and just beyond the pond, you will arrive at the first meadow. If you visit the meadow in late-June through early-July, at the height of the flower season, you will feel as if you were immersed in a soft-toned water color. Whenever I am in this meadow, I long to spend a day with a waist loom weaving its beautiful colors into a many-hued tapestry. The first color I would choose would be purple from the Meadow Penstemon *(Penstemon rydbergii).* In a good year, it creates a purple wash backdropped by the blues of polemoniums, the reds of paintbrushes and the yellows of senecios. In a dry year the flowers are few and grasses dominate the scene, and while still lovely, the palate is limited to varying shades of green and gold.

My tapestry would also include the Alpine Shooting Stars *(Dodecatheon alpinum)* that bloom by the hundreds in sun-filtered lodgepole pine gardens, with

189

pink, reflexed petals. Pink also colors the meadow with the flowers of Bog Mallow *(Sidalcea oregana).* Its dense, spike-like cluster of blossoms appear above lobed, maple-shaped leaves, on stems about 2 feet tall. If you didn't know the name of this plant, could you tell what family it was in just by looking at the flower? Notice that it has the same fused reproductive column as the White-veined Mallow, that we saw earlier along the trail.

This open meadow is also appreciated by other weavers. Red-wing Blackbirds *(Agelaius phoeniceus)* gurgle and trill their songs from nearby trees before swooping through the meadow to gather insects in flight. Look also for chickadees and blue jays as well as for the occasional Mountain Bluebird *(Sialia currucoides),* that adds a vibrant blue to the meadow's color.

The Glandular Bog Saxifrage

If you visit the meadows in mid-June through July, look for the straight, stiff stems of the Bog Saxifrage *(Saxifraga oregana)* that grow up to about 2 feet tall. Its white flowers bloom along the tops of the glandular-pubescent stems. If you have any doubt about what glandular-pubescent means, check the stems and it will become quite clear. Sticky drops of liquid sit on the tips of the densely growing hairs. The best way to understand botanical terms is, of course, to observe their usage in the field. As you sit in the field, look up flowers that you can easily identify and then read their descriptions in a book, like Norman F. Weeden's, *A Sierra Nevada Flora,* that uses more technical terminology. In this way you will soon painlessly learn the botanical terms.

The Bog Saxifrage is a member of the Saxifrage Family, a family that can most easily be identified by its 2-clefted ovary. This can be clearly seen in the saxifrage after fertilization, when the ovary turns reddish and forms 2 small but prominently pointed beaks.

The saxifrage flowers bloom in succession along

Bog Mallow

the stem from lower to upper, so on one plant you will usually be able to see the whole process from bud to flower to seed. If you look at the upper flowers and then at the lower ones, you will notice that the 10 orange anthers lie appressed to the white petals in the freshest flowers. After the anthers ripen, they rise up and away from the petals to release their pollen. Then the pistil ripens and opens, ready to receive pollen. This process is similar to the mallow, discussed earlier on the trail, but notice how the form of the reproductive parts differs.

Finding a New Meadow Rue
In wet areas near the Bog Saxifrage, look among the willows for a species of meadow rue that we have not seen on previous hikes. The Few-flowered Meadow Rue *(Thalictrum sparsiflorum)* is closely related to Fendler's Meadow Rue *(T. fendleri)*, but unlike Fendler's, with its different male and female flowers on separate plants, the Few-flowered Meadow Rue has perfect flowers, or both male and female reproductive parts in one flower.

The blossoms are made up of tiny, white sepals that take the place of petals to surround the yellow-green reproductive parts. The scent of the flower is attractive to small flies, while its stems, that grow up to about 3 feet, lift the barely-noticeable flowers above the lush foliage of the surrounding plants to catch meadow rue pollen grains carried by the wind.

Another treasure, that you might find among the lodgepoles and willows, are the satiny pink flowers of the Bog Wintergreen *(Pyrola asarifolia)*. They bloom in mid-July along the top of leafless, 4 to 12 inch stems above basal leaves, that remain green all winter beneath the snow. Both the sepals and petals are a deep red-pink and are as colorful in bud as in bloom, making them easy to spot.

Creek Gardens of the Common and the Rare
As you continue walking north, you will come to the major creek that feeds the meadow, and in late-June

through July, you will find many flowers. Lining its banks in yellow will be Seep-spring Monkeyflowers *(Mimulus guttatus),* while the white Sierra Rein Orchid *(Habenaria dilatata)* is usually found in abundance among the trees next to the gently flowing creek. Its tiny, 1/2 inch long flowers grow densely along the 1 to 3 foot tall spikes, as they emit the sweet fragrance of vanilla.

As you hike up the creek, look for a very special flower that I have found no where else in Tahoe. Gladys Smith, in her book, *A Flora of the Tahoe Basin and Neighboring Areas,* states that this flower is, "Said to range as far south as Placer County in the Sierra Nevada, this handsome endemic was looked for during the field work of the flora but never found. When it was at last discovered, it was not in Placer County where I had searched, but about the shores of Echo Lake in El Dorado County." The Sierra Corydalis *(Corydalis caseana)* can now be enjoyed in Placer County! It blooms profusely in and along the creek for several weeks from late-June through July and, like the steer's head that we saw on Castle Peak, it is a member of the Fumitory Family.

But unlike the ground-carpeting steer's head, the corydalis grows up to about 4 feet or more tall, with a great profusion of gray-green leaves. Its flowers, which emit a wonderful, grape candy fragrance, grow densely along the stalk. The pinkish petals are purple-tinged and carry a long, single spur, so that the flowers resemble swimming whales perched upon tiny stems.

Arnicas Bloom in Wooded Gardens

If you leave the wet meadows and creeksides to explore the woods, look for an arnica that we have not found on our other hikes. It blooms from June to July with yellow, daisy-like flowers above fragrant leaves. The Heartleaf Arnica *(Arnica cordifolia)* is easy to identify by its pairs of heart-shaped leaves that grow along the flower stem and by its yellow ray flowers.

This is also one of the few places at Tahoe where

the yellow subspecies of Crest Lupine *(Lupinus arbustus ssp. calcaratus)* blooms. We discussed it on the Sagehen Creek West hike; it grows here in the same environment, in sunlit openings at the base of Lodgepole Pines.

Lodgepole Pines *(Pinus contorta, var. murrayana)* are common throughout Tahoe, and in fact are one of the most widespread of trees. They have an amazing range, growing from sea level up to about 11,000 feet and from Alaska to Mexico.

Lodgepoles exhibit two different forms. In stands where the trees grow close together they rise straight, tall and thin. Because of this, they were used by Native Americans as poles for their tepees or lodges (hence the name) and as frames for their travois, a drag-sled used to carry possessions when they moved camp. At higher elevations, where the trees are widely spaced, they take on a variety of contorted shapes, as if finally able to express their individuality.

The Cycle in a Meadow

As you head back through the meadow to return to your car, take a moment to stand and look out across the flowers and grasses. Notice that the meadow is ringed by lodgepoles and white firs. Both of these trees are part of a slow process that, in some cases, changes lakes into meadows.

When the last glaciers retreated over ten thousand years ago, they left behind scoured-out depressions that, over time, filled with water. Over thousands of years, stream erosion on mountain sides carried soil into the depressions, coating lake bottoms and lining shorelines with life-giving nutrients to support both the plant and animal life that was slowly colonizing these alpine lakes.

Over time, as streams deposited more and more soil into the lakes, new shorelines moved farther into the lake. Grasses, sedges and other water loving plants were the first to colonize the lake's edge because of their tolerance for boggy environments. As the previous shoreline moved farther into the lake,

193

because of newly deposited soils, the wet soils of the old shoreline became drier, enabling new plants to migrate into the old shoreline areas. In time there was enough soil to support plants with larger root structures and the conifers and shrubs began to move in.

Lodgepoles, which have the highest moisture tolerance of any conifer, were the first conifers to colonize the drying shorelines of these lakes. They were accompanied by the deciduous aspens, willows and alders, that thrive in wet environments. These plants further helped in the conversion of wet to dry meadows by absorbing and then transpiring thousands of gallons of water into the atmosphere.

As the many different plants went through their seasonal cycles, shedding their leaves and needles, they created new soil to support more plant life. The various root systems also helped stabilize and retain the life-giving soil by forming a maze that prevented it from being washed away by rains or outlet creeks.

After thousands of years of these various factors working together, or as creeks changed their courses and no longer fed the lakes, some of the lakes began to dry up to form meadows. In time, as a meadow dries, it may be invaded by other, less water-tolerant trees, like the white firs which you see near the meadow's edge. Some meadows become dry enough to be completely invaded by other conifers, shrubs and herbaceous plants, until one day all trace of the old lake and meadow is gone.

While some lakes are gradually converted into meadows and woodlands, new lakes are being formed elsewhere by landslides, faulting or other activities. Newly formed creekbeds carry water to the new depressions, and as the water table rises in these new areas, trees and other vegetation die off, and a new lake is formed.

A Cycle that Connects Us with All Life
The process of death and rebirth in Nature is a continual cycle. Imagine the meadow once as a lake or

perhaps as it may be in the future, as a dry woodland. Look out at the plants and imagine them breaking forth from the soil each spring to flower and set seed before withering in the fall.

We of course are a part of this cycle. We are made up of materials that have been recycled on the earth since the beginning of time. The atoms that make up the cells of our bodies may have once been part of the wings of a butterfly, the petals of a flower or the water in a cascade.

We are an important part of the cycle. Our ability to impact the cycles of life has dramatically increased, as our population has grown and as our technologies have become more complex. We have begun to impact the world in ways that will dangerously affect future generations of both plant and animal life. We owe it to these future generations to start demanding that our political and corporate leaders take responsibility for the environmental damage that is being done to the water, air and soil. Additionally, each of us in our own lives, must begin making decisions that minimize our negative impact upon the world. As Duane Elgin points out in his excellent and timely book, *Voluntary Simplicity,*

"Our passage through life is not a neutral process. How we live our lives matters greatly. Each of us makes a difference. Just as boats of various designs leave very different wakes in the water behind them, so too do various approaches to living send out different waves of reverberating influence into the world. The disruptive wake that has been left by nearly two centuries of aggressive industrialization now threatens to swamp Western industrial nations and perhaps even the entire earth. In our highly interdependent, increasingly vulnerable world...we can no longer afford to be oblivious to the impact of our way of living on the rest of the world."

Whether it is by recycling our throw-aways, by

growing or buying our food organically, by supporting environmental organizations, by reducing our consumption or by leaving a wake of love and beauty behind us, we will leave the world a richer place, because we have been here. And I believe that is the dream of each one of us.

Paige Meadows

A Place to Enjoy in All Seasons

One day	
One way	*2 miles*
Trail begins/ends	*6400'/7000'*
Total gain	*600'/600'*
Topo map USGS Tahoe, Calif.	
Wildflower Season	*June through August*

Paige Meadows are a series of meandering, open meadows that form large, sun-filled openings between the forests of conifers and aspens. The meadows come into bloom in early-June, with gardens of yellow buttercups, which are soon followed by pink shooting stars, the scattered blues of camas lilies and swaths of purple penstemons. As summer progresses, the various flowers and grasses go to seed, welcoming birds that sing with delight until the brisk days of fall once again herald their southward journey. Winter brings a new experience, one of cross country skiing and snowshoeing through flat expanses of white, with the thrill of an occasional sighting of a coyote moving with a rhythmic gait through the blanketed landscape.

Graceful Cinquefoil

Trailhead Directions

Heading south from Tahoe City on Highway 89, drive 2.3 miles, and just after passing the Sunnyside Re-

197

sort, turn right onto Pineland Drive. Heading north on 89, turn left onto Pineland Drive 1/10 mile before Sunnyside. When Pineland Drive forks, take Twin Peaks Drive to the left and continue another 1.5 miles, until you arrive at the unsigned logging road on the right. Note that Twin Peaks Drive changes to Ward Creek Blvd. There is parking available on either side of the road. I have described this as a 2 mile hike, even though the first meadow is reached within 1 mile, because the meadows as a group are not reached until you have hiked for about 2 miles.

The Trail Begins

The trail begins on the old logging road and climbs steadily uphill through lovely white fir and lodgepole pine forest. Sunlit openings among the conifers give rise in June and July to the golden, daisy-like flowers

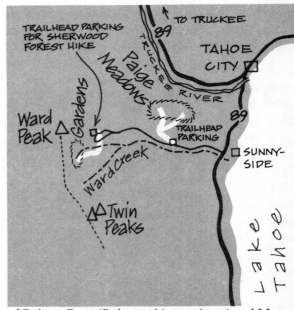

of Balsam Root (*Balsamorhiza sagittata*) and Mountain Mule-ears (*Wyethia mollis*). Among these large flowers grow the small "trumpets" of Scarlet Gilia (*Ipomopsis aggregata*), blooming red along upright stems above finely divided gray-green leaves.

If you leave the trail to wander through these sunny gardens, you'll find Jessica's Stickseed *(Hackelia jessicae)* blooming in early-July with blue forget-me-not flowers. Notice that the flowers have a contrasting raised ring of white in the center; this raised ring is a sure clue to members of the Borage Family.

In the same dry areas, don't pass by the pink, ball-shaped flowers of Pussy Paws *(Calyptridium umbellatum)* without touching the blossoms. If you gently squeeze one of the little flower clusters, you'll see how this plant received its name.

Pussy Paws live in hot, dry and sandy environments and have become adapted to such environments in an interesting way. In the early morning, when temperatures are cool, the flowers rest upon the dry ground. But by mid-morning, or early afternoon, they will have risen several inches above the soil. This movement, which helps the plant cool off by breaking contact with the hot ground, is caused by tension in the stems due to an increase of water pressure within the cells.

The flower clusters radiate outward, beyond the spoon-shaped, leathery leaves. In late-summer the soft, little "paws" are replaced by brown, papery ovaries that hold hundreds of tiny, black seeds that are gobbled up by chipmunks and other small rodents.

As you hike past these dry areas, in July, the intense blue to blue-violet flowers of Nuttall's Larkspur *(Delphinium nuttallianum)* will catch your eye. The plant grows about 4 inches to a foot tall, with only a few leaves and flowers on each stem. Its upper petals are white and veined in blue-violet. The lower 2 petals are bi-lobed, and the sepals are the same intense blue.

Pussy Paws

As you wander along the trail, you may come upon the yellow flowers of the Nodding Microseris *(Microseris nutans)* that bloom from June to July. The microseris, which can be easily identified by its nodding buds and dandelion-like flowers, is a member of the Composite Family. It is composed of ray flowers only, with each petal capable of producing a new plant.

The 4-petaled flowers of the Sierra Wallflower *(Erysimum perenne)* bloom in June and grow clustered at the top of a stem that usually grows 12 to 18 inches tall. Wall flowers are members of the Mustard Family, a large family of plants that includes cabbages, broccoli and radishes. Mustards can be identified by their 4 petals that form a cross, which was the source of their old family name, *Cruciferae*. (The Mustard Family now goes by the designation of *Brassicaceae*). If you look closely at the flower, you'll see that it has 6 stamens with 2 of these shorter than the other 4, as is typical of this family. Be sure to bend down and inhale its fragrance — it's heavenly.

A Silky Tent on Yellow-flowered Shrubs

As you wander through these chaparral-dotted hillsides, look for silky-spun coverings on the branches of the creamy yellow flowered shrubs of the Bitter Brush *(Purshia tridentata)*. These grayish white "webs" are made by the Tent Caterpillar *(Malacosoam pluviale)*, whose moths prefer members of the Wild Lilac and Rose Families as nurseries for their young.

If your timing is right, the tents will be filled with masses of squirming, brown caterpillars — a sight, that if not endearing, is at least interesting! In the fall the pale brown, striped-winged moths lay their eggs in encased rings around the stems. In the spring the larvae appear and spin their silky shelters among the branches before emerging to feed on the leaves.

Views of Twin Peaks

As you continue to climb, you'll arrive at an opening along the trail, with dramatic views of Twin Peaks and a distant saddle. On the Sherwood Forest hike, you'll climb to that saddle, after wandering through flower-filled meadows of golden mule-ears and lavender lupine.

After about 1/2 mile, the trail begins to level out and you'll come to small seep areas of Crimson

Columbine *(Aquilegia formosa)*, Giant Red Paintbrush *(Castilleja miniata)* and yellow Arrowleaf Senecio *(Senecio triangularis)* interspersed with wooded, sun-filled slopes of bracken fern.

In dry areas beyond the seeps and among the sagebrush, look during late-June through July for the red flowers of the Wavy-leaved Paintbrush *(Castilleja applegatei)*. This paintbrush is easily identified by its wavy margined, 3-lobed leaves. Its red leaf bracts are 5-lobed in the upper flowers and surround the yellowish, tubular flower in the center.

Wandering through the Main Meadow

In another 1/4 mile, you'll arrive at a fork in the road. Head to the right for about 1/2 mile, until you arrive at the sign reading, "Closed to Motor Vehicle Travel." After climbing over the dirt pile that blocks off the meadow, follow the trail through mats of white Macloskey's Violets *(Viola macloskeyi)* and yellowish orange Tinker's Pennies *(Hypericum anagalloides)*.

In a few hundred yards, the first meadow comes into view, as a large, open, grassy area, ringed with conifers, aspens and willows. In early-June, Water Plantain Buttercups *(Ranunculus alismaefolius)* spread fragrant carpets of yellow throughout the meadow.

If you head to the left just after entering the meadow, you should find wonderful gardens of monkey flowers *(Mimulus guttatus and M. primuloides)*, shooting stars *(Dodecatheon alpinum)*, paintbrush *(Castilleja miniata)* and other flowers. Look for them hidden between the willows and the dryer slopes of lodgepoles, in June and July.

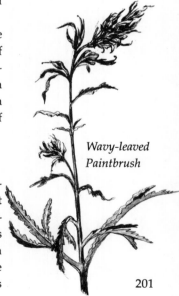

Wavy-leaved Paintbrush

A Vernal Pool for Frogs and Flowers

If you hike the meadows in June, check out the vernal pools at the north edge. In a dry year, you won't find any water, but in a wet year water sits in depressions, formed from an old logging road that has been made deeper through the years by erosion. In a wet year, the pools are home to hundreds of little Tree Frogs *(Hyla regilla)*, who sing to their hearts

201

content, as evening approaches.

The vernal pool also gives rise to the white flowers of Indian Potato (*Sagittaria cuneata*). They float along the surface, their 3-petaled blossoms growing in whorls of 3 along the stem. The Indian Potato has male flowers at the top and female flowers below. Look for the clusters of stamens in the center of the upper male flowers and the numerous pistils in the lower female flowers. After pollination the female flowers swell into a head of black seeds, called achenes, with small and sharply pointed vertical beaks. The long stemmed leaves of the Indian Potato are sagittate, or arrowhead-shaped, and float on the water's surface, forming beautiful shadows on the soil below.

Indian Potato is widely distributed throughout the western United States from Alaska down to the Sierra. Its starchy tubers, that grow at the ends of the rhizomes, were popular with Native Americans, who gathered them with digging sticks or with their toes. They then boiled them or roasted them in earthen ovens between layers of coals and leaves, to be enjoyed with fish or meat. Ducks and geese also appreciate this plant, diving to the bottom of ponds to dig up the smaller tubers.

After leaving the pools, follow the logging road in a westerly direction, where in late-June through early-July, you should be on the look out for the lovely, little, purple flowers of Porterella (*Porterella carnosula*). Once you spot a few along the road, you'll then spot hundreds more scattered throughout the grass on either side of the road.

Life in a Meadow Community
If you leave the road and head through the grass, you may encounter a slithering garter snake hunting for insects, frogs or mice. Though the meadow may seem quiet, except perhaps for the songs of red-wing blackbirds and chickadees, there is more to a meadow community than meets our eyes at first glance. If we could see through the grasses and soils, and if our

ears could pick up the subtle noises, we would be amazed at the abundant life.

Thousands of invertebrates live among the grasses in various stages of maturity, from larvae to adult. Pollinating insects circulate through and above the grasses, and other insects live by busily consuming one another.

Some meadow creatures spend all or much of their time beneath the grasses. Moles pass their entire lives underground, forming vast networks of tunnels. Pocket gophers also form tunnels — when winter comes they move closer to the surface forming mounds that remain standing after the snows melt in the spring. And hundreds of meadow mice and other small rodents scamper through the grasses foraging for seeds and herbs, before returning to their underground burrows to store food, sleep, mate and rear their young.

If you sit quietly among the trees at the meadow's edge, you may spot the Belding's Ground Squirrel (*Citellus beldingi*) along the edges of the meadow, where it sits upright looking out of its burrow. When alarmed, it sends out a squeaky little warning cry, before quickly dropping back into its hole.

It is the abundance of these animals that attracts the Coyotes (*Canis latrans*) that can often be seen gracefully and intently moving through the open areas. A Coyote is about the size of a large dog, but it moves in a way that no domestic animal does. It expresses a dignity and wildness that is thrilling when seen up close. I was once quietly walking through the shrubs at Pyramid Lake, feeling totally at one with my surroundings, when a Coyote passed within a few feet of me, chasing a rabbit. He was so intent on the rabbit that he took no notice of me. A few minutes later he passed back through the small opening, again only a few feet from me, without ever seeing me or indicating that he did.

Coyotes are powerful, cunning animals, long honored by Native Americans for their wisdom and trickery. They can comfortably cruise at speeds up to 25 miles an hour, or at 40 miles an hour for short distances, and can reportedly leap on prey 14 feet away. They are one of the few large animals that has extended its range since the arrival of the white man.

These animals may pair for several years, or like wolves, even for life. They mate in the winter, and the young are born in spring in dens that have been dug into the slopes of mountains, dry riverbanks or other areas. The young are born fully furred and are tended by both parents during the summer until fall, when they leave to start their own lives.

One of the most thrilling sounds at night in the mountains is the wild yelping of coyotes. As I listen to them at night, from my home in Squaw Valley, it is a joyful reminder to me that there are still wild ones living their own lives by their own rules, even though their domain has been invaded by man.

Flowers among the Grasses

As you wander through the meadow in July, look for the pink flowers of elephant heads *(Pedicularis groenlandica and P. attollens)*. Interspersed with them will be thousands of the tufted blossoms of the Bistort *(Polygonum bistortoides)* that sometimes turn the meadow into a sea of white.

Look also for the three different species of cinquefoils that bloom in the meadow in July. Cinquefoils are members of the Rose Family — notice that they have 5 petals and a large number of reproductive parts. The flower design of all cinquefoils is lovely — between each petal, a pointed sepal protrudes to create a star-shaped pattern.

The cinquefoils in this meadow can be identified by their leaves and yellow flower color. The Sticky Cinquefoil *(Potentilla glandulosa)* has pinnate leaves and pale yellow flowers, while the Graceful Cinquefoil *(P. gracilis)* has palmate, toothed leaves and bright yellow flowers. (See the Summit Lake hike for a description of pinnate and palmate leaves.) Drummond's Cinquefoil *(P. drummondii)* grows closer to the ground than the other two species and has

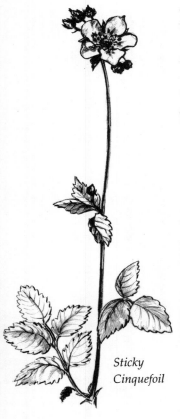

Sticky Cinquefoil

bright yellow flowers and hairy, dark green leaves. Its pinnate leaflets are usually so crowded that they seem at first glance to be palmate.

The word cinquefoil comes from French and means "five leaved" in reference to the 5 leaflets of certain species. Potentilla means "little potent one" and is a reference to the powerful medicinal quality of tea brewed from the leaves of certain species.

Flowers in the Wet Meadow Areas

As you wander to wetter areas in the middle of the meadow, look for the low-growing flowers of the Toad Lily *(Claytonia chamissoi)* blooming in late-June. These plants are easy to locate by their red runners that root on the soil's surface. Their white blossoms are made up of 5 shiny petals, with only 2 green, cup-like sepals, which you can see by tilting the flower. Two sepals are typical of members of the Purslane Family, which is an identifying feature, because most flowers have the same number of sepals as petals.

The flower is especially lovely because of its red anthers that contrast exquisitely with its pure white petals. The anthers are appressed to the petals before maturation, after which they rise to insure that their gift of life will be received. Notice too that the stigma is bright red and opens into 3 lobes when it is ready to receive pollen. In looking at various toad lilies, can you determine what is happening in the flower? Is it ready to receive or release its pollen?

While you're in the same wet area, look for another flower that is similar in size to the Toad Lily but has 6 to 10 white petals, instead of the Toad Lily's 5. Unlike the Toad Lily, which blooms several to a stem, the Nevada Lewisia *(Lewisia nevadensis)* usually carries a single flower atop each stem. By checking the sepal number, you'll see that it is also in the Purslane Family, for it only has 2 sepals.

Continuing on to the Adjacent Meadows

After reaching the west end of the meadow, walk

through the aspens and lodgepoles and wander into the adjacent meadow, which in July of a good year will be solid purple with Meadow Penstemons *(Penstemon rydbergii)*. And near the meadow's edge in small drying vernal pools, look for more lovely blossoms of the Porterella.

If you continue in a southwesterly direction, you will find other meadows. As you wander along the edges and among the trees, look for the red and yellow, nodding flowers of Crimson Columbine *(Aquilegia formosa)* and the orange, 6-petaled flowers of the Alpine Lily *(Lilium parvum)*.

In wooded clearings between the meadows, I often find another special sight, white Yampahs *(Perideridia bolanderi)*, that "float" in the afternoon breezes above a sea of the delicate, lavender flowers of Bridge's Gilia *(Gilia leptalea)*.

Enjoying the Cycle of Seasons

I encourage you to explore the meadows and gardens on your own to find special areas, but do take a compass, because the configuration of the meadows is such that it is easy to become disoriented.

I also encourage you to return to the meadows throughout the year to experience the changing seasons. It is one of Tahoe's most accessible and popular meadows and a place to which I return regularly to experience its different moods. In the spring and summer, I wander its meadows to find old favorites, to lie and lazily daydream in a sunny field of golden buttercups, or to find shelter from the heat of an August afternoon in a damp and shaded grove of lilies.

When I return in winter, to ski through its isolated woodlands, I like to imagine all the flowers resting away beneath the blanket of snow. I think of them encased in millions of tiny seeds, or lying dormant in swollen root stocks, waiting for spring's warmth, to once again emerge from the soil with vibrant color and delicate fragrance to provide life for millions of insects and enjoyment for us.

Sherwood Forest

A Verdant Garden Backdropped by Lake Tahoe

One day	
One way 1.5 miles	
Hike begins/ends 6600'/8300'	
Net gain/total gain 1700'/1700'	
Topo map USGS Tahoe, Calif.	
Wildflower Season Late-June through August	

Sherwood Forest is a magical place, where one can follow a stream to its source and along the way discover crimson columbines nodding their vibrant heads in the misty spray of a waterfall. Below the cascades, bright pink rock fringe bloom in luxurious carpets along the creek's edge, while farther down, a little hummingbird noisily defends its nesting site. Near the top of the ridge, rose-pink onion flowers brighten the dry, rock-strewn slope, while in the lush meadow below, arnicas dance yellow against a backdrop of the blue waters of Lake Tahoe.

Trailhead Directions

See previous hike for directions to the Paige Meadow sign. Continue past the sign, until you arrive at the Sherwood Forest lift, which is on the backside of Alpine Meadow's ski area, where the road loops back. There is plenty of parking along the shoulder.

Mule-ears

207

Cross-country through an Expanse of Yellow

After parking, look west before you begin to hike and you will see your destination — a series of green ledges cut into the mountain slope below the ridg-

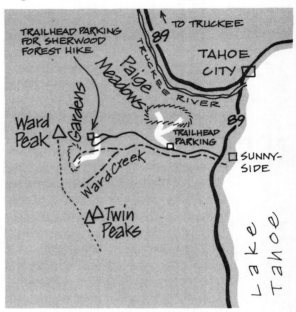

eline. (The Pacific Crest Trail runs north/south along the ridgeline, above the uppermost ledge.) Since there is no trail to the ledges, you will be traveling cross-country up the unnamed creek that flows into Ward Creek. You can locate this tributary, along the northern boundary of sections 20 and 21, as shown on either the topographic map or the Forest Service map for this area.

The flower-covered slopes, beyond the lift, normally begin blooming in late-June. The beauty of these slopes, which are dense with vegetation when sheep grazing has not been allowed, is a tribute to the ecological sensitivity of the developers and management team of Alpine Meadows Ski Area. The lush slopes in summer, demonstrate that winter recreation can be compatible with summer use, when owners and managers of a ski resort show respect for the natural environment.

From late-June to mid-July, the slopes in the bowl usually become covered with the golden, daisy-like flowers of Arrow-leaved Balsam root *(Balsamorhiza sagittata)* and Mountain Mule-ears *(Wyethia mollis)*. But in drier years, or if there is a late-season frost, the flowers may only scatter their color over the hillsides.

Understanding a Daisy

Most people, in looking at mule-ears and balsam roots, would describe them as daisies, and of course everyone is familiar with daisies. Or are they? Most people think of a daisy as a single flower with a circle of petals surrounding "things" in the center. But once you "understand" the flower, you will see that it is not just one flower but a collection of many.

Take a moment to really look at one of the flowers. If you closely examine one of the surrounding "petals," you will see that it carries a thread-like structure at its base. This structure is a single pistil, the female reproductive part. In a daisy-like flower, the petals are actually separate flowers, called "ray flowers", which carry their own set of reproductive parts. (In most flowers, if you pull off a petal, a pistil is not attached to it.)

Now take a moment to look closely at the center of the flower and you will see that it is made up of hundreds of tiny, 5-petaled, tubular flowers. Botanists have named these center blossoms "disk flowers." Notice that the disk flowers along the outer edge of the central circle open first, while those in the center are still tightly in bud.

The reproductive parts tell an interesting story about these flowers. The yellow, thread-like structure that rises out of the center of each, opened, disk flower is the pistil. Compare different flowers and you will see that in some, the pistil appears as one thread, and in others, it is 2-lobed; can you tell what is happening?

To prevent self-pollination, when the anthers are ripe, the stigma is tightly closed and looks like a

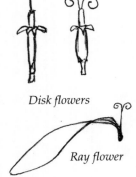

Disk flowers

Ray flower

thread. When the stigma is receptive, it opens into 2 lobes to receive pollen. If you look very closely at the pistil, you will find that it is surrounded by a yellow swelling. This swelling is made up of stamens that are fused to form an anther tube. When the pollen is ripe, it is released into the center of this tube. Then the pistil, which is still tightly closed, moves up the tube, like a piston, pushing the pollen ahead of it. As the stigma, or tip of the pistil, rises up and out of the stamen tube, pollen is released onto the upper edge of the tube, where it is picked up by visiting insects.

After the pollen has been released, the pistil then becomes receptive and opens into the 2-lobed structure that you observed earlier. The ripened pistil, in the ray flower, is identical to that of the disk flower. Your hand lens will help you to see these structures.

A Perfect Composite Flower
The tubular flowers in a daisy are called perfect flowers. This is not a qualitative term, but rather a botanical term, referring to the fact that the flower has both male and female reproductive parts. While the disk flowers are perfect, the ray flowers are imperfect, for they carry only the pistil. Thus an imperfect flower is one that carries only the male or female reproductive parts, which does sound rather imperfect!

All daisies and daisy-like flowers are members of the Composite Family because they are a composite of many flowers in one flower head. (Botanically speaking, "true" daisies are only those of the *Erigeron* genus.) The composites are the largest family of vascular plants, with 20,000 species world wide. Not all composites have both ray and disk flowers, some have only disk flowers, like the thistle, and some have only ray flowers, like the dandelion. Next time someone brings you a bouquet of Marguerites, you can thank them for bringing you a thousand flowers!

Dry Environment Adaptations
Take a moment to view these tiny parts with your hand lens, and then step back and view the whole

mule-ear or balsam root plant in the context in which it grows. What do the plants look like that grow near it? What are the similarities between them and how might these similarities insure survival in this dry habitat?

Notice that the leaves of the mule-ear, and many of the other plants, are thickly covered with hairs to deflect evaporative winds and reflect sunlight, but notice too that they are much larger than the leaves of the surrounding plants. Small-leaved plants predominate in dry environments, because this leaf form minimizes evaporation of precious water. Large leaves are thus usually associated with wet environments where water is abundant and evaporation is not a problem.

The large leaves of the mule-ear and balsam-root deviate from this norm and expose these plants to high water loss. Can you see how these plants have adapted to reduce this loss? Notice that the leaves are covered with fine white hairs, and they grow vertically. This vertical position reduces the amount of leaf surface presented to the sun, which helps to reduce water loss. (These plants also have 6 foot long tap roots to help them search deeply for water.) Notice how many other leaves in this dry environment also grow vertically or are covered with a protective, downy covering.

Now look at the leaves of wet environment plants and you will find that most are horizontal and few are covered with downy hairs. Since water is abundant in wet habitats, horizontal leaf surfaces present no problem and in fact, function to absorb more sunlight, allowing the plant to photosynthesize with little restraint.

In the fall, the leaves of mule-ears decompose into lacy "skeletons" that look like scruffy, tan doilies. You will find them lying on the ground, where they were compacted into the earth by snow from the previous winter. Incidentally, when you see entire hillsides covered with mule-ears, it is a good guess that the soil is volcanic.

Hiking Uphill through Dry Gardens

As you hike among the mule ears and balsam roots, look for the red, tubular blossoms of the Scarlet Gilia *(Ipomopsis aggregata)* and the blue, forget-me-not flowers of the Jessica's Stickseed *(Hackelia jessicae)*, that usually bloom in early-July. As you wander among these flowers, on a warm summer day, stop for a moment and close your eyes to inhale the heady fragrance of Sagebrush *(Artemisia tridentata)* and Mountain Pennyroyal *(Monardella odoratissima)*.

As you enjoy this minty fragrance, open your eyes and look down at your feet at the little belly flowers that are tucked in among the larger plants. They usually bloom from late-June through July, carpeting the ground in soft color. The smallest of all will be the yellow composite called Tiny Tarweed *(Madia minima)*. The tarweed only grows about 4 inches tall and carries 1/8 inch wide flowers that are easy to identify because they only carry 1 to 5, scraggly-looking, ray flowers. If you check out its disk and ray flowers, you will see that they have the same shaped reproductive parts as the larger mule-ears and balsam root. Its common name, tarweed, comes from the pungent odor of its glandular leaves. If you check this out for yourself, you won't ever forget its name! This powerful odor helps to protect this tiny flower from predators.

The delicate, rose-tinged blossoms of the Spanish Clover *(Lotus purshianus)* also bloom at ground level. Their tiny, pea-shaped flowers rise above the trailing stems. Can you find the banner, keel and wings of the flower? Check out the Sagehen Creek West hike if you are not clear on these parts. Once you can spot this flower form, you will have no trouble identifying members of the Pea Family.

While you are down on your knees looking at the Spanish Clover, look in the same area for the Hairy Owl's Clover *(Orthocarpus hispidus)* which blooms in yellow on plants only a few inches tall. Its odd little flowers are tubular with an inflated, pouch-like, lower lip. Its upper lip, which is called a galea, is erect and pointed and encloses the stamens and stigma. Its flowers grow compactly, with each flower barely extending beyond the leafy, red-tipped bracts that surround it. Its slender leaves are vertical, and hairy along the edges, and grow on hairy, reddish stems.

Its genus name, *Orthocarpus,* is derived from orthos for "straight" and karpos for "fruit," which describes the seed capsule. Calling this plant a clover is misleading for it is a not a true clover. It is a member of the Figwort Family, which is characterized by tubular, 2-lipped flowers, with sepals united into a lobed tube. True clovers are members of the Pea Family. Whoever gave this plant its common name was confused as to its true identity — a true clover flower has the banner, keel and wing shape.

Hiking along the Creek
After checking out these drier environment flowers, hike south toward the creek and follow it uphill toward the garden ledges. If you stay south of the creek, you will be on public land and free to explore the different creekside gardens along the way. As you scramble up the creek, you will find the typical, wet environment plants of the pink Lewis' Monkeyflower *(Mimulus lewisii)* and the large Elephant Head *(Pedicularis groelandica).* Look too for the yellows of the Seep-spring Arnica *(Arnica longifolia),* the Seep-spring Monkeyflower *(Mimulus guttatus)* and the Arrowleaf Senecio *(Senecio triangularis).*

In wandering along the creek, you are also likely to come upon the active, little Rufous Hummingbird *(Selasphorus rufus).* It makes its nest in trees or shrubs near the shore. Most books will tell you that the Rufous does not breed at this elevation, but our local bird expert, Michael Jeneid, has confirmed the sighting of a nest here.

The male is a reddish brown, with a bright orange-red marking on its neck, above its white chest. The female has a green back and is reddish brown on the rest of her body. Both males and females have separate feeding territories, which they defend vigorously, although the female leaves her area temporarily to visit the male, when it is time to mate. She then builds a tiny, cup-shaped nest in trees or shrubs and lays 2 small, white eggs.

The Rufous migrates south in the fall, spending the winter in Mexico before flying north again in the spring. In summer, it is known to travel as far north as Alaska, where it breeds before heading south again to grace the streams and meadows in our part of the Sierra.

Slopes of Pink and White below the First Ledge

After scrambling up a steep slope and through the darkness of dense trees, you will arrive at an open hillside in the sunshine where in a good year, you will be treated to some of the best displays of the pink White-veined Mallow *(Sidalcea glaucescens)* in all of Tahoe. Never have I seen such a display of this flower, nor did I truly appreciate how lovely it was, until I found it here by the thousands. (This flower was discussed on the Antone Meadows hike.)

In this same area, look also for the Mariposa Lily *(Calochortus leichtlinii)*, that sometimes can be found blooming in profusion from late-June through July. Its 3 white petals are broadly rounded, and form a shallow bowl, that is about 1 1/2 inches across. At each petal's base is a hairy, yellow, nectar gland with a dark maroon spot.

Its common name, Mariposa, is Spanish for "butterfly" and refers to the beautiful markings on the petals. Notice too that this lily has green sepals. Many lilies have sepals that are the same shape and color as the petals, instead of being green, as in the Mariposa Lily.

Calochortus means "beautiful grass," and although it is a lily rather than a grass, its lovely flowers bloom above grass-like leaves, and so it was given the common name, "beautiful grass." If you look for its leaves, you may have trouble finding them, because they have often withered by the time the flower appears.

A Plant that Strangles its Host

As you wander through this dryish area, look for the orange, twining stems of a parasitic plant called Dodder *(Cuscuta sp.)*. It can usually be found here growing on the stems of paintbrush or sagebrush. Since the Dodder lacks chlorophyll, it lives by parasitizing other plants, and the process by which it does this is interesting.

In spring its capsules split in half to release a seed that sends a tiny rootlet into the ground. As the stem grows, it searches for a plant to encircle. If it finds none, it soon withers and dies. If it finds a plant, it encircles it and grasps it tightly with thread-like suckers. These suckers grow out of the stem of the Dodder and are called *haustorias*, which is Latin for "drink."

After the haustorias penetrate the tissues of the host plant, the Dodder's roots begin to die and are useless within a day or two. Soon the orange stems begin climbing counter-clockwise to the top of the host plant. After the Dodder is secure in its new environment, it produces clusters of tiny, white, bell-shaped flowers, which after fertilization, produce seeds and begin the process anew.

Botanists believe that at one time the Dodder may have been able to photosynthesize, but that over time it lost this ability as it became successful as a parasite. Though its chlorophyll was eliminated, it did not lose all of its past, for it is recalled each time an embryo sends a tiny tap root into the earth to be sustained for a short period until it finds a host. The Dodder, as a perennial, is able to live for many years on its host plant, but as it increases in size, it may eventually kill its host, which then causes its own demise.

Mossy Gardens of Lavender Broomrape

As you approach the first flat ledge, which is about mid-way up the mountain, look for a small wet area where you will find the white, umbel flowers of Yampah *(Perideridia bolanderi)*, in July, delicately floating above the pink blossoms of Bridge's Gilia *(Gilia leptalea)*. This tiny garden is exquisitely beautiful and worth the time to search for it.

If you look among the mossy rocks at the top of the garden in July, look for the lavender or pale yellow flowers of the Naked Broomrape *(Orobanche uniflora)*. These small, parasitic plants grow only a few inches tall, with each tubular flower sitting atop the single stem.

The Blue Waters of Tahoe

Just beyond this dry area, you'll find a large, wet meadow. In mid-July through August, it explodes into color from lavender lupine *(Lupinus polyphyllus)*, bright red paintbrush *(Castilleja miniata)* and pink elephant heads *(Pedicularis attollens and P. groenlandica)*.

As you wander among the flowers, take a moment to kneel down among the yellow, daisy-like flowers of Soft Arnica *(Arnica mollis)*, that bloom here in profusion from July through early-August. Feel their fragrant, downy-soft leaves, and check out the ray and disk flowers to compare them to the mule-ears.

Also check out the fragrant leaves and the square-stems of the Horsemint *(Agastache urticifolia)*, that bloom nearby in July on plants up to about 5 feet tall. Its pale lavender, tubular flowers rise out of purple sepals that are united into a tube. *Agastache* comes from Greek for "many ears of grain" and refers to these tight clusters of flowers.

If you look closely at each horsemint flower, you'll see that it has 5 petals united into a tube with the lower petal longer than the others. Its 4 stamens, which carry pink to lavender anthers, come in pairs of unequal length. Its coarsely toothed leaves, which emit a strong minty fragrance, are arrowhead-shaped and can be brewed into a powerful tea. Standing in these gardens in July, looking out toward the royal blue waters of Lake Tahoe, among gardens of mints, orchids and lilies, I'm sure you'll feel very happy to be alive!

Horsemint

216

Creekside Flowers Carpet the Rocks in Pink

After "inhaling the view," be sure to walk along the creek below the waterfall for several hundred yards to look for the gorgeous, pink flowers of the Rock Fringe *(Epilobium obcordatum)*

In most years they carpet the rocks in solid pink, from mid-July through August. Beneath the flowers, small oval leaves grow densely along the stems, covering the rocks in a lovely tone of gray-green.

The 4 petals, which are 2-lobed and heart-shaped, form a flower that is about an inch across. The sepals are reddish pink and the lovely, dark pink stigma is velvety and 4-lobed, when receptive. Can you surmise what the advantage of this velvety texture might be?

The velvety stigma helps insure that the pollen grains will adhere to its surface until pollination occurs. After pollination, the inferior ovary, which can be located as a swelling in the stem below the flower, will elongate as its seeds mature.

If you follow the creek up the mountainside, you'll find clusters of Crimson Columbines *(Aquilegia formosa)* nodding their gorgeous blossoms in red and yellow at the edge of the waterfall. In among the rocks near the columbines, look also for bright pink penstemons *(Penstemon newberryi)* and the yellows of sulphur flower *(Eriogonum umbellatum)*. While you do so, be careful where you walk, as this is a fragile community.

As you climb higher toward the source of the stream, it will gradually fade into the rocks, and the surrounding soil will become dry. In August, when there has been ample snowfall, these slopes remain damp well into summer and become covered with the flowers of the Pink Star Onion *(Allium platycaule)*. Its rosy pink blossoms grow in dense, ball-shaped umbels that nestle in long, curling, strap-like leaves, with each petal marked by a dark mid-vein.

The photography in these gardens is spectacular

Rock Fringe

217

in late-afternoon; as the sun begins to set, the flowers become backlit and the gardens become intense with color. Of course it is at its best during a storm when the translucent light creates an intensity of color from every direction. Visiting Sherwood Forest for the day is wonderful, or you may wish to continue on along the Pacific Crest Trail that lies along the top of the ridge. If you head south, you will venture into Desolation Wilderness; if you hike north, you'll eventually arrive at Castle Peak.

Barker Peak and Surrounding Gardens

A Bouldered Summit and Creekside Flowers

🧍🌲♿

One day	
One way 2 1/2 miles	
Trail begins/ends 7500'/8166'	
Net gain/total gain 666'/666'	
Topo map USGS Tahoe, Calif.	
Wildflower Season June to September	

Highlighted Flowers
- Jessica's Stickseed
  (*Hackelia jessicae*)
- Ballhead Phacelia
  (*Phacelia hydrophylloides*)
- Mountain Mule-ears
  (*Wyethia mollis*)
- Crest Lupine
  (*Lupinus arbustus*)
- Dwarf Chamaesaracha
  (*Chamaesaracha nana*)
- Woolly Sunflower
  (*Eriophyllum lanatum*)
- Whitney's Locoweed
  (*Astragalus whitneyi*)
- Granite Gilia
  (*Leptodactylon pungens*)
- Western Spring Beauty
  (*Claytonia lanceolata*)
- Brewer's Mitrewort
  (*Mitella breweri*)

B arker Peak rises out of the surrounding landscape as a gray, rock-strewn cone. Its flanks are decorated with evergreen shrubs and clumps of flowers that snuggle in the talus slopes seeking protection from the wind. Barker is one of our most easily reached peaks with lovely views of Lake Tahoe and the snow-capped mountains of Desolation Wilderness. On the summit, a small stone "bench," perfect for two, offers a comfortable resting spot after the final climb to the top. From this stony perch, you can look down upon Red-tailed Hawks as they soar and play on the late afternoon updrafts or listen to the protective calls of a male quail as he gathers up his brood.

Trailhead Directions
The road up Blackwood Canyon begins at the Kaspian sign, a well marked turnoff several miles south of Sunnyside on Highway 89. Both the turnoff and

Velvety Stickseed

219

the road up the canyon (which parallels Blackwood Creek) can be located on a U. S. Forest Service map. One of the delights of reaching Barker Peak is the drive up Blackwood Canyon. In June the roadside

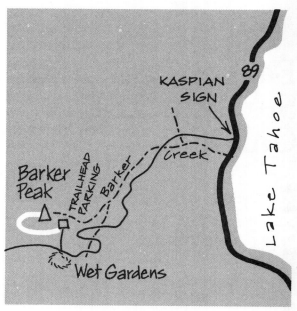

becomes blue-purple with Torrey's Lupine (*Lupinus sellulus*) and lime-green with newly sprouting aspen that line the creek nearby. In fall, the aspen and willows turn bright yellow, and the small, grassy meadows become golden in the backlit light.

After turning off Highway 89 at the Kaspian sign, drive 2.5 miles, until the road makes a sharp left to cross Blackwood Creek. As the road begins to climb, you will pass wonderful hillsides and creekside gardens, alive with orchids, columbines, and other wet environment flowers. The flowers begin their show in late-June and are at the height of their bloom in July. The display continues through August, with gilias and goldenrods blooming on into September. Creek after creek cascades off the hillsides nurturing these rich gardens — any one of which would offer a delightful flower-filled day of exploring, for those who enjoy leaving the beaten path.

The Trail Begins

About 2 miles after crossing the bridge, you will begin to catch glimpses of Barker Peak, which from the road looks unimpressive. Yet once you have hiked through its glorious gardens and discovered the little treasures nestled among its rocks, you will never view it as drab again, for even from a distance, you will "see" the richness that lies sheltered on its flanks.

After driving 7.7 miles from Highway 89, you will arrive at Barker Pass, where you will take the dirt road to the right, 20 feet up to the parking area near the "Barker Pass Trailhead" sign. Next to the parking area is a little meadow easily accessible to wheelchairs where a day could be spent sketching, reading and just enjoying. For those climbing to the peak, the trail begins on the path by the Pacific Crest Trail sign. (Don't take the logging road to the right.)

Dryish Hillsides of Flowers

The trail wanders along the south slope of Barker Peak through sagebrush hillsides of Scarlet Gilia *(Ipomopsis aggregata)*, purple Showy Penstemon *(Penstemon speciosus)* and some of the grandest Leichtlin's Mariposa Lilies *(Calochortus leichtlinii)* that I have ever seen. At Tahoe, these lovely white lilies most often bloom at ground level up to about 8 inches tall, with leaves that wither by the time the flowers appear. But here you will find them growing up to 18 inches tall, with gorgeous clusters of large, robust flowers and long, linear leaves that last through the blooming period.

As you pass through wooded areas, look for the Ballhead Phacelia *(Phacelia hydrophylloides)* with its violet-blue to whitish flowers that are so densely coiled in a cyme, that they form a blooming ball out of which protrude hundreds of little fuzzy-looking reproductive parts. This is a great place to see this flower. It is not common along the trails at Tahoe but blooms here abundantly.

The Mechanisms of Seed Dispersal

After you leave the woods and arrive again at open sagebrush slopes, look for both the Jessica's and Velvety Stickseeds *(Hackelia jessicae and H. velutina)* that bloom with blue, forget-me-not flowers on stems up to about 2 feet tall. The name stickseed refers to the little barbs on their small, round seeds that cling to clothing or to the fur of passing animals. Look at the little barbs through your hand lens and you will see why they adhere so tightly to passing objects. Each little barb has a set of reversed hooks at the end which form a lovely design under the magnifying glass.

Jessica's Stickseed can be differentiated from two other species of stickseed that commonly grow in the Tahoe area *(Hackelia nervosa and H. velutina)* by the distribution of the barbs on the seeds. In Jessica's Stickseed, they grow in vertical rows around each seed, while on the other two species, the barbs are distributed across the entire seed's surface.

I'm sure most of you know the Hackelias best by their little, brown seeds that so tightly adhere to your socks after a day of hiking that you have to pull each one out before you can throw your socks into the laundry. This gripping power enables the seeds to migrate to new areas to start new colonies.

Plants have devised many ingenious ways of dispersing their seeds. Some produce little sails so that they may be easily carried by the wind to far away places. Others, like some members of the Pea Family, produce seed pods that twist so tightly as they ripen and dry that the tension causes the pod to burst open, thrusting the seeds out and away from the parent plant.

Other plants, like the cherry, produce a seed that is surrounded by a sweet, fleshy fruit which carries a substance that actually prevents seed germination until the seed is consumed. The fruit attracts animals who, in eating it, destroy the inhibiting chemical in the fruity covering, allowing the seed to germinate. By the time the seed has been eaten and voided by the animal, it has been carried to a new area away

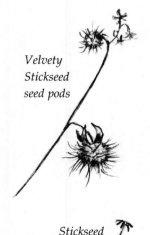

Velvety
Stickseed
seed pods

Stickseed
barb

from the parent plant. This gives it an opportunity to begin its new life in an area where there may be less competition from larger parent plants. In the cases of birds, seeds may even be carried across oceans to new continents, and, indeed, many plants have migrated around the world in this fashion.

Sometimes animals do more than just distribute seeds. Bats, and other animals, after passing the seeds through their digestive tracts, eliminate them in their dung as a sort of ready-made fertilizer packet to nurture the seed after germination. Darwin even discovered a certain seed in the Galapagos Islands that will not germinate until it passes through the digestive tract of one particular species of tortoise! The digestive juices break down the seed casing which then allows germination to occur.

Dispersal of seeds provides for colonization of new areas where there may be less competition from parent or other plant populations, but dispersal is not always in the best interests of a young plant. Orchids, which are dependent upon special soil fungi, deliberately drop their seeds to the ground at the base of the parent plant to guarantee that the young orchid will grow in soil where the fungi are present.

The peanut plant doesn't send its seeds to far-away places either but instead takes responsibility for planting its own seeds. In a practical "lets get it done" manner, the flower stem grows downward after fertilization and pushes the seeds into the soil where they await the coming rains to begin germination.

Crest
Lupine

Golden Mule-ears and Fragrant Lupine

After passing through flowery, open slopes and occasional groves of trees, you will cross a creek and then arrive at an open hillside covered with acres of golden Mountain Mule-ears (*Wyethia mollis*) and Arrow-leaved Balsam Root (*Balsamorhiza sagittata*), interspersed with fragrant, lavender Crest Lupine (*Lupinus arbustus*). These flowers are usually in full bloom by late-June to early-July on the hillside.

As you hike through this area, look along the edge

223

of the trail for the white flowers of Dwarf Chamaesaracha *(Chamaesaracha nana)*. From a distance they can be confused with morning glories, but up close these members of the Nightshade Family have an entirely different look. The leaves are oval-shaped with a covering of white, downy hair, and the petals are spotted green at the base. In the fall, yellowish berries appear, offering nourishment to passing animals.

As the trail climbs toward the saddle through this glorious garden, you will have lovely views of Desolation Wilderness, which makes this a great area for scenic flower photography. As the trail nears the crest of the saddle (to the west of Barker Peak and just before the dense grove of conifers and alders), leave the trail and head a few hundred feet up to the saddle.

From the saddle, there will be beautiful views of Lake Tahoe to the north, Desolation Wilderness to the south and looming to the south-east, you will see the rock-strewn slope that leads to Barker Peak. The saddle is a good place to enjoy lunch, since it is less windy than the top of the peak.

A Community of Golds, Reds and Purples

As you wander south-east along the wide saddle toward Barker Peak, you will pass through gardens of color from ground-hugging, cushion plants like the Creeping Phlox *(Phlox diffusa)* that form lavender and white carpets along the ground. One of the joys of Barker Peak is that you can experience an alpine-like community of cushion plants without having to climb the extra 2,000 feet to experience a "true" alpine environment.

"Cushion plant" is a broad term for plants that grow so low to the ground, for wind protection, that they form cushions. Although Barker does not host a "true" alpine community, I suspect that these plants consider themselves to be true alpine mountaineers. It is man who has defined the alpine community at Tahoe to be at the 10,000 foot elevation. For all practical purposes, these plants behave the same here as they do on the top of 10,776 foot Mt. Rose, except that they grow a bit less compact, because their exposure is less severe.

You will know when you arrive at this community, because you will be above timberline (above where the trees grow), and the ground will be covered with patches of color, if you hit the blooming season at the right time, usually in mid-June to early-July. This part of the trip is definitely for those with tough knees because to enjoy the flowers, you must drop down to their level. Using your hand lens will awaken you with awe and respect for these gentle and tenacious mountaineers.

Now is the time to pull out your Niehaus guide (referenced in the Overview section) so that you can identify the plants that I am about to briefly mention. I won't go into detail, since I have described them on other hikes, but I want to list them so you can easily identify them here.

One of the plants you will find is the Alpine Aster (*Aster alpigenus*) with its single, pink-to-purple, daisy-like flower that grows on an almost bare stem, above a basal clump of leaves. Both its stem and the leafy cluster that holds the flower head are covered with hair — a useful way to help identify this species of aster.

Look also for the intriguing Whitney's Locoweed (*Astragalus whitneyi*) which grows near the aster. You can identify it by its small, purplish pea flowers that give rise to large, inflated seed pods which are tan and mottled with purple. As discussed on the Castle to Basin Peak hike, this plant can create strange reactions in animals that eat the herbage.

Also keep your eyes open for the intensely yellow, daisy-like flowers of Woolly Sunflower (*Eriophyllum lanatum*). The plants grow in clumps, about 6 inches tall. Their "petals" or ray flowers droop slightly, are toothed at the tips, and have a light orange marking at the base. Their stems and leaves are covered with white, woolly hairs.

Look also for a cute, little plant called Butterballs

(Eriogonum ovalifolium) — some botanists actually do have a sense of humor! Its tiny, whitish flowers are clustered so tightly, they form a little ball that is about 1 inch in diameter. The flowers sit upon leafless stems that rise out of a mat of white-woolly, oval leaves. After fertilization, the flower cluster turns red and becomes quite noticeable and very lovely contrasted against the leaves.

Another plant, with congested blossoms, is the Ball-head Gilia *(Ipomopsis congesta)*. Its small, white, tubular flowers form a tight, rounded head which is even more compact than the Ballhead Phacelia, seen earlier along the trail. Its flowers are lovely up close, so be sure to look at them through your hand lens.

One of the least noticeable penstemons at Tahoe grows among these cushion plants and in among the boulders near the summit. It is called Hot Rock Penstemon *(Penstemon deustus)* and is usually found in dry, hot areas among the rocks. Its tan-to-white, tubular flowers grow around the stem in whorls and are only about 1/2 inch long. The petal lobes are marked with red-to-brown lines. Its small, leathery leaves were mashed raw, and the extracted juice was used as a medicine for venereal disease among Native Americans. Its roots were dried into a powder and used by the Shoshones to help heal sores.

Boulder Scrambling to the Summit

As you scramble (or slowly climb!) up the bouldered sides of the mountain, look for colorful flowers tucked in among the rocks or boldly blooming above them. The red trumpet flowers of the Scarlet Gilia appear in scattered groups among the paintbrush and mule-ears. You will also find a gorgeous pink version of the gilia that prefers these higher elevations. It used to be considered just a color variation of the Scarlet Gilia, but now has been declared a separate species and has been given its own name, *Ipomopsis tenuituba*. This change is so new that it does not yet have a common name, so here is your chance to grace it with a name of your own.

Also blooming robustly, among the rocks in July, will be the white-to-purplish tinged flowers of the Granite Gilia *(Leptodactylon pungens)*. Its stems and leaves are very glandular. Check this out with your hand lens and then gently squeeze the stems or leaves to release their pungent fragrance. The leaves are divided into many narrow lobes making them prickly to touch. If you confuse this plant with the phlox *(Phlox diffusa)*, it will be easy to tell them apart if you realize that the leaves of the phlox are not prickly or pungent.

The Granite Gilia's genus name, *Leptodactylon*, is derived from the Greek word *leptus* for "narrow" and *dactylon* for "finger" in reference to the leaves. Its species name, *pungens*, is Latin for "penetrating or prickly." This gilia grows more happily here than in any other place, that I know of at Tahoe.

Rock Gardens of Crimson Columbine
One of the biggest surprises to greet you as you reach the top are the large clusters of Crimson Columbine *(Aquilegia formosa)* that, amazingly enough grow in among the rocks. This columbine is usually found in wet meadows, along creeks and in damp wooded areas. Its seeds must have been brought here by a bird or other animal, and there must be enough spring snow melt to sustain its healthy growth because it has spread profusely throughout the area.

A more typical plant for this environment is the Mountain Pride *(Penstemon newberryi)* which blooms with vivid pink, tubular flowers above leathery leaves in among the rocks. You will also find the yellow tufts of Sulphur Flower *(Eriogonum umbellatum)* and the reds of the Wavy-leaved Paintbrush *(Castilleja applegatei)*.

If you continue heading east along the ridge, you will soon arrive at the very top to find the little stone slab that forms a "bench" upon the rocks — a delightful resting spot from where you can scan the horizon and look down upon soaring Red-tailed Hawks.

Birds that Frequent Barker

Red-tailed Hawks *(Buteo jamaicensis)* are beautiful birds with a wing span of at least 4 feet. In flight, their tails span outward and in the adults are a very noticeable reddish brown. They are commonly seen at Tahoe circling the open skies as they look for rabbits, squirrels and other small prey. When a hawk spots its prey, it dive-bombs downward and grasps it in its vise-like claws. If the prey is small enough, the hawk will carry it to the safety of a tree-top to consume it in peace. Red-tails build their bulky, twig nests at the top of trees or on rock ledges high up on cliffs. They lay 2 to 3 eggs that are whitish with brown spots.

Another bird you might see on this hike is the Mountain Quail *(Oreortyx pictus),* but unlike the hawk, it spends most of its life on the ground in the shelter of shrubs. In late-afternoon, as you sit on top of the mountain, you will often hear the calls of the male as he gathers up his brood. Both the males and females have a long, straight, black head-plume. The more brightly colored male is grayish blue on his head, neck and chest, while his throat is a lovely chestnut. They are about the size of doves and are easy to recognize because of the topknot.

Quail live among the shrubs for protection and consume berries, grass seeds and other herbs, along with the insects that they find among the grasses. They pair in early-April and begin nest building in mid-May. Their nests are hollowed out of the ground, under shrubs, and are lined with grasses, pine needles and leaves. They produce 5 or more pale red eggs.

After the eggs hatch, the parent quail can often be seen protectively herding their tiny young across a path to the shelter of a nearby shrub. Usually the male stands guard, after checking to see that the way is clear, until his family has reached safety. If the quail are threatened, the male lets out a call, and the chicks and female squat down in the grasses to hide while the male flaps around in the air, as if injured. To confuse a pursuer, he will fly several hundred feet away from his brood, making as much noise as possible. When the pursuer has been thrown off the track, the male dives into a shrubby area to seek his own protection. When the weather turns cold, quail migrate by walking in small groups down to lower elevations to wait out the winter below the snow line.

Returning to the Trailhead

After enjoying the top, you may return to the trailhead by scrambling down the rocks on the east side of the peak where you'll find gorgeous gardens of paintbrush, stickseed, senecio and gilia. Alternately, you may head down in a more northerly direction. Once you reach the damp wooded areas, look for the delicately pink, candy-stripped flowers of Western Spring Beauty *(Claytonia lanceolata)*. These little plants carpet pine-needled forested floors soon after the snows melt, usually in early-July.

The more gentle way to descend the mountain is to return the way you came or to return cross-country down the south side once you are west of the heavy, rock area. Carry a compass if you plan to leave the trail because it would be easy to drop below the parking area and become confused, in your enthusiasm to get out. It is always quicker going down than up!

Finding the Creekside Garden Trailhead

After returning to the trailhead, you needn't call it a day because within 1/2 mile there is another wonderful wet area of "brand new" plants that are usually at the height of their bloom in early-July. If you walk down from the parking area to the road that brought you in, you will see a dirt logging road below you, that heads east. Between the main road and the logging road, you will also see a Pacific Crest Trail sign next to a trail that parallels both roads. It reads, "Miller Creek and Desolation Wilderness."

For those in wheel chairs, the logging road is the best way to travel to the creekside gardens, as it is both smooth and level. Others will want to walk along the narrow, wooded trail and then perhaps return by way of the logging road. Though you may be tired from climbing to the summit, the 1/4 mile hike to the first wet garden is level and is well worth the short jaunt.

A Garden of Belly Flowers

Before heading along either the trail or the logging road, be sure to check out the seep area that lies between the trail and the logging road. It is about 25 feet beyond the trail sign. This small, mossy garden is usually filled with belly flowers by early-July. As you lie down on your belly, look for the shiny, white petaled Toad Lily *(Claytonia chamissoi)* with its red runners that radiate outward along the surface of the boggy soil.

Near the Toad Lily, look for the papery, pink flowers of the Bowl Clover *(Trifolium cyathiferum)*. Each flower head is made up of a cluster of flowers that turn brown with age. They are easy to identify because they sit in a bowl-shaped receptacle. Look closely at one flower and you will see that it has the typical pea flower form, although the tip of the sepals is unusual for a pea flower because it is spiny and branched.

One of the tiniest plants that grows here is the Hairy Owl's Clover *(Orthocarpus hispidus)*. Its yellow flower is tubular and inflated into a little sac. The flower rises out of red tipped, finely lobed bracts. Each plant is only a few inches tall and lives its life as an annual, as do all owl's clovers.

In the dry areas near the seep, you will also find other belly flowers carpeting the ground. Look for the delicate, lavender blossoms of Bridge's Gilia *(Gilia leptalea)* and the tiny, pink tubular flowers (with bright yellow throats) of Slender Phlox *(Phlox gracilis)*. Nearby you will also find the small, pink-to-purple tubular flowers of Tiny Trumpet *(Collomia linearis)* that grow in head-like clusters above leafy bracts.

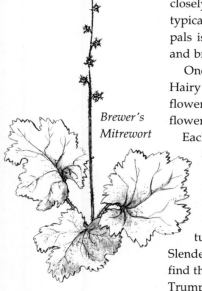

Brewer's
Mitrewort

Look also for the Entire-leaved Allophyllum *(Allophyllum integrifolium)*, whose white flowers rest on or just above the ground. It has lovely blue anthers and a pink mid-vein, that flows down each petal into the flower tube.

The sweet, innocent looking, blue and white flowers of the Blue-eyed Mary *(Collinsia torreyi)* grow near the intense pink blossoms of Torrey's Monkeyflower *(Mimulus torreyi)* in dry, sandy soil. Both plants were named in honor of John Torrey, who was a physician and a professor of chemistry and botany from New York. He botanized in California, in 1865, and is responsible for describing many of the plants collected along the West Coast on early expeditions of that period.

Creekside Gardens of Strange Mitreworts

After leaving this garden of belly flowers, by either the trail or the logging road, you will cross creeksides of orchids, elephant heads and monkeyflowers which bloom near tall larkspurs, lupines and senecios from July through early-August. The trail above the logging road will take you, in about 1/2 mile, to a lush garden of the tiny, strange flowers of Brewer's Mitrewort.

Brewer's Mitrewort *(Mitella breweri)* can be spotted by its slightly hairy, basal leaves which are a deep green and maple-shaped. It grows right at the edges of stream banks, in among other taller flowers. Once you spot its leaves, look for stems that are about 18 inches tall that support tiny, 1/4 inch wide, green flowers that grow along the upper part of the stem. Its flowers are so inconspicuous that it would be easy to walk by and never realize what you were missing. Many of Nature's gifts are discovered only when we take the time to slow down and appreciate the detail around us.

Your hand lens will help you to see its strange flowers, which come into bloom from mid-June to mid-July. Its petals are the green, thread-like, pinnate structures that radiate outward. The anthers

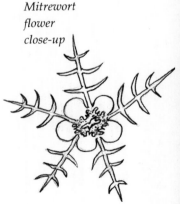

Mitrewort flower close-up

231

are the little white structures that lie on the sepals between the petals. The greenish white stigma sits in the center of the flower at the base of the petals. If it is late-summer when you hike the trail, you will be able to see tiny, black seeds still cupped in the sepals. Its common name, mitrewort, is derived from the shape of the seed capsules, which resemble a bishop's cap. *Mitre* is Latin for such a cap, while wort is old Angle-Saxon for plant.

Look also for the shiny, green leaves of the One-sided Wintergreen *(Pyrola secunda)* growing alongside the mitrewort. The tiny, white, wintergreen flowers are urn-shaped and droop to one side of the main, nodding flower stem. Wintergreens were discussed on the Donner Lake hike.

For those who want to continue onward, many more gardens lie ahead, along with one special little flower. The Naked Star-tulip *(Calochortus nudus)* has white to pale lavender blossoms and grows from a few inches up to a foot tall. It can be found in meadows or in openings in the woods and is worth the treasure hunt to find it.

Highlighted Flowers
- Alpine Lily
  (Lilium parvum)
- Leichtlin's Camas Lily
  (Camassia leichtlinii)
- Sundew
  (Drosera rotundifolia)
- Bog Wintergreen
  (Pyrola asarifolia)
- Thimbleberry
  (Rubus parviflorus)
- Scarlet Gilia
  (Ipomopsis aggregata)
- Bridge's Gilia
  (Gilia leptalea)
- Whisker Brush
  (Linanthus ciliatus)

General Creek

An Old Native American Camp Site

One day

Level loop	3 miles

Elevation   6,200'

Topo map USGS Tahoe, Calif.

Wildflower Season   June Through July

The General Creek loop trail travels to a boggy, sun-filled meadow that houses an intriguing plant that dines on insects. Fringing the meadow's edge are luxuriant growths of orange alpine lilies, pink shooting stars, lavender lupines and tiny, dark blueberries. The leisurely trail also parallels a creek, through sun-filtered gardens of blue camas lilies and large-leaved thimbleberries, before returning through a dry, woodland park brightened with lavender gilias, yellow composites and white yampahs.

Trailhead Directions

The General Creek Campground is on the west side of Highway 89 in the Sugar Pine Point State Park, which is about 9 miles south of Tahoe City and about 18 miles north of the South Tahoe Y. The area offers excellent camp sites, and the creek is stocked with Brook, Rainbow and Brown Trout. Be sure to pick up a trail map at the campground entry booth.

Sundew

233

General Creek in a Wheelchair

The Wheelchair access in General Creek is excellent (although you will miss the sundew meadow). It travels along a level logging road for about 3/4 mile before the road becomes too rocky for general wheelchair travel. Those with nubby tires may find it possible to cross the creek and return to the campground through the open, park-like area. It just depends upon how heavily the creek is flowing and upon how adventuresome you feel! There are also a series of trails through the campground, so regardless of what you decide, I think you'll enjoy visiting the area.

The Trail Begins in a Washo Summer Camp

For at least two thousand years up until the 1920's, the General Creek area was a major summer gathering ground for the Washos, who traveled over the Carson Range to Tahoe each spring, from western Nevada, to fish in the lake's waters and to gather and hunt in the surrounding mountains.

To the Washos, the lake was a sacred body of water, the center of their physical and spiritual life. On this hike we will honor their way of life by going back in time to experience a small part of what the General Creek area might once have been like. But first we will visit the meadow where an intriguing, insect-consuming plant lives.

Hiking the Trail

To find the meadow, hike southeast down through the woods, out of campground 17. In about 200 feet you'll reach the meadow, which is one of the few places in Tahoe to find the insectivorous sundew.

Before reaching the meadow, you will pass through waist-high, colorful gardens of Large-leaved Lupines (*Lupinus polyphyllus*), Alpine Lilies (*Lilium parvum*), Sierra Rein Orchids (*Habenaria dilatata*) and Alpine Shooting Stars (*Dodecatheon alpinum*). You'll also find the lovely, blue, star-shaped flowers of Leichtlin's Camas Lily (*Camassia leichtlinii*). Its close relative, the Quamash Camas Lily, was found on the Sagehen East hike. (See that hike for a discussion of the importance of the bulbs of this lily to the Washos and other native peoples.)

After arriving at the meadow, walk toward the central, boggy area. On the way, you will pass the low growing, grayish green shrubs of the Western Blueberry *(Vaccinium occidentale)*. In June, pinkish urn-shaped flowers hang downward from the branches. The flowers are replaced later in the season by small, dark blue berries. These berries were gathered by the Washos and eaten raw or dried for later use. If you visit the meadow in the fall, the leaves of the blueberry will have turned a gorgeous crimson red.

The Insectivorous Sundew

When the meadow begins to grab your feet, as if to suck you into the mire forever, you will be in the right area to find the Sundew *(Drosera rotundifolia)*. It grows among the grasses at the edges of the tiny creeks that meander through the meadow. It can also be found in areas where downed trees have created water-filled depressions after rotting away. You must look carefully, as their rounded leaves are only the size of a finger nail and difficult to locate. The leaves grow in a basal cluster surrounding a stem that, in July, gives rise to small, white-to-pink flowers.

When you find the leaves, look closely and you will see that each leaf carries bright red hairs that glisten at the tips with a red, sticky liquid. The sticky liquid and long hairs help to entice and trap insects. Though the green leaves of sundews carry out photosynthesis, botanists believe that these highly-modified leaf hairs developed, because their sparse roots live in nitrogen-poor, boggy soils. The insects that they trap provide the nitrogen needed in their diet.

If you look closely at one of the leaves, you will see that its tentacle-like hairs are longest at the leaf edge and shortest in the central portion of the leaf. This helps the plant engulf its prey, after the insect lands on the sticky leaf. After realizing it is trapped, the insect struggles to get free, which stimulates the

235

longer hairs to bend inward, completely entrapping the insect until it is finally released from its struggle by death.

As the long outside hairs bend inward, they move the insect to the center of the leaf where acid-secreting glands digest it. If more than one insect should land on the plant at the same time, the hairs divide into separate sets, encircling and entrapping each insect. Within two to three days the hairs re-open, and the insect's shell is blown away. After this, the glands release more sticky fluid and glisten anew, red and inviting, to await another unwary visitor. The name *drosera* comes from the Greek word for "dewy," and *rotundifolia* means "rounded leaf."

The sundew's gland-hairs are so sensitive that they can be stimulated by a piece of human hair only 1/5 millimeter long and 1/1000 gram in weight, yet they are unaffected by the stimulus of a raindrop. Most likely, through chemical means, these plants have the ability to distinguish food from non-food, which they do quite successfully. It was recorded in England that a two acre patch of sundews captured and consumed six million cabbage butterflies when they alighted on the leaves during an annual migration.

Man has long been aware of the sundew and has used it to his benefit. In Portugal there is one species that grows 5 feet tall and because of its size, it is collected by farmers and hung in their cottages to act as a natural flypaper. Orchid growers throughout the world use a large-leaved, tropical species in their greenhouses to trap insects to prevent damage to their orchids.

Leaving the Meadow
After spending time exploring the meadow, you can leave from the point where you hiked in and head east on the sandy trail that parallels the meadow and the creek. Along the way, in late-June, you will find wonderful, wet gardens of monkeyflowers, elephant heads, senecios, columbines and corn lilies. In these wet areas at the base of conifers, look for the satiny,

pink flowers of the Bog Wintergreen (*Pyrola asarifolia*) which was discussed on the Donner Lake hike. It blooms in mid-July with lovely drooping flowers.

After the small sandy trail dies out, head uphill to the main logging road to look for plants along the way that were appreciated by the Washos and other American Indians. If you are unsure of the plants mentioned, pull out your botanical guide.

As the Washos Lived

The Washos lived intimately and gently upon the land, integrating plants into their daily lives in a way that went beyond just seeing plants as tools, clothing, shelter and food. They saw plants not as "things" but as "plant people" who gave up their lives so that the Washos might live. The Washos responded with gratitude, honoring plants as little "brothers and sisters" who were different but equal in the scheme of life.

Western man generally views life differently and has chosen to place plants and animals in a hierarchy, with man at the top. Yet it is green plants that produce the carbohydrates and oxygen needed to sustain all life. Our definition of the highest form of life is merely a restatement of the attributes which we possess. If we were to choose the criterion of "life sustainers," plants would come out on top.

Native peoples do not define life in terms of hierarchies and have thus lived with greater sensitivity to the earth, expressing themselves more wisely and harmoniously upon the earth. I think we would all be richer if we learned from native peoples that such hierarchies are of the ego, and that plants are not commodities put here for our exclusive use, but rather are made up of a life essence similar to our own. It will enrich us if we recognize them as separate entities with gifts to give. Our responsibility is to receive their gifts with appreciation, to use our intelligence to put limits on our consumption and to be gentle in our impact.

237

Going Back in Time

As you wander along the trail, imagine for a moment that you have gone back in time — that it is a warm day in late-summer and you are a young Washo woman gathering the sweet fruits of wild strawberries, currants and thimbleberries, which grow abundantly along the trail.

While you search for berries, you also gather the leaves of onions to add to a salad of indian lettuce, chickweed, dandelion and mustard greens. Later in the season, you will return to gather the bulbs and small black seeds of the onions and brodiaeas that now bloom along the trail. One of your favorite onions is the tall, pink Swamp Onion *(Allium validum)* that grows along the creek's edge. Its long grass-like leaves, with their onion fragrance, provide rich seasoning for several dishes that you are preparing this evening.

As you hike the trail, you are hounded by mosquitos, but it is not a major problem because you can go to dry sandy areas nearby to gather the leaves of Pennyroyal *(Monardella odoratissima)* which you rub on your body. This helps to repel the mosquitos, while you gather more leaves and flowers of the Pennyroyal to later brew into a minty tea, which you will enjoy after dinner as you watch the alpenglow over the lake.

As you wander through dry areas, you spot the tall stalks of Woolly Mullein *(Verbascum thapsus)* in full bloom with yellow flowers. Your grandmother has taught you the value of this plant. For many generations its leaves have been brewed into a tea to help cure colds or they have been seeped in water to produce a steam, which when inhaled, soothes a sore throat or sinus irritation. You have also often seen your grandfather dry its leaves and smoke them as tobacco to soothe the lungs, while your mother often used the large, soft leaves for your baby diapers when you were young. When you come upon the grayish shrubs of Sagebrush *(Artemisia tridentata)*, you gather their

Sierra Currant

leaves to save in baskets for a time of sickness, for you know that tea made from the fragrant leaves brings relief from the fevers and the aches of the flu, while the essence from boiled or burned leaves can be inhaled to relieve general flu symptoms.

As the warm summer breezes carry the fragrances of Sagebrush and Mugwort (*Artemisia ludoviciana*), you are reminded of the special times when these plants have been used by your people in sacred ceremony to purify body and soul. Since you also use Sagebrush for other purposes, you gather an extra handful and put it in your basket for later use in shampoo to help blacken your hair. You will also dry some of the leaves and later grind them into an antiseptic diaper powder for your baby brother.

The Tools and Weapons of the Men

As you wander through the woods, looking for rose hips for tea, you come upon many stately old Sugar Pines (*Pinus lambertiana*). As you search their bark for the sweet chewable sap, a cone falls enabling you to gather the few sweet seeds that remain. While you are extracting the seeds, your brother comes walking through the woods. He has been out gathering material for the tools and weapons that he has been making this summer.

After searching out the elderberries, cottonwoods, willows, and cedars that grow abundantly throughout the area, he takes their small branches and carves them into fire drills or flattens them for use as bases for the drills. You have often seen him and the older men vigorously rotate the drill between their palms, until the friction magically creates a tiny burning coal which, with the right timing and gentle blowing, ignites the tinder that sits at the base of the drill.

You have helped gather the tinder, which comes from the dried and shredded inner bark of cottonwood and fireweed (*Epilobium angustifolium*), which both grow along the creek. The fluffy seed heads of the yellow flowered goldenrod (*Solidago sp.*) and the purplish pink thistle (*Cirsium andersonii*), which grow in drier areas along the trail, also make valuable tinder by helping to increase combustion.

Your brother is also gathering incense cedar branches to make a new bow, while he chooses straight, small branches from the wild rose to make arrows. It will be many years before he is skilled enough with his bow to hunt large game. Because your people's bows are short with a limited range, game must be closely approached by a hunter with highly skilled techniques. For now, he will hunt jackrabbits and other small game, but someday he will kill his first deer, and perhaps when he grows in stature, he will have the honor of bringing in a bear to your people.

The Fine Art of Washo Basketry

As you come to the creek to take a drink from its cool, sweet waters, you find willows growing so densely that you cannot see the water that you know flows behind the shrubs. Early this spring you and some of your friends, who arrived at Tahoe before the young children and the elders, gathered the new spring shoots that grew unbranched out of the base of the willow.

For years you have been working with your grandmother to learn to make beautiful baskets. This summer she will help you make a very special one with your own design. It will be made from yellow willow and red dogwood shoots and from the black roots of the bracken fern. Such a basket, you know, is important for many uses, from the gathering and carrying, to the storing and cooking of food. You remember, as a child, being amazed at how your mother and grandmother cooked acorn mush in the baskets with red hot rocks without burning the containers. As you got older, you also learned to keep the rocks moving without burning the baskets until the mush boiled and completed its cooking.

As the years pass, another Washo woman, named Dat-so-la-le, is born. She weaves baskets on the shores of Tahoe at the turn of the century, and, with the help of a trader, she becomes highly acclaimed in the white world for the complexity and beauty of her baskets. Her baskets offer both art and function in its highest form and many years later become valued well above $10,000 each, though Dat-so-la-le herself earned little compared to the value they would later bring.

Dat-so-la-le died in 1925, at the age of ninety-six. The Gatekeeper's Cabin in Tahoe City has displayed her baskets on occasion, along with a permanent collection of other Washo and Paiute basketry. Dat-so-la-le's baskets can be seen on permanent display at the Nevada State Historical Society Museum in Reno and the Nevada State Museum in Carson City.

At the present time the Washos are in the planning stages to develop a Cultural Center on the West Shore of Lake Tahoe to honor their ancestors and to tell their own story. The center will be constructed on approximately 40 acres of Forest Service land near Taylor Creek, land used in ancient times as a meeting place for Washo tribal leaders. For now you can visit the excellent Washo exhibit at the Tallac Historic Site.

Returning to the Present

As you continue to look for the plants that the Washos used to make their lives comfortable, you will soon come to where the logging road crosses the creek. At this point you can cross the creek and loop back, returning by way of the sandy open "park."

Others may wish to cross the creek later, after walking another 1/2 mile or so to the junction with the Lily Lake trail. At this junction, the loop trail turns left, as the map on the post indicates, and crosses a wooden bridge. After walking through a gorgeous, leafy meadow of shoulder-high larkspurs, lupines, monkshoods and bracken fern, the trail crosses a second larger bridge and then arrives at the dry woodland area.

If your timing is right, usually in late-June to early-July, this area will be carpeted with the tiny belly

241

flowers of Bridge's Gilia *(Gilia leptalea)* and Whisker Brush *(Linanthus ciliatus)*, which were mentioned on the Shirley Canyon hike. Growing above them will be the flowers of Yampah *(Perideridia bolanderi)* floating in the slightest of breezes. Its sweet tubers were relished by the Washos, as well as by other Native Americans throughout the western states.

A Final Reflection

As you wander through these gorgeous wet and dry gardens or as you stop to picnic on some sandy little beach along the banks of the creek, I hope you'll take some time to reflect on how fortunate we are to be able to enjoy the General Creek area. Years ago, beginning in the 1890s, there were those who cared enough to protect General Creek, and other areas at Tahoe, from development so that we, the future generations, would be able to experience the beauty and wildness of Tahoe's backcountry.

But as they did for us, so must we do for future generations. Development is still going on in the Tahoe Basin. It has been reported by Dr. Charles Goldman that Tahoe has lost 25 percent of its clarity in only 14 years. Even with our awareness of the problem, the lake continues to lose its clarity at the unacceptable rate of 1.5 feet per year. Over the last 20 years the lake has lost over 23 feet of clarity. It has been estimated that this represents an aging of the lake, in only 20 years, of what normally would have taken 50,000 to 100,000 years.

The measurement of clarity was begun in 1967, after heavy development had already started to take place in the Tahoe Basin. There is no record of the loss of clarity before 1967, but I remember swimming along the shoreline in the late-1950s. There was no algae on the rocks, only royal blue waters with a surface, like clear glass, that magnified the boulders below. Now the rocks on most areas around the lake are covered with brown algae, and the sandy bottom is strewn in some places with broken glass and beer cans. A visit to the shoreline, north of Sand Harbor

Whisker Brush

242

on the east shore, will show what the lake once looked like. There are Washos still living today who remember the way the lake once was but who no longer come to its shores because it breaks their heart to see what has been done to its waters.

Even with these problems, the lake is still a beautiful and thrilling sight, and we must keep it that way, while we work to reverse the trend toward loss of quality. The positive news is that there are many today who are working hard to educate visitors and residents alike to help prevent further deterioration. The League to Save Lake Tahoe has spearheaded the preservation movement by pressing for protective legislation. The Tahoe Research Group, a University of California at Davis scientific team, under the leadership of Dr. Charles Goldman, has been gathering data on their research vessel on the lake for 20 years.

Some individuals have quietly donated their undeveloped land in the basin to the League to Save Lake Tahoe Land Trust while others have sold their land through a federal program set up by the Santini-Burton Act in 1980, which sets aside public funds to purchase environmentally sensitive lands in the Tahoe Basin.

The people of California and Nevada are also doing their part. The California Tahoe Conservancy's Land Aquisition Program has been funded with $85 million to acquire new lands and to do environmental protection work in the basin. Nevada has set aside $31 million in a similar program.

On a smaller, but no less important scale, other aware individuals have begun pulling out their lawns (fertilizing lawns and ornamentals adds to the nitrogen content in the lake and feeds the growth of algae) to return to native, drought tolerant flowers and shrubs. Local nurseries and governmental groups, like the Tahoe Regional Planning Agency, offer a wealth of information on the planting of natives.

It is difficult in our daily lives to see how we can personally stop the environmental damage being done to areas that we cherish. But it is clear that by working together we can stop the destructive trend. In joining and supporting organizations like the League to Save Lake Tahoe (P. O. Box 10110, South Lake Tahoe, CA 95731, 916-541-5388), by refusing to allow greed and self-interest to dominate decisions, by keeping tabs on our elected local representatives, by doing our part to return our gardens to native vegetation and by teaching our children to honor and respect Nature, we can and will make a difference.

For as Chief Seattle once said, "This we know. The earth does not belong to man; man belongs to the earth. . . Whatever befalls the earth befalls the sons of the earth. Man did not weave the web of life; he is merely a strand in it. Whatever he does to the web he does to himself..."

Highlighted Flowers

- Mountain Pride
  (*Penstemon newberryi*)
- California Fuchsia
  (*Zauschneria californica*)
- Western Eupatorium
  (*Eupatorium occidentale*)
- Explorer's Gentian
  (*Gentiana calycosa*)
- Red Mountain Heather
  (*Phyllodoce breweri*)
- Cassiope
  (*Cassiope mertensiana*)
- Sierra Saxifrage
  (*Saxifraga aprica*)
- Sibbaldia
  (*Sibbaldia procumbens*)
- Mountain Pennyroyal
  (*Monardella odoratissima*)

Fontanillis Lake

Hiking to the Source

🚶 (to Eagle Lake)

Strenuous day/overnight
One way   5 miles
Trail begins/ends   6580'/8500'
Net gain/Total gain   1920'/2300'
Topo map USGS Fallen Leaf Lake, Calif.
Wildflower Season   June to September

Fontanillis Lake is a narrow body of cold, pristine water that feeds the thundering cascades of Eagle Falls far below. In early-spring, its shoreline harbors snow-formed ice caves that offer chilling shelter to tiny clumps of wildflowers. The waters of Fontanillis are the final destination for a hike that climbs past lovely Eagle Lake, through hillsides of white cassiope and red heather, past thrilling patches of blue gentian and beneath craggy walls that offer magnificent views of Lake Tahoe.

Trailhead Directions

From Tahoe City, take Highway 89 south for 16 1/2 miles to the Eagle Falls Picnic Area. From the South Lake Tahoe Y, drive 8.8 miles to the Picnic Area. The Emerald Bay/Eagle Lake Trail begins at the west end of the parking lot by a wooden map that describes the trail. Be sure to fill out your wilderness permit, available in a box by the map.

*Red
Mountain
Heather*

245

After parking in the Eagle Creek Picnic Area, walk across the street and take a few minutes to sit near the side of magnificent Eagle Falls. Be careful to stay safely back from the falls as it is easy to slip on wet rocks. Such an accident took the life of a woman recently, but with good judgement the area is safe.

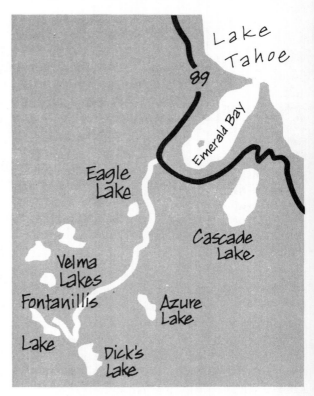

As you look out at the sprays of tiny water droplets, take a few minutes to imagine the journey that one droplet might have taken to reach this place in time with you, before its final fall into the blue waters of Lake Tahoe. Your hike up to Fontanillis Lake will be a much simpler re-tracing of that journey, a hike to the source of it all.

The Trail Begins
After returning through the parking lot and picking up the trail on the west end of the picnic area, you'll

head up Eagle Creek Canyon along a rocky, switch-backed trail. In the canyon below, you'll see Eagle Creek on the final leg of its journey to the falls.

As you look up at the rock walls above the trail, look for the vivid pink blossoms of Mountain Pride *(Penstemon newberryi)*, the yellows of Sulphur Flower *(Eriogonum umbellatum)* and the soft pinks of Alum-root *(Heuchera rubescens)*, that bloom in July. Later in August and September, the rocky trail will be bright-ened by the red, tubular flowers of the California Fuchsia *(Zauschneria californica)*.

Arriving at Eagle Lake

After crossing the bridge, by the cascades on Eagle Creek, you will be able to look back to see the deep blues of Emerald Bay and Lake Tahoe. You'll then pass through shaded forests of white firs and jeffrey pines and across open chaparral slopes, before you arrive at a wooden post that directs you to the right, to Eagle Lake, or to the left, toward Dick's Pass.

The short spur trail to Eagle Lake will take you to the lake's shore by the outlet creek. You may want to picnic at the lake's edge and take a mid-morning swim before continuing along the trail toward Dick's Pass, or you may want to spend the day at Eagle Lake. The lake is a nice destination for young chil-dren; it is an easy, short hike and the shallow, level shoreline near the trail is safe for wading.

Returning to the Trail

If you choose to continue on, after enjoying the lake, return to the junction and pick up the Dick's Pass trail. It will take you past more chaparral-covered slopes, where you might hear the cries of Clark's Nutcracker *(Nucifraga columbiana)*. The nutcracker is the size of a small crow; it has a light gray body and black and white tail feathers which are easy to spot when in flight. Its loud "khaaa" sound also makes it easy to identify.

The nutcracker prefers the high mountains near timberline and is a common sight above 9,000 feet, as it flits about noisily searching the cones of nearby conifers for seeds. Inside its mouth is a special cheek pouch which enables it to hold several seeds, while it greedily gathers more; nutcrackers also eat carrion or catch insects in flight.

Mating occurs in March, while the mountains are still blanketed with snow, and nest building soon follows. Their nests are shaped like a deep bowl and are constructed out of bark and twigs and placed in conifers. The female lays 2 to 4 eggs which are pale green and lightly spotted. The young hatch in April and May and by June leave the nest to join their parents on forays.

As you continue the climb, you'll pass by several shrubs. Those of the Mountain Maple *(Acer glabrum)*, which grow well over 6 feet tall, are perhaps best appreciated at noontime when they take on a translucent, silvery radiance from the backlit light of the overhead sun. You'll also find the evergreen shrubs of the Sierra Chinquapin *(Castanopsis sempervirens)*; look for a roundish bush that is about 4 feet tall.

The chinquapin blooms along the trail in August with separate male and female flowers. The male flowers grow in catkins out of the axils of the leaves and emit a strong odor which will clearly let you know the shrub is nearby. The female flowers appear out of tiny, leafy bracts at the base of the male flowers, and, like the males, they lack petals. The round-tipped leaves are oblong, a gray green above and a downy golden or pale rust beneath. The fruit appears, by September of the second year, as a spiny burr that encloses 1 to 3 bitter nuts.

The chinquapin belongs to the same family as the Oaks. Its name Castanopsis comes from the Greek words *kastanea* for "chestnut" and *opsis* for "resemblance" because of the similarity of some members of the genus to chestnut trees. *Sempervirens* means evergreen, as this shrub stays green all winter under the snow. Chinquapin is a Native American word for this shrub.

A Plant of Pink Fuzzies

Another August blooming flower, that grows on rock ledges along the trail near the chinquapin, is the Western Eupatorium *(Eupatorium occidentale)*. Its pink, fuzzy flowers are not very fancy from the trail, but if you take a moment to look at them through your hand lens, you'll be treated to a lovely sight. The best way to describe the flowers is that they have jubilant pistils. Now if that doesn't get your attention, nothing will!

The 2-parted pistil twists and flares out, as if to express joy, and all the reproductive parts are a soft pink to lavender. The anther tube surrounds the pistil, as is typical in members of the Composite Family, (as discussed on the Sherwood Forest hike). Its blossoms are made up of tubular, 5-petaled disk flowers and lack ray flowers. Scraggly pappus, another clue to this family, surrounds the base of the petals. Its triangular-shaped leaves are serrate and emit an odor that is unpleasant, but the flowers themselves are sweetly fragrant.

The eupatorium was named in honor of an ancient king, called Eupator Mithridates, who ruled over Pontus. According to Pliny, the Roman naturalist and writer who lived one hundred years later, this plant was named to honor Eupator, because he used a species of eupatorium as an antidote for poison. Eupator became known for claiming that he had become immune to poisons by taking them in small dosages over a period of time.

In the eastern United States, certain species of eupatorium are called Joe-pye weed after a Native American who taught the colonists how to use the plants for relief when suffering from typhus fever.

Creekside Banks of Explorer's Gentian

After returning to the trail, you'll traverse a boulder strewn section, cross a creek and then parallel two more creeks. If you are hiking the trail in August or September, look in these areas for the exquisite, blue flowers of the Explorer's Gentian *(Gentiana calycosa)*.

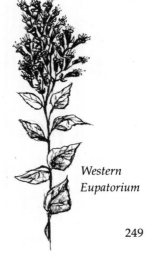

Western
Eupatorium

249

Its tubular flowers are an intense deep-blue, and its petals carry a spattering of white or green dots. Its dark, purplish blue buds are as lovely, and as sensual, as the blossoms. The buds seem determined to be admired in this stage for they sit tightly closed for weeks before bursting into full bloom. With the coming of nightfall, or on dark, stormy days, the flower closes to protect its precious pollen, saving its beauty for only the most glorious of sunny days.

In the same area, you'll come upon the shrubs of both the Mountain Spiraea *(Spiraea densiflora)*, which blooms pink in July, and the Labrador Tea *(Ledum glandulosum)*, which blooms white, with azalea-like leaves. As you pass through this lush, seep area of alders and bracken fern, you'll come upon a wonderful rock wall to the right of the trail. This natural sculpture is stained red, black and green from the minerals carried in the water which flows down its face and from the lichen and moss which spot its surface. In June, as the snows above slowly release their waters, tiny cascades flow across the little ledges and down the smooth rock face.

Soon, you'll arrive at a saddle where Pinemat Manzanita *(Arctostaphylos nevadensis)* and Red Mountain Heather *(Phyllodoce breweri)* grow, carpeting the ground. At this point, the trail descends through solid Thimbleberry *(Rubus parviflorus)*, where off to your right, and far down the slope, you'll see a brackish pond with pond lilies growing near its shore.

Soon the trail crosses a tiny creek with ferns and mossy rocks. When you arrive at this spot, look for the leafy green plants of the Enchanter's Nightshade *(Circaea alpina)*, that bloom in August, with tiny white flowers. Its flowers are inconspicuous and are made up of 4 petals and 4 reflexed sepals. After pollination, the flowers are followed by tiny, pear-shaped, bristly fruits which are lovely seen through a hand lens.

Joining the Bayview Trail

After crossing another creek, and a large granitic slab

Exporer's
Gentian

with western white pines growing out of the rocks in tiny bits of soil, you will arrive at the juncture with the Bayview-Velma Lakes Trail. The Bayview Trail is another nice way to approach Fontanillis. Its lake views and scenic granite spires are a delight, but its trail is steeper initially and a bit longer.

As you continue heading toward Velma Lakes and Dick's Pass, along the sandy trail, you will pass wonderful old junipers, their reddish orange bark forming wooden sculptures, in magnificent twisted forms, on the granitic platforms. Soon you will arrive at the juncture with Velma Lakes and Dick's Pass. At this point, head toward Dick's Pass, past the lodgepole pines that seem to sprout out of the granite.

A Place to Take a Break

After crossing the creek, that unites two small ponds, you'll come to a wonderful spot where you may want to spend the day or evening. White granitic walls backdrop a series of grassy, meandering ponds, and in the late-afternoon light, or if a storm is approaching, satin ripples form undulating lines on the water's surface.

Along the shores of the ponds in July, you'll find monkeyflowers, shooting stars and elephant heads as well as the rose-pink flowers of Bog Laurel *(Kalmia polifolia)*. If you look closely at the laurel's saucer-shaped flowers, you'll spot something interesting; each of the 10, thread-like filaments is bent down into a little pocket in the petal. This pocket cups the anther, holding it in place, until an insect lands on the flower. The pressure of the insect causes the anther to be released from the pocket and slam into the insect's body. If the anther is ripe, it insures that the insect will not leave the flower before it is dusted with pollen. Try this with a pine needle; the action is so quick, it's hard to follow.

Its species name, *polifolia,* comes from the Latin words *polio* which means "to whiten" and *folia* for "leaf," which refers to the whitish coating on the underside of the leaf. Its genus name, *Kalmia,* is in honor of Peter Kalm who was a student of Carl Linnaeus, the Swedish naturalist. Peter botanized throughout eastern North America in the mid-1700's but first gathered this plant on the island of Sitka in Alaska. The Bog Laurel blooms in boggy soils throughout much of the United States and up through Canada to Alaska and the Yukon.

Hillsides of Red Heather and White Cassiope

As you continue along the trail, you'll soon arrive at the most spectacular displays of red heather and white cassiope in all of Tahoe. Red Mountain Heather has flowers which, oddly enough, resemble the Bog Laurel, although they lack the little petal pockets. Its flowers bloom on shrubs which grow up to about a foot tall with needle-like leaves which grow densely along the branches.

The white Cassiope *(Cassiope mertensiana)* blooms in profusion along the trail. Its white, bell-shaped flowers carry tiny, red, sepal-caps and nod at the tips of ground-hugging branches which carry needle-like leaves. It was one of John Muir's favorite flowers, and one he hunted a long time in Yosemite to find in bloom. Its beauty so moved him that he once exclaimed, "No evangel among all the mountain plants speaks Nature's love more plainly than cassiope."

Its name comes from the Greek myth of Cassiopeia who was the wife of Cepheus, King of the Ethiopians, and the mother of Andromeda. According to the legends, Andromeda was taken from her mother and chained to a rock in the sea where she was to be devoured by a sea monster. Later she was rescued by Perseus and lived happily ever after. What this has to do with this lovely flower I can't imagine, except that it so often grows in and among the rocks. But rather than being chained to the rocks, it flows lavishly and freely over them, perhaps symbolizing the freeing of Andromeda. Its less dramatic species' name, *mertensiana,* is in honor of Franz Mertens, a German botanist who lived from 1764 to 1831.

Finding a Tiny Member of the Rose Family

After passing through this glorious heather and cassiope garden, you'll begin the last steep climb up to the saddle by Dick's and Fontanillis Lakes. To help keep your mind off this last tiring section, look along the edge of the trail for the small, ground-hugging plants of Sibbaldia *(Sibbaldia procumbens)*. The tiny, inconspicuous flowers are pale yellow, and as typical of members of the Rose Family, the flower has 5 petals which alternate with the green, pointed sepals. Its sepals are twice as long as the miniature, pointed petals and are thus more prominent.

The Sibbaldia's basal leaves come in sets of 3, and if you look closely, you'll see that both surfaces of the leaves are covered with white hairs to retain heat and reflect intense solar light. Notice too that its ground-hugging growth helps it to stay out of the wind. These adaptations allow the Sibbaldia to survive up to 12,000 feet in rocky, alpine gardens. This little flower may be unobtrusive, but it is a successful world traveler that has circumnavigated the globe, for it appears in mountain gardens throughout the world.

As you look for the Sibbaldia, look also for the tiny white flowers of the Sierra Saxifrage *(Saxifraga aprica)*. They grow in little clusters atop a 1 to 5 inch tall, solitary stem. A basal rosette of oval, purplish leaves spreads out along the rocks beneath the flower stems. It has a charming, unobtrusive manner and brings me great delight whenever I come upon it.

Exploring the Ice Caves

Upon reaching the saddle, the trail joins the Pacific Crest Trail and heads south to a sign that will guide you toward Dick's Lake. After a 1/4 mile downhill saunter to Dick's Lake, you'll see one source of the water droplets that you saw cascading down Eagle Falls. If you hike around the north shore of the lake to the outlet creek, you can have fun following it past the ice caves (in early-July) to the shores of Fontanillis Lake. Be careful in walking through the caves,

253

because, with the warming temperatures of spring, it would be easy to fall through the soft snow banks, which, if deep enough, could trap you in the stream below.

Hillsides of Fragrant Mountain Pennyroyal

As you explore the lake-side gardens, you'll find many species of flowers, but one of the most fragrant is the Mountain Pennyroyal (*Monardella odoratissima*). Each "pincushion" cluster of flowers is supported by a green receptacle of leafy bracts that sit atop stems which are about a foot tall. Its mint-scented leaves and square stems make it easy to identify as a member of the Mint Family.

Each little tubular flower is 2-lipped, with the upper lip being 2-lobed and the lower lip 3-lobed and bent horizontally. The green sepals, surrounding the flower, form a lobed tube. Pennyroyals, like most mints, have 4 stamens which are inserted on the corolla tube in 2 pairs of unequal length. If you look at the base of the forked stigma, you will find a fleshy ring, which secrets nectar to reward visiting insects.

Fontanillis is one of Tahoe's most beautiful alpine lakes. It offers gorgeous views of Lake Tahoe, while the Velma Lakes shimmer in the sunlight on the slopes below. I once hiked to Fontanillis with my daughter, Jennifer, on a 5 day family trip through the backcountry, which began at Meeks Bay and ended at Horsetail Falls, by Twin Bridges. She was only about 7 years old, but she loved the trip. I don't recommend that particular route, because hiking in the rocks above Horsetail Falls is treacherous. Instead, an exhilarating, but comfortable, family trip would be one which begins at Meeks Bay and ends with the last night spent on the shores of Fontanillis Lake. That way, the final hike out will take you to the shores of Eagle Lake for one last cooling swim, before the final leg of the leisurely, downhill section to the Eagle Falls Picnic Area.

Pennyroyal

Cascade Falls to Snow Lake

A Cross Country Excursion through Lupine Hillsides

Highlighted Flowers

- Broadleaf Lupine
  (Lupinus latifolius)
- Bog Wintergreen
  (Pyrola asarifolia)
- Alpine Lily
  (Lilium parvum)
- Brewer's Mitrewort
  (Mitella breweri)
- Sierra Rein Orchid
  (Habenaria dilatata)
- Bog Orchid
  (Habenaria sparsiflora)
- Fireweed
  (Epilobium angustifolium)
- Thimbleberry
  (Rubus parviflorus)
- Star Solomon's Seal
  (Smilacena stellata)
- Pretty Face
  (Brodiaea lutea)

One day/overnight	
One way 2 1/2 miles	
Begin/end 6910'/7390'	
Net gain/total gain 480'/600'	
Topo map Fallen Leaf Lake, Calif.	
Wildflower Season June to September	

C ascade Falls to Snow Lake is an area of contrasts — from dry, chaparral-covered slopes of manzanita to small, luxuriant gardens of orchids and ferns. In some places, slowly moving waters form languid emerald pools, while in others, wild, untamed waters cascade over boulders and down sheer granite walls.

Snow Lake lies in a granite basin, fed by cascades that bring life-giving water to small gardens near the lake's edge. Its isolation guarantees privacy, but requires a cross-country trip across creeks, over boulders and through forests. Thoreau once said, "Our life would stagnate if it were not for the unexplored forests and meadows which surround it. We need the tonic of wilderness. We can never have enough of it." If you're one who "can never have enough," come find your wilderness tonic at Snow Lake.

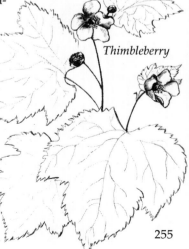

Thimbleberry

Trailhead Directions

From Tahoe City, take Highway 89 south, 2.2 miles to the William Kent Visitor Center, where you can pick up your wilderness permit, which is required to hike in Desolation Wilderness. Then continue another 17 1/2 miles to the Bay View Campground, which is a mile south of Eagle Falls. From the South Tahoe Y, take Highway 89 north, 3.2 miles to the Lake Tahoe Visitor's Center to pick up your wilderness permit. Then continue for another 4.6 miles to the Bay View Campground.

The Trail Begins

After parking at the west end of the campground, walk thirty feet or so to the "Bayview Trailhead Sign." There you'll see two trails, one to the right, which heads toward Fontanillis Lake, and the other to the left, which leads to Snow Lake. At the first fork in

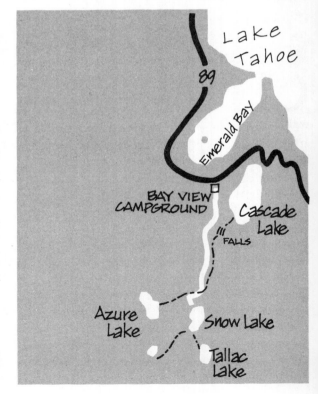

the trail, stay to the right until you arrive at the "T." At this point head left and begin climbing up the rocky "steps" which will take you to the chaparral-covered slopes above Cascade Lake. Within 1/4 mile of the trailhead gorgeous views of Lake Tahoe and Cascade Lake will open up to you.

Chaparral and Lupine Hillsides

The best time to enjoy the trail's beginning is early-to mid-July, when the slopes below Maggie's Peaks, still damp from snow melt, support the growth of thousands of Broadleaf Lupine *(Lupinus latifolius)*. Its fragrant blossoms cover the hillsides above and below the narrow trail in a swath of purple which flows in flowery delight between the chaparral.

Chaparral is a general term applied to leathery-leaved, evergreen shrubs, such as manzanita and ceanothus, which dominate dry hillsides in certain areas of California. The word is derived from the Spanish chaparro, which means "evergreen oak." (Chaps, the leather leg coverings that cowboys wore to protect themselves from brush, also came from this word.)

Before arriving at the lupine hillside, you'll pass through dense chaparral growths of Tobacco Bush *(Ceanothus velutinus)*, Greenleaf Manzanita *(Arctostaphylos patula)* and Huckleberry Oak *(Quercus vaccinifolia)* that bloom in June.

The Tobacco Bush's glossy, dark green, leathery leaves emit a resiny fragrance on warm afternoons, while the tips of the branches carry clusters of white, wild-lilac flowers.

The Greenleaf Manzanita has shiny, reddish brown, exfoliating bark and dark green leaves. It branch·tips give rise to clusters of pink, urn-shaped flowers.

You can identify the Huckleberry Oak by its leaves; they are smaller than the other two shrubs and are a dull green. From its branch tips, inconspicuous, tannish, male flowers hang downward in catkins. You may find brown acorns, from the previous year, still clinging to its branches, and later in September and

257

October, you'll see the new acorns, green and round which, as they mature, elongate and turn brown.

Strange Swellings Called Galls

If you search the branches of the Huckleberry Oaks, you may find a few 1 1/2 inch wide, tan balls clinging to the branches. These strange looking balls are not fruit, as some people think, but rather galls produced by a tiny paper gall wasp called, *Trichoteras vaccinifoliae.*

Galls are tumor-like growths in plant tissue caused by the chemical and/or mechanical stimulation of an invading insect or plant. The formation of galls is still not completely understood, but the process in the Huckleberry Oak is thought to begin when a female wasp pierces stem tissue with her ovipositor and inserts her eggs. At the same time as she lays her eggs, she also injects a chemical, rich in nucleic acid, protein and carbohydrates, which causes a change in the genetics of the cells of the surrounding plant tissue. As the cells divide, they form a "house" around the egg and then provide food and shelter to the growing larva.

If, during spring, you cut a fresh gall open, with a sharp knife, look for the larva in the spongy plant tissue in the center. From this central tissue, radiating outward, will be dozens of spokes supporting the gall casing. The larva both lives within and eats this plant tissue in the center of the gall. It produces its own food in this little self-contained house by secreting an enzyme which changes the starch in the plant tissue to sugar. It then consumes the sugar to sustain its growth until it pupates.

Later in the season, the wasps, which are about the size of fruit flies, emerge from the galls and fly away. The life cycle of gall-producing wasps is interesting, for in some species, there are two generations each year. One generation may be composed of females only. They emerge from the gall and lay eggs. From those eggs, male and females hatch to later emerge, mate and lay the eggs which will give birth

Huckleberry Oak Gall

to females, who again start the cycle anew.

In some species it is believed that there are only females who clone themselves to carry on the family line and, in other cases, it may take several years for the adult male or female wasps to emerge, instead of the usual one year.

Some galls are created by mites, aphids or even fungi. If you check out the manzanitas in the area, you'll find red swellings along the margins of some of the leaves. These are also galls, formed by an aphid called *Tamalia coweni*. When the galls are opened, the mothers and offspring can often be found incased within a white, cottony wax.

Galls may be formed from any type of plant tissue, from buds, to flowers, to leaves, to stems or even roots. Each gall is created by a specific invader, on specific plant tissue, on a particular species of plant. Some galls take on gorgeous shapes, like little cones, sea urchins or fuzzy white balls. Some drip so heavily with honey that bees and ants feed upon them.

Galls usually don't hurt the host plant unless they become too invasive, then they can weaken the plant making it susceptible to disease or invasion by parasites. The French grape industry was almost ruined in the 1800's by an aphid gall on the leaves and roots of the vines. By 1875, 1/3 of the vineyards had been destroyed — the industry was finally saved when American rootstocks were grafted onto the French plants.

Fire in a Chaparral Community

The chaparral community is interesting, not only for its galls and the little creatures they shelter and nourish, but also for its cycle of regeneration after fire. When a summer fire roars violently through a community, leaving its blackened swath, we lament the ugliness and apparent senseless destruction, but with the melting snows of spring, a miracle occurs.

New life bursts forth from blacked stumps, as young sprouts appear from chaparral root crowns below the soil's surface. These root crowns are "designed" to resist fire and sprout soon after, giving the plant a definite edge over other herbaceous species, that must sprout from seed and then compete with the chaparral's heavy root system for nourishment. The rapid growth of new shoots in the chaparral allows the plant to quickly re-establish itself, while at the same time it provides immediate food for the area's wildlife.

Within a short time, the blackened hillsides are made vibrant by the flowers of seeds which may not have bloomed on the hillsides for many years. They are released from their dormancy when their seed covers, scarified by the fire, break open to allow germination in the now fertile soils of these sunny, ash-nurseries. Many seeds, like those of the manzanita and ceanothus, can actually live dormant for decades, waiting for the heat of fire and the chemical stimulation of ash to break their dormancy.

Nutrients, which until the fire occurred, were locked up in the leaves and structures of the dense chaparral, are returned to the soil as ash to nurture the new and varied herbaceous plant life that springs up. In addition, toxins, previously released into the soil over the years by many of the chaparral species to inhibit competition, are destroyed by fire and so no longer prevent the growth of new herbs and young shrubs.

With the dense chaparral stands gone, abundant sunlight is able to reach the soil to aid in seed germination and to support sun-loving wildflowers and grasses. After a winter of ample moisture, the hillsides come alive with the color and life of thousands of new flowers.

Several years after the fire, grasses begin to dominate the hillsides. A few years later, the shrubs begin to grow more densely, crowding out the grasses by blocking sunlight and grabbing nutrients. The cycle continues until conditions are once again ripe for a fire. Renewal by fire is so important to the viability of the shrubs of this community that some, like the Tobacco Bush, can actually self-ignite on a hot summer day due to a flammable substance in its leaves.

Montane chaparral lives in a slower growing community than that found in lower elevation areas, for here the depth of snow and the shorter growing season make survival and rebirth more delicate and the destruction of animal habitats more serious. (Studies have shown that most animals either escape from a burning area or survive in tunnels under the ground.) Here the burn-rejuvenation cycle includes a longer transition from herbs to shrubs to conifers and may take a hundred years or more.

The Lodgepole Pine *(Pinus contorta, var. murrayana)* is one of the first trees to sprout after a fire in this community. Many of its cones remain closed for years on mature trees, until the fire's heat melts the resin and allows the seeds to be released. The evenness of large stands of lodgepole, frequently seen throughout Tahoe, often are an indication of a previous fire.

A Swath of Purple Lupines

The chaparral community has its own beauty, but it is a delightful surprise to find the monotony of these evergreens broken by the purple blossoms of the Broadleaf Lupine *(Lupinus latifolius)*. This lupine is not commonly found at Tahoe and would be easy to confuse with the Large-leaved Lupine *(Lupinus polyphyllus)* which commonly grows along the trails.

These species look almost identical to one another, but there is a way to tell the two apart, if you look closely at the keel. (See the Sagehen Creek West hike for an illustration of the pea flower structure.) In *L. latifolius* the upper edge of the keel is ciliate, or lined with tiny hairs; in *L. polyphyllus* this area is glabrous or without hairs. Check this out for yourself because both species bloom in this area. Lupinus polyphyllus is common in wet areas, where it grows alongside larkspur, monkshood, monkeyflowers and rein orchids.

Some of you may not care about so small a differentiation, but if you stop to check out this detail, you will find yourself slowing down and feeling a greater appreciation for the beautiful structure of a lupine flower. As with so many things in life, if we just glance and walk on, we miss so much.

The Flying White Manes of Cascade Falls

After passing the lupine, you'll soon hear the sound of Cascade Falls as it plunges into the lake below. At this point, head cross-country toward the sound of the falls, to Cascade Creek, just above the main falls. After passing through the lovely shrubs of pink flowered Spiraea *(Spiraea densiflora)* which bloom in June, you'll arrive at the creek, from which you can head up to the mini-falls. Here the waters splash off falling logs and flow over gigantic boulders, which remind me of John Muir's enthusiastic description of the waters in Yosemite's streams,

> "At the height of the flood, in the warmest June weather, they seem fairly to shout for joy, and clash their upleaping waters together like clapping of hands; racing down the canyons with white manes flying in glorious exuberance of strength, compelling huge sleeping boulders to wake up and join in the dance and song to swell their chorus."

After enjoying these flying cascades, head west along the creek, past large sunbathing-sized slabs of granite and past deep green pools, until you pick up the trail again.

Gardens of Lush Growth

As you leave the creek, to return to the trail, look for lush gardens of orchids, camas lilies, monkeyflowers, larkspurs and mitreworts. In a good year here, and in other wet areas along the trail, you'll also find hundreds of orange Alpine Lilies *(Lilium parvum)*. These flowers are lovely in the fall too, when their seed chambers split into 3 parts, looking like a brown star-flower.

In shady wet areas, often at the base of lodgepole

pines, you'll find the satiny pink flowers of Bog Winterngreen *(Pyrola asarifolia)* in July. Later in the season, along the trail, look for the tall stalks and flowers of the deep pink Fireweed.

In among these plants, look also for the white, star-shaped flowers of Star Solomon's Seal *(Smilacena stellata)*; they grow in a raceme of a dozen or so flowers. Its species' name, stellata, means "set with stars." This flower also goes by the common name, False Solomon's Seal, which refers to the shape of its leaves, which resemble a plant called Solomon's Seal. The true Solomon's Seal has round scars on its roots, left by the stems after they wither in the fall. The scars resemble the seal of King Solomon. Solomon ruled Israel in late 900 B. C. and became famous for his wisdom and fairness. His seal was made up of two interlaced triangles which, with time, in honor of him, have come to represent ultimate wisdom or the mystic union of the soul and the body.

After returning to the trail, you'll continue through a dry, rocky area and then enter damp woodland gardens of Thimbleberry *(Rubus parviflorus)* and bracken fern. In June and July, the large, white flowers of the Thimbleberry will be in bloom, and by August and September, the plants will carry "pincushion" receptacles of tiny red fruit.

In the same areas, you'll again find the shrubs of Mountain Spiraea, and when you do so, look carefully at the leaves and see what you notice. At least some of the leaves should be affected by a gall midge, with the ponderous name of *Rhabdophaga salicifolia*. This creature causes a rolling of the leaf edges toward the mid-vein. Within each roll or gall is a single chamber that houses several bright orange larvae. Beyond this, scientists know little of the life cycle of this little fly.

Gardens of Color among the Rocks
As you continue along the trail, you'll crest over the top of huge granite slabs which house showy displays of pink penstemon, white phlox, yellow tufts

Star Solomon's Seal berries

of sulphur flowers and fragrant yellow wall flowers, in late-June through July. By August, these rock areas become bright with the red blossoms of California Fuchsia *(Zauchneria californica)* and the intense blues of Explorer's Gentian *(Gentiana calycosa).*

Continue paralleling the creek after the trail dies out, crossing over to the left side when convenient to do so. In this way, you can't help but follow the left fork of the creek when it splits off to Snow Lake, instead of the right one to Azure Lake. As you wander into sunny openings, in dryish sandy areas, be sure to look for the thousands of creamy yellow Pretty Face *(Brodiaea lutea)* that carpet the ground. Some of Tahoe's largest displays of Pretty Face bloom here. Its tubular flowers radiate outward from the main stem in umbel fashion. Each petal and sepal is marked with a dark mid-vein, making the flower look as lovely in bud as when in full flower.

After arriving at Snow Lake, you may want to relax a while with lunch, before you wander through the wet gardens which line the creek along the southwest shore of the lake. They can be reached after crossing the "dance room floor" slabs of flat granite, that show exfoliation from ancient glaciers that once slowly moved through the canyon.

As you enjoy lunch, you can look out across the lake to a waterfall at the south end that flows out of Tallac Lake, 600 feet above. Snow Lake is a delightful place to enjoy an afternoon or several days. Because there is, as yet, no trail to the lake, you will be unlikely to meet another soul, which makes it a perfect place, if solitude and gentle wilderness are what you seek.

Pretty
Face

Osgood Swamp
Botanical
Preserve

The Beauty of Diversity

🏃

One leisurely day	
One way Level 1/4 mile	
Elevation 6500'	
Topo map USGS Fallen Leaf Lake, Calif.	
Wildflower Season June through August	

Highlighted Flowers

- Common Wintergreen
  (Pyrola minor)
- Blue-eyed Grass
  (Sisyrinchium idahoense)
- Mountain Yellow-eyed Grass
  (Sisyrinchium elmeri)
- White Brodiaea
  (Brodiaea hyacinthina)
- Hiker's Gentian
  (Gentiana simplex)
- Green-stipuled Lupine
  (Lupinus fulcratus)
- Hansen's Monkshood
  (Aconitum hansenii)
- Yellow Pond Lily
  (Nuphar polysepalum)

Osgood Swamp is a small area of rich botanical diversity, supporting over 140 species of wildflowers — from small insectivorous sundews to large yellow pond lilies and intense blue gentians. In the 1960s, private owners created a twelve foot channel through the swamp to drain it, doing serious damage to the flora and fauna, but fortunately in the 1970's the land was acquired by the Forest Service.

The Forest Service restored the breached morainal dam and, in doing so, brought the water level in the swamp back to its natural state. With this restoration, the plants and animals have returned, and the area is now designated as a Wildlife Refuge and Botanical Preserve (closed to dogs and all vehicles). I applaud the Forest Service for their sensitivity in returning the swamp to its natural state and for their creation of the preserve, and I encourage each of you to visit this unique area to celebrate what

Brewer's Lupine

265

can be done when someone cares.

Trailhead Directions
Osgood Swamp lies at the foot of Meyers Grade off Highway 50. Going west on 50, drive 1.2 miles past where Highway 89 South exits. Going east on 50, drive toward the bottom of Meyers Grade until you spot the old avalanche blasting platform to the left of the highway, at the turnout. Checking the topo map, you'll find Osgood Swamp located in Section 31, just north of Lower Echo Lake.

For those who would like a plant list of the swamp, it is available for a small fee through the Northern Nevada Native Plant Society, Box 8965, Reno, Nevada 89507. It was prepared by Wilma Follette and was published in Newsletter 8, pages 6-9, October 1982.

The Jaunt to the Swamp
After parking in the turnout, head down the chained-off road for several hundred yards, until you arrive at a sandy opening where the road takes a sharp turn to the left. Walk north, 20 feet across the sandy flat, to the old logging road, which is blocked off by a small post. Just past the post, head toward the willows and continue north for a few hundred yards, or so, on a faint trail through a wooded area of lodgepoles. When you merge with a sandy stream-bed, follow it to the right through lush plants, and within 20 feet or so you will run into the little, sun-filled clearing of Osgood Swamp.

In the wet, rich soil from June through August, flowers bloom in all sizes, shapes and colors, against a verdant backdrop of green, while the melodies of songbirds greet you as you leave the canopy of lodgepoles, enticing you to linger all day in the tranquility of this small, gentle meadow.

Encountering the Old and the New
As you wander around the edge of the swamp, look for the wet environment flowers that we have seen

on other hikes, such as, the pinks of Alpine Shooting Star *(Dodecatheon alpinum)*, the blues of Leichtlin's Camas Lily *(Camassia leichtlinii)* and, close to the ground, the yellows of the Primrose Monkeyflower *(Mimulus primuloides)*.

Along with the familiar, you may also encounter a few new and intriguing species. In boggy, shaded places, look for the Common Wintergreen *(Pyrola minor)*, which is similar to the four different wintergreens that we encountered on the Donner Lake hike. This species has white to pink, 1/4 inch wide flowers that bloom in a short, compact raceme. (In a raceme, the flowers grow off the main stem with individual flower stems.) The plant grows up to about 6 inches tall and supports basal, rounded leaves with long leaf stems. Unlike many species of wintergreens, its style is straight and does not protrude so far out of the flower. Its stigma is made up of 5 tiny lobes that are lovely in detail.

As you wander among the grasses, look for two gorgeous members of the Iris Family, the Blue-eyed Grass *(Sisyrinchium idahoense)*, that we saw on the Sagehen West hike, and a new species, the Mountain Yellow-eyed Grass *(Sisyrinchium elmeri)*, with lovely, yellow-orange petals that are darkly veined.

Brodiaeas may be more common in grassy foothill elevations, but if you visit Osgood in July, look for a gorgeous one in bloom, called the White Brodiaea *(Brodiaea hyacinthina)*. Each stem carries umbels of 5 or more, papery-white flowers with a green mid-vein along each petal lobe. Its anthers are white to blue and rest upon white filaments that resemble small petals. In older books, you'll find this flower listed as Triteleia hyacinthina; it has since been renamed and placed in the Brodiaea genus.

On other hikes, we have seen the whitish lavender blossoms of the Alpine Gentian *(Gentiana newberryi)*, and we have come upon the blue, tubular flowers of the Explorer's Gentian *(Gentiana calycosa)*. Here's your chance to find another species of gentian, which blooms in just as lovely a dark blue as the Explorer's

267

but with smaller flowers. The Hiker's Gentian *(Gentiana simplex)* has flower lobes that are as long as the flower tube, with solitary flowers blooming at the ends of leafy stems.

A Lesson in the Pea Family

In various environments at Osgood, you will also find several members of the Pea Family, which represent at least two different genera and three different species. This will give you a chance to see what these plants have in common to cause them to be grouped into the same family or genus. On previous hikes, we have discussed the characteristics of the Pea Family — the typical flower shape of banner, wings and keel and its compound leaves which are either pinnately or palmately-lobed.

To compare the various species of lupines that grow at Osgood, wander through dry open areas, at the fringes of the swamp, to see if you can find a plant growing low to the ground in fragrant mats with soft, silvery haired, palmate leaves. It will have dense racemes, which are only about 1 to 2 inches long, and each flower will be blue-violet with a white-to-yellow spot on the banner. This is the Brewer's Lupine *(Lupinus breweri)*, which we found on Mt. Rose.

Now search in similar dry-to-dampish areas for a taller lupine, which has large stipules (leaf-shaped bracts) growing in the axil of its leaf stems. Notice the similarities and differences between these two closely related species. The Green-stipuled Lupine *(Lupinus fulcratus)* is taller. Instead of carpeting the ground in mats, it grows up to about 3 feet high with erect, leafy stems. Its flowers are in a looser, longer raceme but are almost exactly the same shape as those of the Brewer's Lupine. Its leaves are larger but have the same palmate form that is typical of all lupines.

Now take a few minutes to look in grassy areas and see if you can find another member of the Pea Family but one which is different enough to be placed in a separate genus. What was the characteristic you

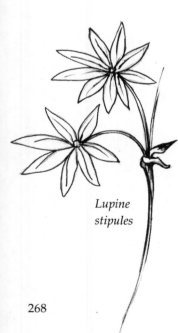

Lupine
stipules

chose to narrow down your search — was it the flower or the leaf or a combination of both?

The flower I hoped you would find is the Long-stalked Clover *(Trifolium longipes)*. Most of you are familiar with clovers, and think that you know what the flower looks like, but I wonder how many of you, who are new to botany, have ever looked closely enough at a flower head to realize that it is made up of the same little pea-shaped flowers that you found in the previous two species of lupines. (See the Sagehen Creek West hike for a drawing of the pea flower shape.)

Within the Pea Family, there are two different genera: the lupines, of the genus *Lupinus* and the clovers, of the genus *Trifolium*. Clovers differ from lupines in the shape of their flower clusters and in the number of leaflets in their palmate leaves. Lupine flowers bloom in racemes, while clovers bloom in rounded heads. Lupines generally carry 4 or more leaflets, in each palmate leaf, while clovers carry only 3 leaflets per palmate leaf. While these flowers carry the same family heritage, each, through the passage of time, has chosen its own pathway of self-expression.

Two Intriguing Plant Forms

As you continue walking through wet areas, look for the shoulder-high plants of the bluish purple flowered Monkshood. It has a unique way of reproducing itself. If you examine the plant closely, you will discover tiny round objects, called bulbils, growing in the axils and on the surface of some of the leaves. Bulbils are vegetative buds that fall to the ground to root and form clones of the parent plant.

Botanists have not decided whether this characteristic "makes" this plant a form of the Monkshood *(Aconitum columbianum)* or a separate species *(Aconitum hansenii)*, but regardless of where it is finally categorized, it is intriguing that some monkshoods have developed this form of asexual reproduction, while others have not. This form has only been

269

recorded growing in El Dorado and Mariposa Counties.

Another unusual plant is the Buckbean *(Menyanthes trifoliata)*. You'll find its white flowers blooming above sets of 3 fleshy leaflets. It grows in standing water, so you'll have to walk into the water to look closely at the flowers, but it's worth slogging through the mud to do so. The blossoms, which grow in a tight raceme, are star-shaped, with 5 to 6 petals. The surface of each petal is covered with white, thread-like strands and makes one wonder what evolutionary advantage this may have given the buckbean, or are these strands merely a playful whim of Nature?

The Gift of Diversity

After checking out the buckbean, go back to drier ground and find a special spot to sit, where you can look out across the meadow at all the different flowers — those blooming at the forest's edge, those in the damp transitional zone between swamp and forest and those with their "feet" in the water. Allow your mind to float over the whole scene, to become absorbed in the incredible diversity surrounding you — in the various sizes, textures and shapes of leaves; in the forms and colors of flowers; in the markings and shapes of their petals; in the intricate and varied structures of their reproductive parts.

Imagine that you can look beneath the earth's surface at all the different root forms — the swollen bulbs of lilies, the coral-shaped roots of orchids, which live in a symbiotic relationship with mycorrhizal fungi, the massive root system of a pine tree or of a single rye plant, whose total system of root hairs has been found to extend to an astounding 6,372 miles!

All this beautiful and miraculous diversity just to achieve the ends of survival and reproduction. One might think that after all the millions of years that plants have been on this earth that they would have narrowed themselves down to the few most efficient forms and processes necessary to "get the job done." Yet with the passage of time, we see more diversity

— with the most primitive of flower forms, such as those of the buttercup, continuing to exist and live cooperatively side by side with the more complex forms, such as those of the orchid or lily.

What does such diversity tell us about the world and about our own lives? What lessons are there in it for the raising of our children?

As parents, we are entrusted with the vulnerable souls of our children. Will we honor their individuality or will we encourage them to conform? Reinhold Messner, who climbed 29,000 foot Mt. Everest, without oxygen or sherpa guides, once said,

> "I believe that although we are the same basically, we are also very different. There is a right way of life for each one of us. Whoever finds his own way and has the courage to follow it can't go far wrong. It's just that most people get talked out of being who they really are."

Perhaps plants are lucky that they don't have ears! But we do, and we can "listen" to their message, for life always speaks the truth about itself — we simply have to learn at what level to listen. If we listen to them, plants will teach us that diversity leads to beauty, to vitality, to creative problem solving and to abundance. Of all the life forms, it is the plants that can best teach us to celebrate and honor our individuality and to "not get talked out of being who we really are."

So as you hike through the meadow today, searching for the different plants that grow in the grasses and streams, think about the wonderful diversity of the trees and flowers here in Osgood Swamp and also think about the wonderful diversity among people — how you, in your own way, express that diversity through your own individuality. If you truly honor those special qualities that make you unique, you will know the sweet joy of being and living who you really are.

Highlighted Flowers

- Yellow Pond Lily
  (Nuphar polysepalum)
- Alaska Rein Orchid
  (Habenaria unalascensis)
- Quamash Camas Lily
  (Camassia quamash)
- Elephant Heads
  (Pedicularis groenlandica)
- Seep-spring Monkeyflower
  (Mimulus guttatus)
- Narrow-leaved Lotus
  (Lotus oblongifolius)

Benwood Meadow

Pink! Pink! Pink!

弗

One way 1/2 mile	
Trail begins/ends 7400'/7520'	
Net gain/total gain 120'/120'	
Topo map USGS Fallen Leaf Lake, Calif.	
Wildflower Season June through August	

I f you love pink, head for Benwood Meadow in late-June or early-July and you will be treated to one of the most spectacular displays of shooting stars in all of Tahoe. Along the way, you will also find an unusual species of rein orchid, a small lake dotted yellow with pond lilies and stalks of sticky pinedrops growing reddish brown out of graceful bracken fern. The pond and leisurely walk make this a fun hike for young children and the elderly, and the gorgeous meadow is a wonderful place to spend the day photographing.

Trailhead Directions

After arriving at the green roofed maintenance station on Highway 50 at Echo Summit, take the unmarked black-topped road on the south side of the highway. Within 50 feet, you will arrive at a sign that reads, "Lake Tahoe Basin Summer Homes." Drive past scattered cabins and after .3 mile, you will see a green water tower on the left,

Nude Buckwheat

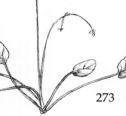

273

where the road veers left. The Pacific Crest Trailhead sign is across from the water tower. There are a few places to park, but if they are taken, you can go back down the road to a gravel road off to the left which leads to a straw-covered parking area. Be sure not to park in driveways leading to the cabins.

The Trail Begins

After parking near the watertower, pick up the trail by the sign on the post that reads, "Pacific Crest Trail, Showers Lake." Wind your way southward through the large boulders and over dry, open areas and,

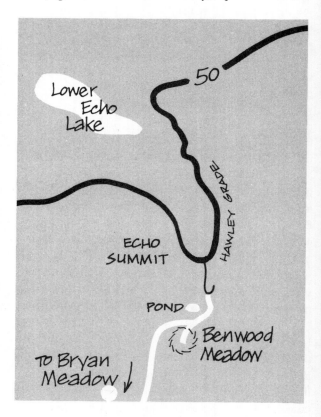

while doing so, look for the flowers of the Nude Buckwheat *(Eriogonum nudum)*. They grow in small tufts at the top of leafless (naked) stems that grow 2, or more, feet tall. The small white flowers, with their bright red anthers, are beautiful up close with a hand lens. Don't pass this one by without taking a moment to look closely at it. What seems nondescript from a distance is a real treat up close.

After about 1/4 mile, you'll descend to a small lake where you will find the floating flowers of the yellow Pond Lily *(Nuphar polysepalum)*. It is a lovely sight to come upon the large, floating leaves and bright yellow blossoms of this lily. It blooms from July through August, with flowers which are at least 2 to 3 inches wide. They float on the water's surface among the large, oval, heart-shaped leaves. Beneath the surface, many of the leaves lie coiled and are a deep purple; after rising to the surface, they open and become a dark, leathery green.

If you look at the flower, you will see the large, disk-like stigma that rises above the numerous stamens, that are bent down out of the way. The large, yellow sepals are often tinged in red and are surrounded by another ring of greenish sepals, while the small, narrow petals lie hidden, down by the stamens. The seeds, which follow the flowers in the fall, are a rich source of food for water fowl. They were gathered from California to Montana by Native Americans, who parched them and ground them into a flour, while the Klamath Indians of southern Oregon collected the seed pods by boat and then roasted them in fire to make a kind of popcorn. The rootstocks, which cling to the soil on the pond's bottom, also were eaten in soups and stew or were ground into flour after being dried.

While exploring the edge of the pond, look for the brown, sticky plants of Pinedrops *(Pterospora andromedea)*, that bloom in July and August, beneath the trees among the ferns. They grow about 2 feet tall, with drooping, urn-shaped flowers. Pinedrops was discussed on the Donner Lake hike.

As you wander around the lake, you will arrive at a small, outlet creek at the southeast end. If you check your topo map, you'll see that it flows down over steep Hawley Grade and eventually into Grass Lake

Pinedrops

several miles away. In the 1850's, Hawley Grade was a major toll road for emigrants and miners crossing the central Sierra.

Finding a Tiny Green Orchid

After crossing the outlet creek, take the westerly trail, which gently climbs through extensive areas of Pinemat Manzanita *(Arctostaphylos nevadensis),* out of which grow hundreds of red flowers of the Wavy-leaved Paintbrush *(Castilleja applegatei).* As with other manzanitas, its bark is a reddish brown and it exfoliates into straggly, paper-thin pieces. Its urn-shaped flowers, though usually white, are sometimes pink and are similar in size to the pink flowers of the larger Greenleaf Manzanita *(Arctostaphylos patula),* beside which it often grows.

As with the Greenleaf Manzanita, this smaller manzanita hosts the same gall-making aphid that creates red folded swellings along leaf edges. In the fall clusters of red berries hang downward, easily accessible to small animals. As with other species of manzanita, its berries were brewed into a cider and were dried and added to various grain and meat dishes by Native Americans.

In the same area with the manzanita and paintbrush and just before large areas of the pinemat manzanita, you'll come to a large flat rock, about the size of a small table. Look on either side of the trail in July, in this conifered area, for an unobtrusive, pale green plant. It grows about a foot high and supports tiny green orchids along a thin, leafless stem.

You'll more easily spot the orchid, if you begin your search by looking for its leaves on the brown humus floor. The leaves grow in sets of 2 or 4 and are parallel-veined. They are about 3 to 8 inches long and 1/2 to 2 inches wide, tapering to a point at the tip. From a distance, its slightly twisted flowers seem a bit worn out, but if you look carefully at each one through your hand lens, you'll see, with perhaps a bit of imagination, that it looks like the face of a droopy eared frog!

This relatively rare Alaska Rein Orchid (*Habenaria unalascensis*) was first found by western botanists on the island of Unalaska in the Aleutians and seems to prefer wooded areas that dry up by mid-season. If you get down on your hands and knees, it will reward you with its delicate fragrance.

Lush Gardens at the Meadow's Edge

Within less than 1/4 mile, the trail will drop down to a creek. Follow the creek into the meadow — if you stay on the trail, you may miss the flowers, since the trail only skirts the meadow and then heads south, without actually taking you into the wet meadow.

As you wander along the creek toward the meadow in late-June or July, look for the happy yellows of the Seep-spring Monkeyflower (*Mimulus guttatus*), the graceful, bluish lavender Quamash Camas Lilies (*Camassia quamash*) and the pinks of the cute little Elephant Heads (*Pedicularis groenlandica*).

As you walk in this area, be on the lookout for a flower that we have not yet seen. Its gorgeous pea flowers are two toned — with a yellow banner (veined in purple) and white wings and keel. Directly beneath the umbel of 1 to 5 flowers are 1 to 3 leaf-like bracts. Its pinnate leaves carry 7 to 11 narrow leaflets, while the main flower stem rises out of the axils of the leaf stems. The plant grows from about 6 inches to 2 feet tall and can be either upright or ascending.

It is called Narrow-leaved Lotus (*Lotus oblongifolius*) and comprises another genus within the Pea Family. It is closely related to the *Trifolium* genus of clovers that we discussed on the previous hike, but differs from clovers because its flowers do not grow in tightly clustered heads. Instead, lotus flowers are solitary or grow in umbels, with their individual flower stems rising from a central point as do the spokes of an umbrella.

A Meadow of Pink

After exploring the creek, for these and other flowers, you will arrive at the main meadow, which flows into other smaller meadows, which are interspersed with clumps of willows. In late-June through July, Benwood is usually very wet, or even flooded, and in most years becomes a sea of gorgeous pink from thousands of shooting stars.

There are two species of shooting stars at Tahoe: the Alpine and the Jeffrey's *(Dodecatheon alpinum, D. jeffreyi)*. On previous hikes, we have discussed the Alpine Shooting Star. In this meadow, I want to challenge you by not telling you which species grows here. If you are carrying Norman F. Weeden's book, *A Sierra Nevada Flora,* key out the shooting star in the meadow to determine for yourself what species it is.

Comparing the treatment of these two plants in the Ripper and Niehaus book, *A Field Guide to Pacific States Wildflowers* and in Weeden's book will give you a good feeling for the different approach of the two books. In Niehaus, there are illustrations for almost every flower described, whereas Weeden has very few. On the other hand, Weeden's descriptions are more comprehensive (though more technical), and he has a family, genus and species key. Niehaus only contains a family key. I generally carry both books and find, that together, they form a balanced reference.

A Wildflower Photographer's Delight
Benwood Meadow is a wonderful place to spend the day photographing. Do bring an herbal repellent, and a determined outlook, because the mosquitos in spring can be aggressive. The best days to photograph are not sunny, cloudless days but rather are the cloudy days, when the light is diffused, creating intense colors and eliminating contrasting shadows. It is also wonderful to photograph just after a storm, when the plants glisten under still cloudy skies.

It is also a joy to photograph soon after the sun has risen, while spider webs and flower buds are still frosty from early morning dew. And it is best to arrive before the morning's warmth has had a chance to create those soft breezes that gently caress the early-morning hiker but play havoc with the close-up photographer's ability to focus on a jiggling flower.

In early-morning the light has a golden quality, as it does in late-afternoon. Mid-day, in full sunshine, is usually the least desirable time to photograph, particularly if you are including people in your shots, because the overhead sun will create harsh shadows under their eyes. So mid-day is the time to enjoy a picnic, to have fun keying out flowers and to just loaf.

One piece of equipment that makes flower photography a delight is a 55 mm macro lens. This is a lens that can focus on a scene miles away and then focus on a flower only a few inches away. Another gadget that will drive you crazy, but will give the best results, is a tripod. Adjusting the legs will demand patience, particularly if you are setting up in the middle of a boggy meadow, like Benwood. On the other hand, it will make you slow down and compose your photographs in a way that you will not do if you simply hand-hold your camera. A tripod will also allow you to relax, while you wait for the breeze to stop moving your flower. If you have ever tried to hold your breath, wait for the breeze to stop and ignore the mosquitos biting your back, while the water oozes up your pant leg, you will appreciate what I am talking about!

After enjoying Benwood Meadow, you may want to continue on to its western edge. There you can pick up the trail, which will take you through dry, forested slopes where, if you are hiking late in the season in August or September, you may come across the lavender, daisy-like flowers of the Entire-leaved Aster *(Aster integrifolius)*. You can identify this aster by its purple ray flowers, which radiate outward in a scraggly manner from the central, yellow disk flowers. It grows up to about 2 feet tall, with leaves that are sessile (growing directly out of the stem) or with leaves that are clasping (their bases wrapping around the stem). Its straggly ray flowers and clasping leaves make

Entire-leaved Aster

279

this one of the easier asters to identify.

As you hike through the woods, you will arrive at several creeks that, in July, usually support hundreds of the orange, tubular flowers of the Alpine Lily *(Lilium parvum)*, which were discussed on the Shirley Canyon hike.

Those who want to make this trip a more extensive hike can continue on along the Pacific Crest Trail, past the alpine lilies, south to Bryan Meadow and Sayles Canyon, which are described in the next hike. This would be a great two or three day flower-filled trip, but you would need two cars, or a good hitch-hiking thumb to conveniently complete the journey.

Sayles Canyon to Bryan Meadow

Shaded Glens and Sunlit Meadows

🚶 *(for the first mile or so)*

One day/overnight
10 mile loop
Trail begins/highest point   6880'/8500'
Net gain/total gain   1620'/1620'
Topo map USGS Fallen Leaf Lake, Calif.
Wildflower Season   Late-June to September

Highlighted Flowers

- Lemmon's Campion
  (Silene lemmonii)
- Alpine Lily
  (Lilium parvum)
- Crimson Columbine
  (Aquilegia formosa)
- Enchanter's Nightshade
  (Circaea alpina)
- Fringed Lungwort
  (Mertensia ciliata)
- Corn Lily
  (Veratrum californicum)
- Alpine Shooting Star
  (Dodecatheon alpinum)

Glaucous Larkspur

Sayles Canyon celebrates Nature's abundance with lush gardens that bloom in profusion with shoulder-high blossoms of blues, yellows and purples. Lower down, other tiny flowers spend their days staring up at the world through linear blades of green. In the morning, soft rays of light stream through stately stands of conifers, creating dancing patterns on the lazy trail that meanders along Sayles Creek.

Two meadows are reached on the loop trail through the canyon. One meadow is small and peaceful with weathered old lodgepoles flanking its border, the other large and open with rolling fields of purple penstemon and fall-flowering aster. Along the final miles of the trail's loop, dry slopes of paintbrush, sulphur flower and lupine intersperse with small, creekside gardens of violets.

281

Trailhead Directions

Take the Sierra Ski Ranch exit off Highway 50, 3.1 miles west of Echo Summit or 3.9 miles east of Twin Bridges. After driving south along the road for about 2.1 miles, the road splits. Take the right fork and drive past the ski runs and chair lifts, keeping your eyes open for 6 foot tall plants of the Alpine Lily (*Lilium parvum*) growing alongside the road. One year in early-July, I found 50 flowers on one stalk.

Within 2 miles from where the road splits, you'll arrive at the looped end of the road where you can park and then pick up the trailhead at the upper end of the loop.

The Trail Begins

Early-July is the time to find the canyon at the height of its bloom, while two weeks later Bryan and Round Meadows come into flower. The trail begins in a

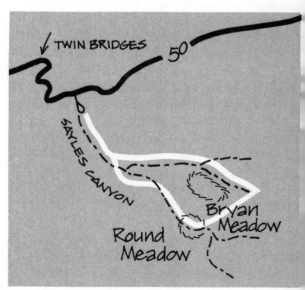

shady, damp forest of columbines, lungworts and alpine lilies and within 1/4 mile opens up to sunlit, bouldered-covered slopes where you'll see the distant ridgelines of Ralston and Pyramid Peaks and the white cascades of Horsetail Falls.

But just before breaking out into the sunlight, you'll arrive at a fork in the trail, with two large boulders on either side — the one to the left is 15-20 feet high and the one on the right about 5 feet tall. Atop the one on the right, a "log-lizard" created by a long-ago fallen tree languishes in subliminal delight. At this point take the trail's left fork until it begins to climb through colorful rock gardens of lupine, paintbrush and penstemon that bloom in July.

Within about 1/2 mile from the trailhead, you'll arrive at another trail split and a post that reads, "3 Round Meadow." On the trail that heads off to the left is a sign reading "Bryan Meadow Trail." This is the beginning of the loop, and at this point I usually head to the right, through Sayles Canyon toward Round Meadow, because for me the canyon and its creekside flowers are the most beautiful part of the hike.

After heading right, you'll soon find yourself amidst the pink, fragrant flowers of Mountain Spiraea (*Spiraea densiflora*), which bloom in July on leafy shrubs. In wet areas, you'll come upon many of the wet environment flowers which we have seen on previous hikes. These lush, shaded, flower-filled gardens are particularly lovely in the morning, as golden shafts of light softly penetrate the forest canopy to highlight the graceful sweep of a lily's petal or to catch the reds and yellows of a nodding columbine. It is also beautiful here in the fall when the yellows of changing aspens, thimbleberries and willows take on a translucent glow in the late-afternoon light.

Crossing the Creek

Soon you'll come to an area where the trail again forks. The left fork ends abruptly at several excellent creekside campsites in little sunlit glens of lilies, lupines and columbines. The right fork, which you will travel upon, fords the creek and continues through more wet gardens of hundreds of yellow Arrowleaf Senecio (*Senecio triangularis*), monkshoods and lush bracken fern.

283

Also growing in this area are many members of the Umbel Family. The large Cow Parsnip (*Heracleum lanatum*), the smaller Brewer's Angelica (*Angelica breweri*) and Gray's Lovage (*Ligusticum grayi*) grow near one another, which will give you a chance to compare their flowers. Cow Parsnip can easily be identified by its huge, 2 foot wide, maple-like leaves and large flat-topped clusters of tiny white flowers. The white flowers of angelica come in smaller clusters, with serrated leaves that are pinnate with a 3-lobed terminal leaflet. Gray's Lovage is similar to the angelica but its leaves are more finely divided.

You'll also see another flower that has the same "look" because it too is a member of the Umbel Family, though its leaves are quite different. The Yampah (*Perideridia bolanderi*) has white flowers in smaller umbelled clusters and grows only about 2 feet tall with linear, lobed leaves.

Some people give the name "Queen Anne's Lace" to any member of the Umbel Family that blooms in white, but that name more commonly refers to the plant, *Daucus carota*, that does not grow at Tahoe. It is not native to the United States but has become widespread here. It has a strong carrot fragrance with a large, flat spray of flowers that moves into a cup-like shape as it ages.

Members of the Umbel Family can be identified by their clusters of small, 5-petaled white or yellow flowers that grow on stems that radiate outward from a central point like spokes on an umbrella. Their compound leaves usually have sheathing leaf bases. This family includes many familiar plants such as carrots and parsley, but should be treated with caution in the wild because two members, the Poison Hemlock (*Conium maculatum*) and the Water Hemlock (*Cicuta douglasii*), grow at Tahoe and are deadly poisonous.

It was the Poison Hemlock that took Socrate's life, and several years ago a hiker at Tahoe died from eating the hemlock, thinking it was a wild carrot. Poison Hemlock can be identified by the purplish spots on its 2 to 6 foot tall stems. Its leaves are so

Gray's
Lovage

finely divided that they are fern-like, and its flowers are white. The Water Hemlock has coarser leaves and can more easily be confused with the other umbels than the Poison Hemlock with its warning spots. It is important to realize that no plant in the wild should ever be sampled unless you can positively identify it as safe.

Another tall, poisonous plant that blooms nearby is the purple-flowered Glaucous Larkspur *(Delphinium glaucum)*. It blooms in July with stalks of flowers that rise above the surrounding plants. Once you locate the plant, be sure to look closely at the flowers in bud. They look just like tiny dolphins perched atop outward-radiating flower stems, hence their genus name, *Delphinium,* which comes from the Latin *delphinus* for "dolphin." This genus has been admired for at least several thousand years and was given its name by Dioscorides, a Greek physician who lived in the First Century A. D.

Each 3/4 to 1 inch long flower has 5 petal-like sepals and 4 smaller petals in the flower center, all of which are a deep bluish purple. The upper sepal extends backward into a nectar spur like a Lark's back toe, which is the source of its common name, larkspur. *Glaucous* refers to the fine, white powder on the stem, which, if rubbed gently, can be removed to expose the green stem — a powder that acts to reflect the sunlight's intensity.

Look closely at the larkspur and you'll notice that the lower flowers are in bloom, while the upper are still in bud. This blooming progression from lower to upper is common in flowers that grow along a stalk and helps to prevent self-pollination. If the upper ones opened first, they would drop pollen onto the ripening stigma of the lower flowers causing self-pollination. As it is, by the time the upper flowers open, the lower are no longer fertile, having already been pollinated, or having withered because of "lack of fulfillment."

Most larkspurs are poisonous. The roots of certain species are narcotic and were brewed into a tea

Brewer's Angelica

by some Native Americans and then slipped to their opponents during gambling games to dull their minds.

Muppet Flowers and Yellow Ballerinas

One little plant that you'll find along the trail is easy to identify even from a distance. The Shasta Clover *(Trifolium productum)*, with its head of downward-drooping pea flowers, looks just like a little, pink muppet. As the genus name indicates, its leaves grow in sets of 3.

As you wander into heavily wooded areas, be on the lookout for a dainty, creamy-yellow flower that nods on stems that grow up to about 18 inches tall. Each blossom looks like a many legged ballerina in a tutu with tiny, yellow dancing slippers. It is a member of the Pink Family and is called, Lemmon's Campion *(Silene lemmonii)*.

In deeply shaded woods, by streambanks in August, look for the tiny white flowers of Enchanter's Nightshade *(Circaea alpina)*. Its inconspicuous little flower has 4 petals and 4 reflexed sepals. After pollination, tiny, pear-shaped, bristly fruits appear that are delicately beautiful when viewed through a hand lens. It is reported that this plant was named by French botanists who believed it was the magic plant that Circe used to try to enchant Ulysses, and thus gave it its genus name, *Circaea*.

After crossing several more creeks and passing through gardens of alders, fern and corn lilies, the trail begins to fade out. Just continue paralleling the creek until you pick up the trail again after a few hundred yards. Looking for ducks (2 to 3 rocks placed on top of each other) and tree blazes (vertical gashes at about head height made in the bark) will also help you stay on course.

After passing through a boulder-covered slope, you will come to a little meadow where the trail dies out in a creek bed. At this point, head southeast through the grass to the creek's edge to where the trail crosses the creek, between the two trees marked

Lemmon's
Campion

with blazes. If the creek is low, crossing is easy; you can continue on through the grass to cross the creek again and then pick up the trail, as you begin the gentle uphill climb to Round Meadow. If the creek is too deep to be forded comfortably, just head upstream, paralleling the creek, until you find a place to cross. If you head southeast after crossing, you'll pick up the trail within 40 or 50 feet.

Arriving at Round Meadow

Within about 5 minutes after crossing the creek, you will arrive at grassy, Round Meadow. In mid-July the purple, whorled flowers of Meadow Penstemon (*Penstemon rydbergii*) and the reds of paintbrushes bloom alongside shooting stars, senecios and lupines, while earlier in July, Marsh Marigolds (*Caltha howellii*) bloom in robust white above shiny, rounded leaves.

Since the trail dies out at the meadow, you'll want to reconnect with it by passing to the north of the willow clump that lines the creek. At the willows, look northeast or straight ahead and you'll see girdled, dead lodgepoles, while way off to your right will be the remnants of an old corral. When you're ready to leave the meadow, head northeast past the girdled trees and through the wet area of corn lilies, where the trail reappears in the grass. Then follow it uphill, through the trees for several miles, until it connects with the Pacific Crest Trail to take you into Bryan Meadow.

Descending into Bryan Meadow

As you drop into Bryan Meadow, you'll arrive at a small, wet area of shooting stars, marsh marigolds and monkeyflowers that bloom from late-June through early- to mid-July. After heading north a few hundred yards past wet gardens of the Sparsely-flowered Bog Orchid and the Sierra Rein Orchid, *(Habenaria sparsiflora and H. dilatata),* you'll arrive at the split where the Pacific Crest Trail heads east and our loop trail heads west.

At this point you'll wander west along the north

edge of the meadow, past the ground-carpeting, blue flowers of Jacob's Ladder *(Polemonium californicum)* that bloom at the base of lodgepoles, until you pass the small white flowers of Bud Saxifrage *(Saxifraga bryophora)*, the larger whites of Coulter's Daisies *(Erigeron coulteri)* and many other species of flowers that bloom in the meadow through August.

The return trail along the north part of the loop is well marked and easy to follow, as it descends across mossy creeks of violets and mitreworts, meanders through pine-needled woods and crosses open, rocky slopes. The views will be expansive and the downward pace exhilarating. Soon you will arrive at the original split in the trail by the Bryan Meadow Trail sign. At this point you have completed the loop! At the sign, take the trail to the right, and you will soon arrive at your car.

Red Lake Peak

Every Flower, a Mirror Reflecting the Creator

One day/overnight	
One way	*2 miles*
Begin/end	*8573'/9300'*
Net gain/total gain	*727'/727'*
Topo maps	*USGS Markleeville, Calif.*
	USGS Silver Lake, Calif.
Wildflower Season	*June through August*

Seen from Carson Pass, Red Lake Peak looks drab and imposing, but that first misleading impression is quickly forgotten amidst the poetic shapes of twisted junipers, in the sunny meadows of wild iris and in the gardens of alpine flowers that brightly bloom among the rocks on the flanks of the Peak.

Trailhead Directions
Take Highway 88 to the Carson Pass parking area, where you can read about Kit Carson's travels through the Sierra and see the stone monolith raised to honor Snowshoe Thompson. After the stop at Carson Pass, drive 2/10 of a mile west to the small turnout on the north side of the road. The trailhead is at the northwest corner of the turnout.

Western Blue Flag

289

The Trail Begins

You will begin the hike among scattered groves of aspens and soon pass by wonderful, old Sierra Junipers *(Juniperus occidentalis)* that sit wedged in among

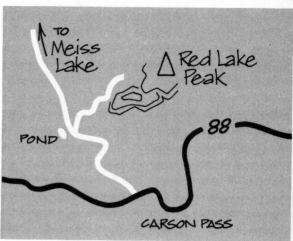

granite boulders, looking like regal patriarchs. John Muir, who had a great fondness for this tree, described it as "A thickset, sturdy, picturesque highlander, seemingly content to live for more than a score of centuries on sunshine and snow; a truly wonderful fellow, dogged endurance expressed in every feature, lasting about as long as the granite he stands on."

The Sierra Juniper *(Juniperus occidentalis)* may live for over a thousand years. At these exposed elevations, it may only grow to about 10 feet in height, but its thick trunk, which is built to withstand years of storm and avalanche, may be well over 5 feet wide. Its tenaciously clinging root system is partially exposed and may be as broad as the tree's crown, giving the juniper a stable platform upon which to pass its days in stoic defiance of the harsh elements.

Its scale-like leaves highlight clusters of sticky, blue berries. These berries were gathered by Native Americans, who placed them near anthills to convert them into fragrant beads. After the ants ate the sweet substance out of the center, the hollowed out berries could be strung! Native people gathered the cinnamon-brown bark in shreds to help line the floors of their homes, and the Paiutes used the wood to smoke their buckskin to soften it for clothing.

Towering Green Gentians

In July, thousands of flowers usually bloom on these slopes, as the trail heads west through rolling hillsides of junipers and aspens. After hiking through the flowers and trees for about a mile, you'll arrive at a trail sign that points the way to Meiss Pass. This sign is a junction with the "Old Meiss Trailhead," which begins 1/4 mile below, off Highway 88. If you approach the trail from that point, it is a mile shorter, but fairly steep, and you would miss a lot of flowers!

At the sign, head toward Meiss Pass, and as you wander along the trail among gilias, lupines and mule-ears, look for towering Green Gentians (*Frasera speciosa*). They grow up to about 5 feet tall, with whorls of long leaves that fan outward, cradling hundreds of elaborately decorated flowers.

The green flowers grow out of the axils of the leaves. Their 4-petaled blossoms carry linear sepals and oval petals that are purple spotted. Two hairy, purple-edged glands sit at the base of the petals, while the enlarged ovary swells enthusiastically in the center of it all.

If there are several plants in the area, look around and see if you notice a difference among them. Some will carry flowering stalks and others will have only a rosette of leaves. These gentians are biennials (or short lived perennials), which means they grow a rosette of leaves one year and send up the flower heads the following year, after which they re-seed and die.

Ground-hugging Thistles

While looking at these tall plants, don't forget to look closely at the ground for plants that grow only a few inches high. One that is somewhat drab at first sight, but interesting up close, is Drummond's Thistle (*Cirsium drummondii*). Its flower heads, which nestle in a basal rosette of spiny leaves, are as prickly as the leaves that cradle them and, because of this, provide protective shelter for small insects.

Drummond's Thistle is a member of the Composite Family and, like all thistles, is made up of disk flowers only. Check this out for yourself; you will see that each flower head is composed of numerous, tubular, 5-petaled flowers. Drummond's Thistle is very similar to the Dwarf Thistle *(Cirsium foliosum)* and, in some books, is referred to as the same species.

The Graceful Flowers of Mountain Bluebells
Within a few hundred yards, the trail crosses several small washes which usually abound with masses of drooping, blue, bell-shaped flowers that are pink in bud and fade to pink again as they age. Look closely at the edges of the sepals and you will see that they are fringed with tiny hairs, which led to one of its common names, Fringed Lungwort *(Mertensia ciliata)*.

This unglamorous common name, for such a lovely flower, came from herbalists in the 16th and 17th Centuries, who believed the plant could cure lung diseases. Wort is an old, Ango-Saxon word for plant. It is also known by the prettier names of Mountain Bluebells and Languid Ladies. Its botanical name, *ciliata,* means "hairy along the edges." *Mertensia* is in honor of Franz Mertens, a 19th Century German botanist.

Soon after these washes, the trail opens up to large, rounded, treeless hillsides, and the flanks of Red Lake Peak loom in the distance. In July, on these barren hillsides, sulphur flowers and stonecrops come into bloom brightening the talus slopes with yellow.

The Stonecrop *(Sedum lanceolatum)* grows among the rocks with large clusters of solid yellow, star-shaped flowers. The genus name, *sedum,* is derived from the Latin *sedeo,* which means "to sit." *Sedum* is easy to remember, for these plants seem to sit with contentment, nestled among the rocks.

As with most yellow flowers, it is difficult to pick up definition when photographing them. In shooting

Mountain Bluebells

with slides, underexpose by 1 to 2 stops, and I think you will be happy with the results.

A Palate of Purple Violets

If you hike Red Lake Peak just after the snow melts in early-June, you will experience the joy of finding thousands of little violets, carpeting the ground in velvety purple. Beckwith's Violet *(Viola beckwithii)* blooms among the grayish green shrubs of sagebrush soon after the snows melt. Its purple, velvety petals are yellow at the throat and rise above linear-divided leaves. If you arrive early enough to see the violets, you may also find the lovely blossoms of Creeping Phlox *(Phlox diffusa)*, spreading their fragrant flowers in carpets of lavender and white.

A Velvety Lupine Lines the Gullies

As you continue hiking, the trail will make one last dip before the steady, uphill climb toward the peak. In a small seep that crosses the trail in the dip, look for the hairiest lupine you'll probably ever see. Lobb's Lupine *(Lupinus lobbii)* grows only a few inches off the ground, and its silky white hairs lie dense and flat against the stems and leaflets. The flowers are a bluish purple, with a white spot on the banner, and give rise to silky haired pea pods in late-summer.

Also keep your eyes open for one of the tiniest plants at Tahoe. This miniature annual has yellow flowers that are only about 1/8 inch wide, and its petals are only about 1 mm long! Brewer's Navarretia *(Navarretia breweri)* nestles on the ground in dry, sandy soil, while its flowers bloom in spiny-bracted heads above the needle-like leaves.

Take a moment to look at this flower to decide if you think it has a 2 or 3-lobed stigma! Your hand lens will help, and if you stop to enjoy its detail, you will relate to it as a separate little individual, rather than simply as a yellow dot. Most people walk by without ever spotting it. I like to stop to offer it the recognition and respect it deserves for managing to thrive in such a dry, wind-swept home.

Beckwith's Violet

293

Meadow Gardens of Lavender Iris

There are many beautiful flowers along the trail, but my favorite part of the hike lies just ahead. After climbing, the trail will begin to level out by a pond, where hundreds of purple iris bloom from late-June to early-July. Irises are one of the loveliest of all flowers.

The Western Blue Flag *(Iris missouriensis)* grows about 2 feet tall and has lavender flowers that are 4 to 5 inches across. The petal-like sepals are pale lavender and are veined in purple to guide insects past the stigma, which is housed in the petal above. The petals are vertical and lack the veining of the sepals, and they are a deeper color. Its ovary can be seen as a swelling, just below where the petals and sepals join the stem.

The process of pollination in an iris is amazing — an example of the specialized co-evolution of insects and flowers. Bees are attracted to the large, colorful, landing-pad sepals and are guided by the purple lines on the sepals to the nectar that lies at the base of the sepal. As the bee approaches the nectar, its back brushes against the petal-like branch of the style, that is above the sepal. This style branch houses the stigma at the tip and shelters the anther below at its base.

As the bee walks under it, the stigma rolls backward to pick up pollen from the bee's back and the flower is fertilized. As the bee approaches the base of the sepal, it picks up pollen from the anther which lies appressed to the base of the style. As the bee backs out after sipping the nectar, it unrolls the tip of the style so that the surface of the stigma now faces upward and cannot contact its own pollen. It is obvious from this intricate process that bees and irises have been in close, beneficial contact for hundreds of thousands of years.

Irises take their name from the classical Goddess of The Rainbow, who flew through the skies as a winged messenger of the gods, with a glorious rainbow for her flowing cloak. Thomas Nuttall, a noted botanist and ornithologist from Phila-

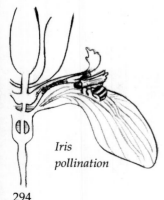

Iris pollination

delphia, first discovered this iris near the headwaters of the Missouri River and thus gave it its species' name. Thomas collected extensively in California in 1835, from San Francisco to San Diego. He added much to the field of botany and many species of flowers carry his name.

Native Americans honored the powers of this iris long before the white man came. They made a poison from its fresh roots to coat their arrow heads, and I'm sure they too delighted in its beauty.

Roses among the Grasses

Two other lovely, though less conspicuous flowers, bloom in this same meadow. They are both members of the Rose Family. The Dusky Horkelia (*Horkelia fusca*) has separate heart-shaped petals that are inconspicuous from afar but quite lovely up close. Pink lines mark the whitish petals, and between each petal is a red-brown sepal; between each sepal is a tiny, red-brown bract. Its pinnate leaves carry finely lobed leaflets and its flower stems, which grow up to about 2 feet, are red and glandular hairy.

The other rose I'd like you to look for has nodding buds, with red-purple sepals, and linear bracts between each sepal. In full bloom, the creamy flowers point upward and after fertilization are followed by swelling styles that are feathery and more showy than the flowers. This plant is called Downy Avens (*Geum canescens*) and is found at elevations from 8,500 to 11,000 feet where you'll often find it in such grassy meadows.

Dusky Horkelia

You will also see a third member of the Rose Family that grows about 2 feet tall with yellow, 5-petaled flowers. The Graceful Cinquefoil (*Potentilla gracilis*) has reddish stems covered with dense, straggly hairs, and its fan-shaped leaves are palmately lobed. Its petals are heart-shaped, and its anthers and pistils are bright yellow.

Alpine Gardens Grace Red Lake Peak

After enjoying these flowers, and the others

295

in the meadow, head northeast up the slope, cross-country toward Red Lake Peak, where in early- to mid-July, you'll usually find one of the most spectacular displays of sub-alpine plants in all of Tahoe. Violets, gilias, lupines and sunflowers bloom in purples, pinks, reds and yellows. You will have seen many of these flowers on previous hikes, but some may be new to you.

One in particular that may attract your attention, in July and August, is Pursh's Woolly Pod *(Astragalus purshii)*. It grows only a few inches off the ground with cute-looking, fuzzy white seed pods. It is closely related to Whitney's Locoweed *(Astragalus whitneyi)*, which was discussed on the Castle to Basin Peak hike. Whitney's Locoweed also grows abundantly here with seed pods that are inflated and spotted purple.

Look also for other ground-hugging plants. The Timberline Phacelia *(Phacelia frigida)* grows with silvery, densely hairy leaves and compact, lavender to white flowers that cluster on caterpillar-like coils. You'll also find Gordon's Ivesia *(Ivesia gordonii)*, which blooms with tiny, narrow, deep-yellow petals that alternate with the larger, triangular-shaped, green sepals. The flowers cluster in a head at the end of stems that are about 6 inches long. The basal rosette of pinnate leaves are long and narrow, with numerous, tiny, lobed leaflets.

A Treasure Hunt for Alpine Composites

See also if you can locate two similar-looking cushion plants of the Composite Family. Both have bright yellow, daisy-like flowers that grow in clusters above hairy, gray leaves. One of them, the Woolly Butterweed *(Senecio canus)*, grows about 6 inches tall with downy covered basal leaves that are oval-shaped and long-stemmed. Check out its phyllaries, which are the green bracts that encircle the bowl beneath the petals, and you will see that they are black-tipped and are arranged in a row without overlapping each other (as is characteristic of this genus).

Now see if you can find the Cushion Stenotus *(Haplopappus acaulis)*. Its yellow flowers bloom atop stems that are only about 4 inches tall at this elevation. The stems grow densely from a woody base. Touch the linear, to spoon-shaped, leaves and you'll feel the bristly hairs that cover the surface. Notice that its leaves remain on the plant, clothing its base, even after they dry out. Check the phyllaries and you'll see that they overlap like shingles and are not black-tipped as in the Butterweed.

After you have checked out these two composites, see if you can locate the Woolly Sunflower *(Eriophyllum lanatum)* which we have discussed on other hikes, and then hunt for a fourth composite that blooms with purple rays and yellow disk flowers. It is a compact little plant with stems and leaves that are shiny because of the stiff, appressed hairs that grow on their surfaces. Because of the reflective hairs, it is called Shining Daisy *(Erigeron barbellulatus)*. Its narrow leaves are usually vertical, to avoid the intense, solar radiation at this elevation. The solitary flower heads rise only a few inches above the basal leaves.

Not all the plants on these slopes hug the ground, others stand tall as if to ignore the conditions under which they live. Pink and red gilias, yellow wallflowers, whorled penstemons and the gracefully drooping flowers of Blue Flax *(Linum perenne)* all celebrate life on these slopes.

A Discovery of Lake Tahoe

If you continue climbing cross-country, up the flanks of Red Lake's 10,000 foot peak, you will be rewarded with magnificent views of Lake Tahoe. It is thought that John Fremont made the first recorded sighting of Lake Tahoe from this peak on Valentine's Day in 1844. The Washos led him to it by drawing a map that showed both the lake and the Truckee River. Although the Indians warned him of deep snow around the lake, he and his men were determined to reach the lake.

To gain a perspective, Fremont and his men climbed Red Lake Peak, until the lake loomed into view. They were astounded by its size and beauty and were delighted by its blue waters, especially after having just passed through the dry, Nevada desert. Fremont wrote in his journal that evening, "We had a beautiful view of a mountain lake at our feet, about fifteen miles in length, and so entirely surrounded by mountains that we could not discover an outlet."

It was not very long ago that Fremont stood in the snow, where you perhaps now stand, and it was not very long ago that the Washos made Tahoe their summer home. I'm sure they too marveled at the beauty of the flowers on Red Lake Peak. In fact, the flanks of the peak are so filled with life, it is hard to remember how drab the mountain looked when the hike first began.

As you sit among the flowers, take a few moments to lie back and enjoy these words from John Muir; they were written as he sat on a similar mountain in Yosemite,

"How boundless the sky seems as we revel in these storm-beaten sky gardens amid so vast a congregation of onlooking mountains! Strange and admirable it is that the more savage and chilly and storm-chafed the mountains, the finer the glow on their faces and the finer the plants they bear. The myriads of flowers tingeing the mountain-top do not seem to have grown out of the dry, rough gravel of disintegration, but rather they appear as visitors, a cloud of witnesses to Nature's love... every flower a window opening into heaven, a mirror reflecting the Creator."

- Western Blue Flag
  (*Iris missouriensis*)
- Large-leaved Lupine
  (*Lupinus polyphyllus*)
- Crimson Columbine
  (*Aquilegia formosa*)
- Mountain Bluebells
  (*Mertensia ciliata*)
- Silverleaf Raillardella
  (*Raillardella argentea*)
- Alpine Paintbrush
  (*Castilleja nana*)
- Sierra Primrose
  (*Primula suffrutescens*)

Frog and Winnemucca Lakes

Sweeping Hillsides of Rainbow Color

𝝠𝝠

One day/overnight	
One way 2 miles	
Begin/end 8560'/8980'	
Net gain/total gain 420'/420'	
Topo map USGS Markleeville, Calif.	
Wildflower Season July through September	

Frog Lake is a serene body of water tucked into a windswept ridge. Near its edge, lavender iris bloom with regal grace, and weathered old pines reach out with swooping arms to offer their gifts of reddish purple, resiny cones. The short stretch of trail past Frog Lake, on the way to Winnemucca, is a blaze of color in July, with the most intense flower displays in all of Tahoe. On the slopes above scenic and icy-cold Winnemucca Lake, dry environment daisies, gilia and paintbrush create soft patches of color among the fragrant gray-greens of sagebrush and pennyroyal.

Trailhead Directions

Take Highway 88 to the Carson Pass parking turnout. The trailhead leaves the parking area near the Forest Service information booth. If you plan to go beyond Winnemucca Lake, you will need a wilderness permit, even for a day hike. It can be picked up

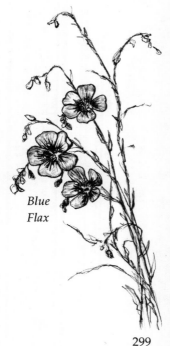

Blue
Flax

at the information booth by the parking area.

The Trail Begins

The hike to Frog Lake is short and enjoyable, and so it is fun for both the elderly and young children. Along the way, you will see many of the flowers that have been discussed on previous hikes, but one that is especially lovely is the Blue Flax *(Linum perenne).*

When you find several of these plants growing together, stop for a moment and look closely at the flowers to see if you notice a difference among them. Though the flowers appear the same in most respects, you may have discovered that in some the style is very long, while in other flowers the style is short. This condition is called heterostyly which means "different styles."

On other hikes, we have discussed some of the structural mechanisms that have evolved in flowers to help reduce the chances of self-pollination; the heterostyly of the Blue Flax is another such mechanism. It works this way: the short-styled flowers produce large pollen grains which are incompatible with the stigma of its own short-styled flower. Therefore, pollen inadvertently brushed onto its own stigma will not cause self-pollination. These short-styled flowers can only be fertilized by long-styled flowers, which produce small pollen grains, and, of course, the reverse is true for long-styled flowers.

After fertilization occurs, shiny brown seeds appear, which are rich in oil — it is from a related species of flax that we extract linseed oil. Flax has long been important to man for its fiber, as well as for its seeds, and has been in cultivation since ancient times. (*Linum* is derived from the Greek *"linon"* for thread.)

Arriving at Frog Lake
Within 1/2 mile, you will arrive at Frog Lake, which has a surprisingly isolated feeling, even though you are but a short distance from a major highway. Hesperochirons, pussy toes and cinquefoils nestle in the grasses near the lake, and usually in early-July the first irises begin to appear.

As you wander among the rocks look for the penstemons, gilias and sulphur flowers which bloom in the sandy soil. Look also for one of Tahoe's prettiest buckwheats. The Mountain Sorrel (*Oxyria digyna*) blooms with inconspicuous flowers, but its flat rounded seeds are tinged in red and from a distance look like clusters of flowers. Sorrel is delicious in salads because of the sour oxalic acid in the leaves.

As you wander along the edge of the lake, you will find the 5-needled Whitebark Pine (*Pinus albicaulis*) that grows low enough at this elevation to show you its tightly closed resiny cones. Under less severe conditions, these trees may grow up to a height of 70 feet, making examination of the cones rather difficult, unless you are very tall!

After the snows melt in late-June, the tree sets flower with male catkins, which are a rose-purple, and female flowers, with bright red scales. The fertilized cones grow very slowly the first year, and they stand erect. By the next summer, they have become horizontal and ripen later in the season.

Whitebark Pines are considered the most primitive of all our native pines, because their cones remain closed until they decay to release the seeds. Even when the seeds are released, the process is inefficient, because the wings on the seeds, which help in the dispersal of most pines, stick to the resiny scales of the cones. When the seeds finally do break away, they usually lack wings and, therefore, fall to the ground close to the parent tree. Clark's Nutcrackers help to offset this failure of dispersal by breaking open the cones in search of seeds and in the process of eating and eliminating them, they distribute the seeds.

The downward swooping branches of these sturdy trees form protective coverings and comfortable beds for animals and man alike. As John Muir once wrote,

"During stormy nights, I have often camped snugly beneath the interlacing arches of this little pine. The needles, which have accumulated for centuries, make fine beds, a fact well known to other mountaineers, such as deer and wild sheep, who paw out oval hollows and lie beneath the larger trees in safe and comfortable concealment."

Nature's Mode of Cooperation
As you leave the shores of Frog Lake, you will continue hiking along a generally level trail. Within about 1/4 mile, you will arrive at sloping hillsides of flowers, which in July come alive with magnificent color. Off in the distance will be Caples Lake, reflecting the sky above. The area is a photographer's paradise, with mornings offering the best lighting conditions and colors most saturated on an overcast day immediately following a storm.

Pausing in these gardens, one can't help but be impressed by the beauty and diversity of Nature, yet there is another quality, often overlooked, which is important to the survival of man and the world —
that of cooperation.

As you stand among the gardens of color, looking out around you, you will see a myriad of insects and flowers living in harmony, sustaining life in one another. Look also at the trees which provide much of the world's oxygen and create homes for animals and protective environments for plants. Think also of the leaves of plants; life would not exist if it were not for the cooperative relationship between the chloroplasts which manufacture life-sustaining sugars and the plants that house them.

Imagine the hundreds of species of soil fungi which cover the root tips of conifers and other plants, extending their root systems so that they are more efficient in absorbing nutrients and moisture from the soil. In exchange, the fungi are housed and fed sugars from the host's roots.

Within the insect world one of the most amazing examples of cooperation is the relationship between ants and aphids, whereby the ants actually domesticate the aphids in exchange for a honey they secrete. The ants hover over and protect the aphids from predators, or from harsh weather, by taking them into their nests at night or by building tiny mud huts for outdoor protection. Some species of ants herd the aphids to plants near their ant hills to make honey collecting more convenient. Other species of ants actually gather up the aphid's eggs and take them to their ant hills to store and protect them throughout the winter. Come spring, they return them to the plants to hatch!

Stephan Lackner in his book, *Peaceable Nature*, points out that most animals live their lives in relative harmony, with about 95% dying from natural causes, rather than from predation and that animals cooperate far more than they compete — even though nature films too often present the opposite picture.

Along with such nature films, interpreters of Darwin's Theory of Evolution have done us a disservice by emphasizing competitiveness, while ignoring the cooperative relationships that abound in the natural world. On the Galapagos Islands, where Darwin did his research, life has maintained its equilibrium and healthy functioning with few predators and with cooperation, not competition, as the norm.

Only through love and cooperation will we begin to re-heal the earth and once again find harmony within ourselves. Seeing healthy competition and loving cooperation as the norm in Nature will help man to realize that "survival of the fittest" and ruthless competition are not the path to a higher quality of life. Observing Nature will help us to see that cooperation is the real pathway to the harmonious life that we all desire.

A Rainbow of Color

As you wander along the trail among the flowers, the intensity of color and diversity of species will stand out. Look for the tall plants of Green Gentian *(Frasera speciosa)* with hundreds of green flowers blooming along the stalks in the axils of the leaves. You will see many of the species discussed on the previous hike, such as irises and mountain bluebells. There are also both species of pink elephant heads *(Pedicularis groenlandica, P. attollens)*, the tall Giant Red Paintbrush *(Castilleja miniata)* and the lavender stalks of the Large-leaved Lupine *(Lupinus polyphyllus)*.

Large-leaved Lupine

Within several hundred yards of entering the flower-covered slope, you will cross a feeder creek. Along its shores, willow herbs, monkeyflowers, lupines and many other flowers bloom in vibrant yellows, reds and lavenders. This is definitely a place to spend hours photographing, botanizing and just plain enjoying.

Continuing on to Winnemucca Lake

As you leave these gardens behind, and make your way to Winnemucca Lake, you will pass hillsides of Alpine Paintbrush *(Castilleja nana)* which bloom in July, and, although they don't look like much from a distance, they are soft and delicate up close. You will also find the tiny, whitish flowers of Shasta Knotweed *(Polygonum shastense)* in July. Its dainty blossoms are lined with pink mid-veins and grow 2 or 3 in the axils of the leaves. The angled, leafy stems of this woody perennial lie upon the ground in dry, sandy places.

In a little more than a mile, you will arrive at Winnemucca Lake, perhaps in time for a picnic along its shores. At the water's edge, you'll find Red Heather *(Phyllodoce breweri)* and Bog Laurel *(Kalmia polifolia)* and, if both are in bloom, it will give you a chance to compare these similar looking flowers, which have been discussed on previous hikes.

Alpine Prickly Currant *(Ribes montigenum)* also blooms at the lake's edge and is wonderful, viewed through a hand lens. Its flowers have 5 tiny, reddish petals and longer, yellowish sepals which form a saucer beneath the petals. Its rounded, lobed leaves are glandular-hairy and fragrant on both surfaces. Be sure also to use your hand lens to look closely at the globular berry. Bright red glands sit exquisitely on the top of shiny, red stalks.

Be sure to check out the lake's outlet creek, which gives rise to wet gardens of marsh marigolds, shooting stars, monkeyflowers, elephant heads and buttercups. The waterfall, at the southwest end of the lake, supports similar flowers, while the rocks near the creek that flows into the lake are decorated with the nodding bells of white Cassiope *(Cassiope mertensiana).* Up in the rocks, on the slopes above and beyond the creek, look for the pink, upright flowers of Sierra Primrose *(Primula suffrutescens).* In some years, the display of pink is breath-taking.

After checking out the flowers in the rocks beyond Winnemucca Lake, you may wish to continue along the windswept ridge that leads to Round Lake and then drop down a thousand feet to flowery Fourth of July Lake. There are campsites along the lake's edge, where you can spend the night as a prelude to an extended trip into the backcountry.

If I were to choose any hike at Tahoe, as an introduction to the glory of its wild gardens,

Alpine Prickly Currant

it would be this hike. The intensity of color, the variety of flowers, the easy trail and the expansive views have created an experience that is spectacular. You will not find solitude, but you just might come upon an old friend hiking along the trail or perhaps meet a new one!

- Sticky Starwort
  (*Stellaria jamesiana*)
- Richardson's Geranium
  (*Geranium richardsonii*)
- Swamp Onion
  (*Allium validum*)
- Ranger's Buttons
  (*Sphenosciadium capitellatum*)
- Fireweed
  (*Epilobium angustifolium*)
- Lady's Tresses
  (*Spiranthes romanzoffiana*)
- Buckbean
  (*Menyanthes trifoliata*)
- Purple Cinquefoil
  (*Potentilla palustris*)

Grass Lake
A Boggy Lake Fringed with Flowers

術 木 ぐ

One leisurely day
A roadside lake at 7500'
Topo map USGS Freel Peak, Calif.
Wildflower Season   July through August

In the boggy waters of shallow Grass Lake, intriguing flowers of various shapes and colors bloom above mud-mired stems, while in less boggy areas, fireweeds glow satiny pink in the late-afternoon light. At the lake's mossy inlet creek, graceful grasses undulate in greens and yellows beneath the surface of slowly moving waters, while nearby, wild strawberries bloom in fragrant damp woods, and dense willow gardens shelter hidden flower treasures.

Finding Grass Lake
Grass Lake is located just west of Luther Pass on the south side of Highway 89. There is plenty of parking off the highway at the west end of the lake, which makes wheel chair access excellent.

Wandering among the Flowers
To those with inquiring minds and open hearts, a day spent among wildflowers is a joyous quest for knowledge and an immersion in pure pleasure. Grass

*Swamp
Onion*

Lake is a wonderful place to immerse yourself in such pleasure, because its proximity to the road allows plenty of leisurely time to explore its gardens and to learn about its flowers. The lake sits in a boggy meadow, fed by creeks that cascade off the surrounding mountains. Many flowers bloom around the lake, but to enjoy those that grow in the lake, it's best to wear rubber boots or shoes that you don't mind getting wet and muddy.

After parking at the west end of the meadow, walk toward the inlet creek, which is a few yards southeast of where you parked. As you do so, look for two starworts growing in the grass near its banks. The small white flowers of the Sticky Starwort (*Stellaria jamesiana*) and the Long-stalked Starwort (*Stellaria longipes*), can usually be found blooming in early-July. Starworts are members of the Pink Family, a family characterized by 5-petaled flowers with "pinked" petal tips and opposite leaves.

The Sticky Starwort usually grows right next to the creek. You can identify it by the V-notch in each petal tip and by the way its flowers rise in pairs out of the axils of the leaves. Its glandular-hairy stems grow from 4 to 12 inches tall with narrow, lance-like leaves. (Glandular-hairy refers to hairs that carry a sticky drop of liquid at their tips.)

The Long-stalked Starwort is about the same height, but its 5 petals are so deeply notched that the flowers look as if there were 10 linear petals beneath the bright red anthers. Its narrow, lance-like leaves grow vertically as opposed to the horizontal leaves of the Sticky Starwort. The solitary flowers bloom atop flower stems which are without hairs or glands.

Wild Strawberry

As you leave the creek to wander through the lodgepole pines, look for the plants of the Wild Strawberry (*Fragaria platypetala*) which carpet the pine-needled floor with white flowers, that carry clusters of yellow reproductive parts. Later, tiny sweet berries will lie hidden under the leaves.

The Way It Used to Be

Wild strawberries were common throughout America in the past. It was recorded by settlers in the 1640's that strawberries grew so thick on the American prairies that the horses' fetlocks seemed covered with blood! Native Americans, and these early settlers, must have known a natural abundance that we can only dream of, now that we have so changed the country's landscape.

John Muir saw untouched landscape when he walked from San Francisco down the great Central Valley to Yosemite in the 1860's. He described the valley, during a time before it was grazed and plowed, in his book *The Mountains of California,*

> "When California was wild, it was one sweet bee-garden throughout its entire length, north and south, and all the way across from the snowy Sierra to the ocean.
>
> The Great Central Plain of California, during the months of March, April, and May, was one smooth, continuous bed of honey-bloom, so marvelously rich that, in walking from one end of it to the other, a distance of 400 miles, your foot would press about a hundred flowers at every step... The radiant, honeyful corollas, touching and overlapping, and rising above one another, glowed in the living light like a sunset sky — one sheet of purple and gold, with the bright Sacramento pouring through the midst of it..."

Imagine the joy and exhilaration of spending every day, during springtime, outdoors among these gardens, as did the early Native Americans. They didn't need to pick bouquets of flowers to brighten their homes; their outdoor homes were covered with one big, living bouquet. You still have a chance to experience a small part of what it must have been like. The hills of The Antelope Valley California Poppy Preserve, which lie east of Santa Barbara between the small towns of Gorman and Lancaster, come alive each spring with a blaze of orange poppies, blue lupines and pink owl's clover.

The preserve is located 10 miles west of Lancaster and is open from about mid-March through late-May. This is a part of every Californian's heritage and a sight that should not be missed. After visiting the preserve, you will see why the early Spanish explorers thought the hills were on fire when their ships first came within sight of California's coast in the spring. The southern California poppies are a deeper orange than those in the north and set the hills afire with their vibrant color. For further information, call the preserve at (805) 724-1180. There is also a wildflower hotline (818) 768-3533, sponsored by the Theodora Payne foundation, which gives updated weekly information on southern California wildflower bloomings, throughout the spring.

Wandering among the Willow Gardens

Though not as extravagant as California's central plain, Grass Lake supports beautiful gardens of wildflowers. Near groves of willows (not far from the stream) and in among the lodgepoles, Richardson's Geranium (*Geranium richardsonii*) blooms in early-July. Its white-to-light pink flowers are veined in purple and grow on plants up to about 3 feet tall.

Ranger's Buttons

Look closely and you will find yellow anthers, edged in purple, sitting above the petals, waiting to distribute their golden, life-giving pollen to visiting insects, while prominent stigmas rise like crane's bills, as if waiting to be fed. After pollination, the petals fall off, and the pistils begin to elongate. The pistil then ripens into the form of a tiny candelabra as its styles are freed from the central axis, as they prepare to release the mature seeds.

In wetter areas among the willows, Swamp Onions (*Allium validum*), grow up to a height of about 4 feet. They bloom with pink flowers in dense heads, with

310

an onion fragrance that permeates the air. Alongside the onions, look for the round, white heads of Ranger's Buttons (*Sphenosciadium capitellatum*). Each "little button" is made up of clusters of tightly packed flowers.

Blooming Progression on a Satiny Pink Fireweed

As you wander through these and other flowers along the meadow's north edge, you'll soon come to stands of one of Tahoe's prettiest plants. The inch-wide, satiny pink flowers of Fireweed (*Epilobium angustifolium*) usually come into bloom by mid- to late-July on stems which grow from about 3 to 5 feet tall.

If you compare the flowers along each stem, you will notice that those at the bottom are in full bloom, while those at the top are still tightly in bud. We have discussed this progression in various flowers on previous hikes, but be sure to check out the stages here too, as they are particularly beautiful in the Fireweed. The white, swooping pistil of the Fireweed opens into 4 parts when it is receptive — notice the difference in its form among the flowers and see if you can determine what stage the flower is in. Usually on the same plant you can find the flower in bud, in full bloom and in seed, which will allow you to observe these important processes of its life cycle.

After fertilization, the ovary, which resides below where the petals join the stem, elongates into a long, thin seed pod which splits lengthwise to release seeds that catch the wind to drift away on feathery wings.

Creating Beauty after Devastation

Fireweed, with its wide-ranging seed dispersal, is one of the first flowers to move into moist, fire-damaged or road-scarred areas, creating beauty out of disaster. It is from this ability to re-populate fire-damaged areas that its common name comes. Also, in the fall, its 3 to 5 inch long, narrow leaves turn fire-red. The leaves, when brewed into tea by Native Americans, were an important source of Vitamin C, and the young shoots in spring were gathered by native peoples and eaten like asparagus.

Its botanical name, *angustifolium*, means "narrow-leaved," and *Epilobium* is derived from the Greek words, *epi*, for "upon" and *lobos* for "a pod," which refers to the placement of the flower parts above the ovary.

An Amazing Pollen Dispersal Method

After wandering around the meadow, walk toward the lake to see the flowers which grow near and in its standing water. The Hooded Lady's Tresses (*Spiranthes romanzoffiana*), with its white orchid flowers, blooms right in the standing water. Its flowers grow so geometrically and compactly along the stem that they look like braided hair. The plants grow up to about 20 inches high with small, upper leaves and grass-like, basal ones.

Its complicated sounding botanical name is easy once you know how it was derived. *Spiranthes* describes the spiral placement of the flowers along the stem, with *speira* meaning "a spiral" and *anthos* meaning "a flower." *Romanzoffiana* is in honor of a Russian count and patron of science who lived in the early-1800's.

This plant has an intriguing method of pollen dispersal. If you look closely at one of the tiny flowers with your hand lens, you will see that the pollen is held in a 2-pronged structure, out of which protrudes a point. When the bee lands on the flower, she makes contact with this pointed part of the structure. It adheres to her forehead and is then carried away with her as she flies to another flower.

After the pollen structure has been removed from the flower by the bee, the pistil (which until now was bent out of the way) pops up exposing the stigma in the exact position that the anther was in before it became attached to the bee's forehead. When the bee flies to a new flower, where the pollen has already been removed, the stigma is now in position to receive the pollen (that is held outward from her forehead), and fertilization takes place.

After pollination, the pollen structure falls off her forehead — apparently having caused no discomfort or damage. It is extraordinary that such a mechanism could have evolved, yet within Nature we see many such amazing examples of co-evolution. Before you wander on, be sure to inhale the delicate fragrance of this lovely orchid.

Other Plants with their Feet in the Water

The Buckbean (*Menyanthes trifoliata*), with unusual white flowers that bloom above sets of 3 leaves, was discussed on the Osgood Swamp hike, but be sure to check it out here, as it grows in profusion with white threads covering its petals.

Another flower that grows right in the water is one that I first discovered here. The Purple Cinquefoil (*Potentilla palustris*) has a typical cinquefoil look, but its sepals are purplish green and its petals are a deep burgundy. Notice that it is easy to identify this flower as a cinquefoil, even though it is not the typical yellow, because of the form of the sepals and petals. This burgundy color, which is unusual in a flower, is repeated in the reproductive parts which cluster in the flower's center. Its pinnate leaves are toothed, and its species' name, *palustris*, means "of the swamp."

The Sundew (*Drosera rotundifolia*), that small insectivorous plant discussed on the General Creek hike, also grows here in boggy areas near the lake's edge. Look for finger-nail sized, rounded leaves which are covered with red, glandular hairs. These hairs trap and digest insects to obtain their nitrogen.

The Yellow Pond Lily (*Nuphar polysepalum*) and many other flowers can be found on the lake and in the meadow, so plan to spend a whole day exploring the unusual flowers that live and bloom here beneath the summer sun.

Living within the Scheme of Nature

While standing in Grass Lake's meadow and looking out across the lake, take a moment to stop and

313

appreciate Nature's gift of wildflowers. It is a gift that we sometimes take for granted, yet what would life be without flowers?

How delicately they express the life force, and how joyfully they appear each spring, after the bitter cold of winter. On windy days they dance in the breezes, celebrating their aliveness with vibrant color and sweet fragrance. They bloom with exquisite beauty whether anyone is there to see them or not. They require no care by man, as do our garden plants — no need to water, fertilize, cultivate. As much as I love to garden, nothing can compare to the freedom I feel in a wild meadow of flowers.

What a mistake it is to over-domesticate our flowers and monoculture our crops and forests and to lose this harmony and balance. If man respectfully studied Nature to understand her ways and applied it to his life, he would stop resorting to frantic, but futile, attempts to poison insects and unwanted plants, and, with wisdom, he would return to a system which works within the scheme of Nature.

One of the greatest gifts we can give to Nature, to ourselves and to our families would be to never again use any herbicide or pesticide and to begin buying (or growing) organically grown produce to support those who care enough to stop poisoning the earth. We are just beginning to realize the dangers of the culmulative effect of these poisons in our food and in the environment. Yet it will be a long time before responsibility is taken by those in standard farming, by the goverment or by most retail outlets. If we care about the health of our families and the environment, we must take responsibility by taking action now. Soon we will fully realize the havoc these poisons have created in our lives, but by then, I fear, it may be too late.

Grass Lake on a Rainy Day

If you are lucky enough, or adventuresome enough to have timed your visit to the lake on a rainy day, you will discover an intriguing adaptation within the plant world. Many plants, like poppies, dandelions and water lilies, close their petals on an overcast day. They do this to protect their pollen from damage by the rain.

But other flowers have a different way of protecting their pollen. As you wander among tall plants in wet areas, look for the white umbel flowers of angelica, cow parsnip or lovage and you may find that some of the individual flowers in each large cluster are tipped 90 degrees. They take on this form in wet weather, when the walls of the stems become limp, a few inches below the flower head.

What is interesting is that not all the flowers have bent stems but only those with ripened pollen. The older flowers, which have already released their pollen, remain upright. Somehow a message travels from the ripe pollen to the stem that says, "Oops better protect me, it's going to rain!" These are not the only flowers which shelter their pollen in this manner from the rain — buttercups and geraniums do the same. Since these plants also grow around the lake, check them out too. As soon as the sun comes out, the stems become stiff again and the flowers, that seemed "damaged" a few hours before, brightly present their vital parts to visiting insects and to the sun's rays.

As you look at other plants in the meadow, ask yourself which of them has developed pollen-protecting mechanisms. Does the flower head always droop, rain or shine, to protect the pollen from overhead rain? Are the pollen-bearing parts enclosed in a tight petal case, as in flowers of the pea family? Or do the petals form a closed, urn-shaped, drooping blossom, as in the manzanita?

Diversity as Nature's Way

Every aspect of Nature is intriguing, from the most subtle of changes or forms to the most obvious or outrageous. A close relationship with flowers can teach us an important lesson, for we are often led to believe that there is one best way to do things or one best way to be.

Yet everywhere in Nature we see diversity — that there is no one way of being. We see it in the various sizes, shapes and textures of leaves, in the forms and colors of flowers, in the markings and shapes of their petals and in the unabashed beauty and complexity of their reproductive parts. It is as if Nature loves both beauty and diversity and in doing so, she offers us a valuable lesson for our own lives and brings us a lifetime of pleasure.

Highlighted Flowers
- Crest Lupine
  (*Lupinus arbustus*)
- Scarlet Gilia
  (*Ipomopsis aggregata*)
- Bridge's Gilia
  (*Gilia leptalea*)
- White-veined Mallow
  (*Sidalcea glaucescens*)
- Mariposa Lily
  (*Calochortus leichtlinii*)
- Sierra Onion
  (*Allium campanulatum*)
- White Lupine
  (*Lupinus albicaulis*)

Charity Valley to Grovers Hot Springs

Resonating Cow Bells among Lilies and Lupines

One day/overnight	
One way 5.5 miles	
Beginning/end 7800'/5900'	
Net loss 1900'	
Topo map Markleeville, Calif.	
Wildflower Season June through October	

The rolling trail down to Grovers Hot Springs begins on dry, flower-swept slopes of pink onions, golden brodiaeas and blue-lavender lupines and soon crosses small ravines with meandering creeks, which give rise to more colorful gardens. Later, groves of aspens offer cool relief from the summer sun as the trail winds its way across boulder perches that look down upon beaver dams and meandering Charity Valley Creek, and in a broad, green valley below, cowboys return from a late-afternoon roundup. The trail ends in a large, grassy meadow, near the hot springs, where the day may end in a soothing soak as a prelude to a hearty Basque dinner in nearby Minden.

Trailhead Directions
From South Lake Tahoe, take Emerald Bay Road south past the airport toward Meyers. Continue on this road, which is designated as

Mariposa Lily

317

both Highways 50 and 89, until just past Meyers, where Highway 89 splits off to the south toward Markleeville and Highway 88. Drive past Grass Lake, over Luther Pass and into lovely Hope Valley. This part of the drive is gorgeous, especially in the spring when the valley is yellow and purple with butter-cups and penstemons. At the "T" in Hope Valley, take Highway 88 to the west toward Kirkwood and then after 2.5 miles, take the Blue Lakes Road to the left. After 6.4 miles, you will arrive at the Forest Serv-ice sign that reads, "Grovers Hot Springs 5.5, Charity Valley Trail."

Tall Mullein Stalks along the Blue Lakes Road

As you drive along the Blue Lakes road in mid-June through July, you will see lupines, gilias and other flowers in bloom as well as the tall, yellow-flowered spikes of Woolly Mullein (*Verbascum thapsus*). Mul-lein is native to Europe, but was brought to America and became well established by the 1800's. Its large, woolly leaves grow erect along the single stem which may be up to 6 feet tall.

If you stop to look at the flowers, you'll see that the bright yellow petals surround a long green style and 5 stamens. Three of the stamens are short and covered with white hairs, while 2 are long and with-out hairs. Notice too that the flower-blooming cycle in mulleins is unusual. The flowers do not mature in progression, as on most stalked plants, but rather they mature in a haphazard way, with a few upper ones blooming, followed by those lower down and then later by higher ones. Each flower blooms for only a day, after which it closes permanently, so its random blooming is unlikely to create problems with self-pollination.

After pollination, each plant may produce as many as 170,000 tiny seeds, which, when mature, fall out of the capsules onto the ground beside the parent plant. For this reason you'll often see many plants growing in one small area. Mulleins need bare, dis-turbed soil to germinate, which is why they are often found along roadsides or in other disturbed areas. The seeds are amazing in that they can remain in the soil in a dormant state for 100 years and then sprout, when conditions are right.

The mullein is normally a biennial. It usually forms a rosette of downy leaves the first year and sends up the thick, flowering stalk the second year, though some individual plants may live for more than two years. A tea made from the flowers and leaves is soothing for a sore throat or congested chest, and its leaves were smoked as tobacco by native peoples to relieve coughs.

Mullein is also known by the name, Quaker's Rouge. Makeup is not allowed by the Quaker religion, but some young girls have found a way around this rule. They rub their cheeks with the leaves — the barbed hairs on the leaves irritate the skin causing reddening of their cheeks, as a kind of natural rouge.

Look closely at the leaves, through your hand lens, and you'll see that they are barbed and interwoven, forming a dense mat. Insects and animals normally don't eat the leaves, probably because the hairs make the leaves unpalatable, but small insects like to snuggle down in the soft, protected center of the rosette.

The Trail Begins

After parking in the turnout which is across the street from the trail sign, walk through the cattle gate by the sign. The trail begins at the gate amidst July-blooming carpets of blue Torrey's Lupine (*Lupinus sellulus*) and hillsides of golden Mountain Mule-ears (*Wyethia mollis*), interspersed with the tall stalks of the Green Gentian (*Frasera speciosa*).

At the base of the large leaves of mule-ears and balsamroots, look for the white flowers of Leichtlin's Mariposa Lily (*Calochortus leichtlinii*). Its petals are spotted black and yellow from the nectar glands at the base. Native people felt that this plant was a special gift from the Great Spirit because it yields life-

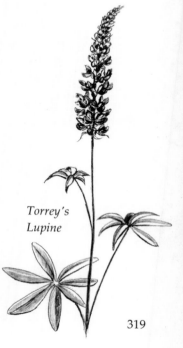

Torrey's Lupine

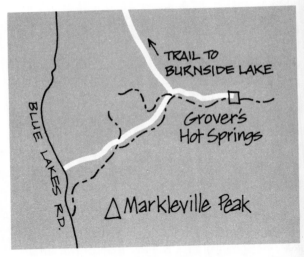

giving food on dry, barren slopes. Its bulb, which was a staple among all the tribes, was roasted and eaten like potatoes. They honored it by calling it the "life plant" which is appropriate not only for the bulb, but for its lovely flowers which give "life" to dry terrain.

Interspersed with the mariposa lily are large displays of the clustered flowers of the Sierra Onion (*Allium campanulatum*). Look closely at the detail of its exquisite, pink flowers with your hand lens — they have some of the feeling of a passion flower. The bulbs of this onion were gathered in the fall and roasted or added raw to season dishes, while its leaves were enjoyed raw in salads or as seasonings in stews.

Enjoying Fall Color
The best time to find these slopes in full bloom is June through mid-July, while the wetter, creek areas bloom through August. I have suggested that the wildflower season on this trail is June through October, because I want to encourage you to visit Charity Valley several times during the season to see the flowers in bloom and later in seed, when the leaves of many of the plants become bright with fall color.

In early-October the aspens and willows turn yellow, and the trail is lined with the red stems and yellow leaves of dogwoods, the large, golden, maple-like leaves of thimbleberry, the brownish yellows of bracken fern and the reds of fireweed. This late in the season the shrubless, open slopes become drab and withered, but the air is brisk and the windy, exposed hillsides are exhilarating.

Returning to July-Blooming Flowers
The daintiest blossoms along the trail in July are those of Bridge's Gilia (*Gilia leptalea*). They carpet the ground in pink-lavender beneath the lacy, umbel flowers of white Yampah (*Perideridia bolanderi*). These two flowers take delight in growing together.

Along the rocky slopes, look for an umbel flower with small yellow flowers. (Its flower stems radiate outward from a central point as do the spokes on an umbrella.) The flowers bloom above lacy, grayish green leaves that are divided into numerous, tiny, linear segments. Its ray flowers are unequal in length and its oblong to oval-shaped seeds have wavy margined edges. Its botanical name is *Pteryxia terebinthina*, and its common name is Terebinth Pteryxia, which is not much help!

Two of the prettiest lupines that bloom along the trail are the fragrant Crest Lupine (*Lupinus arbustus*), that we have seen on many previous hikes, and a new one, the White Lupine (*Lupinus albicaulis*), that blooms in a shrub-like fashion with leafy stems which are bare at the base. Its racemes of white flowers may be up to 12 inches long, with the flowers growing along the stem in a random manner. The banner is marked with a yellow spot, and the flowers fade to brown as they age.

As you wander along these flowered slopes, you'll look down into green grassy meadows which lie at the base of the dark, talus flanks of Markleeville Peak. While off in the distance, the rhythmic music of cow bells resonates up the hillside.

Passing through Aspen Gardens
After crossing several seeps, you'll begin to wind your

321

way down through large boulders. At this point, the trail fades out, but if you continue in the same direction, you will soon link up with it again. After climbing down through the rocks, you'll arrive at groves of crooked-stemmed aspens which will lead you to the small, damp meadows of Charity Valley Creek, which usually bloom lushly through mid-August.

As you approach mossy areas near the banks of the creek, look for small, white, pea flowers which bloom above carpets of deep green. Its flowers are marked with pink lines along the top edge of the banner petals and its tiny keel is purple-tipped. It's easy to identify the Carpet Clover (*Trifolium monanthum*) by its white flowers and by its 3-palmate leaves that are toothed. The flower heads of these, and other clovers of this genus, may be brewed into a tea, and its leaves, which are high in protein, may be eaten raw or cooked.

Within a little less than 2 miles, the trail merges with Charity Valley Creek, where horsetail ferns and red paintbrush lushly grace the creek's edge, drooping over its banks, as if reaching to take a drink from the slowly moving waters. Near this point, the trail narrows down between the willows and is lined with colorful flowers looking like a magical garden, with a little path leading to a secret place.

Are Plants Sensate Beings?

As you wander through these gardens, take a few minutes to sit alongside the creek and look out at the plants that surround you. How do you view the trees and flowers? How do you feel about the possibility that they may have senses which we don't normally attribute to the plant world? In *The Secret Life of Plants*, Peter Tompkins and Christopher Bird suggest that there is a whole new and exciting way of looking at plants.

They discuss research that suggests that plants may be more sensate than we realize. According to the authors, plants grow more happily if they are exposed to classical music or if they are treated with

322

love. The authors also report that plants shrink back from hard rock or dissonant music or when they sense impending danger.

Some of their studies suggest that, in certain areas, plants may have senses that far transcend our own. In the words of Tompkins and Bird,

"Evidence now supports the vision of the poet and the philosopher that plants are living, breathing, communicating creatures, endowed with personality and the attributes of soul. It is only we, in our blindness, who have insisted on considering them automata."

Though I cannot pass judgement on the validity of their experiments, I feel it is an area certainly worthy of scientific research. The danger in closing our minds to such research is that such prejudgment may limit our perception and thus our experience of the world. As Tompkins and Bird point out, Nature's treasures are not discovered by those who take the heart out of science, but by those who are in sympathy with Nature, by those who put the heart back into life. One of the greatest scientists of all time, Albert Einstein, used heart, intuition and scientific methods to open his mind to the universe, to see it in ways never before imagined.

On a simpler level, how beautiful the world would be if there were more people who put the heart back into life, as Kote Lotah's Uncle, who was so in tune with Nature that he would hug a tree when he heard it crying for love. Seem far fetched? Only if our minds are conditioned to reject such notions, and our hearts are closed to such joy.

Majestic Groves of Incense Cedar and White Fir
After returning to the trail, you will continue for about 3 miles, until you arrive at the Burnside Lake trail. Here damp slopes of bracken fern soften the bases of dramatic, rock spires that rise above Sawmill Creek with majesty and power. If you hike the trail late in

the day, you'll often find these magnificent spires glowing golden in the late-afternoon light.

Nearby, groves of incense cedar and white fir tower over the younger trees, like parents nurturing their children. The branches of the young trees point upward, looking like happy children lifting their hands in laughter, while the downward swooping branches of the parent trees seem to offer loving protection to the youngsters in their midst.

The Incense Cedar (*Libocedrus decurrens*) is a lovely tree with rich, cinnamon-brown bark. Its fragrant, scale-like leaves lie pressed tightly against the stems. Its flowers appear on the ends of the branches with its male flowers, which are bright yellow, releasing their pollen in billowy clouds during the summer. The female flowers are a light green and are made up of 6 spreading scales that elongate and hang downward from the branches after fertilization. After the seeds are released, the cones fall to the ground looking like wooden flowers because of their outward, spreading scales.

A Luxuriant Soak at Day's End

After the deep woods of incense cedar and white fir, you will arrive at the big meadow at Grovers Hot Springs. Just beyond the meadow are the hot springs. They are made up of two pools, one for swimming, the other for soaking. The facility is clean and well maintained and offers soothing relaxation after the hike. If you are lucky and have a friend who will drop you or your group off at the beginning of the hike and meet you at the end for a soak in the pools, you won't have to do the return, uphill hike back to your car. After the hot springs you can top off your day with a hearty Basque dinner in Minden.

Lower Prey Meadows

Hidden Creek Gardens of Rare Plants

One day	
One way 1 1/2 miles	
Begin/end 6885'/6737'	
Net loss 148'	
Topo map USGS Carson City, Nev.	
Wildflower Season Mid-May through August	

Highlighted Flowers

- Wright's Buckwheat
  (*Eriogonum wrightii*)
- Snow Plant
  (*Sarcodes sanguinea*)
- Pinedrops
  (*Pterospora andromedea*)
- Sierra Wallflower
  (*Erysimum perenne*)
- Twayblade
  (*Listera convallarioides*)
- Western Baneberry
  (*Actaea rubra*)
- Spotted Mountain Bells
  (*Fritillaria atropurpurea*)
- Sierra Nemophila
  (*Nemophila spatulata*)
- Nevada Pea
  (*Lathyrus lanszwertii*)
- Ox-eye Daisy
  (*Chrysanthemum leucanthemum*)

L ower Prey Meadow lies green, sun-filled and open between forested hillsides. Along its edges, small, grassy side meadows flow into the main meadow forming a network of creeks, flowery gardens and sunlit openings. A tiny, rare orchid hides in the shelter of an alder-lined creek, while in the filtered light of lodgepoles another rare plant blooms in fuzzy white. Intense, red snow plants break up the browns of the forested floor, and a tiny gall fly creates downy swellings on rabbitbrush stems. Ancient horsetails wave their feathery fronds along streambanks at the water's edge, while nearby gorgeous pink pea flowers and blue-purple lupines bloom beneath a canopy of aspens.

Spotted Mountain Bells

Trailhead Directions

The Lower Prey Meadows are on the east shore of Lake Tahoe, just north of Glenbrook. The parking turnout, on Highway 28, is by the gated logging road,

325

15N07, which is 1.8 miles north of the Spooner Lake Picnic Area and 5.4 miles south of Sand Harbor State Park. There is parking for only a few cars in the turn-out.

The Trail Begins
The trail starts at the logging road by the turnout. As you head down the road, you'll pass gray-green

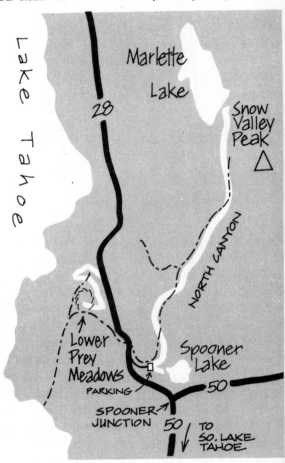

shrubs that bloom with clusters of yellow disk flowers in July. Look closely at the flower heads of the Rabbitbrush *(Chrysothamnus nauseosus)* and you will see that, like some members of the Composite Family, they are made up of tiny, 5-petaled, tubular disk flowers. If you look at the base of an individual disk flower, as is also typical of this family, you will find a conspicuous tuft of white feathery hairs, called pappus. It is the pappus that catches the wind to distribute the seeds after maturation.

The Rabbitbrush is a popular browse shrub for jack rabbits in the sagebrush flats of Nevada where is grows abundantly. Its botanical name is derived from the Greek, *chrysos*, for "gold", and *thamnos*, for "shrub." Its unpleasant name, *nauseosus*, comes from the supposedly bad smell of the twigs, though I don't find them objectionable. In examining the stems, look for white, fuzzy swellings. These are galls, which house the larvae of young insects. The gall-making process is discussed on the Snow Lake hike.

Lovely Pink Buckwheats

On the dry slopes near the Rabbitbrush, look for the delicate pink flowers of Wright's Buckwheat (*Eriogonum wrightii*) in August. This plant grows about 12 to 18 inches high with woody stems and white, woolly leaves, that are wavy at the margins and densely clustered along the lower stems.

After finding it, turn one of the flowers over and you will notice that it lacks green sepals. Buckwheats do not have petals. Instead, their sepals are colored and shaped like petals. The lack of green sepals and the tiny flowers, that bloom in tight clusters, are clues to members of the Buckwheat Family.

Look closely at the flower and you'll see that its sepals are marked with reddish brown mid-veins. Its 9 stamens are topped with bright red anthers, and its style is 3-clefted. Notice also that 3 brown bracts grow just below the flower cluster; these bracts are helpful in keying out this species. Wright's Buckwheat is a common Great Basin plant and occurs in many places along the trail.

The Startling Red Snowplant

After about 1/4 mile, you'll come to a panoramic view of Lake Tahoe, where the trail splits. If you were to take the right trail, you would arrive at the lake's edge. If you head to the left at the split, which is a 180 degree turn, you'll be heading toward Prey Meadows.

As you hike down the sandy trail, look in the woods for the sticky, tan, urn-shaped flowers of Pinedrops *(Pterospora andromedea)*. They bloom in August and were discussed on the Donner Lake hike. Earlier in the season, in June, you'll find the startling, red flowers of the Snow Plant *(Sarcodes sanguinea)*. The lack of green leaves and the sunless location in which both plants grow is a clue that neither plant depends upon photosynthesis for survival.

Instead, these plants live in the same, close, mutual relationship with soil fungi as does the coral root orchid, which was discussed on the Summit Lake hike. Because of the delicate balance between it and the mycorrhizal fungi that coat its roots, the Snow Plant is limited in its ability to spread and reproduce; it was the first wildflower in California to be protected by law, with a $500 fine for anyone caught picking it.

The Snow Plant resembles a fat, red asparagus — even its thin, bract-like leaves glow red as they twist around the 30 or more bell-shaped flowers. The intensity of the Snow Plant's color may seem out of place, but the red pigment helps it to absorb whatever warmth may be available in early-spring, as the plant begins to emerge out of the forest duff.

The Snow Plant's common name is a bit misleading because, though it may appear early, it rarely grows through snow, since it needs warm soils to emerge. Its name may have come from someone who found it dusted by a late-season snowstorm. Its botanical name, *Sarcodes sanguinea*, is derived from Greek, for "flesh-like" and "blood-like" respectively. The first of the early explorers to collect it was John Fremont, who gathered it near North Tahoe along the Yuba River in 1853. Its botanical name was given to it by a famous American botanist, John Torrey, who was responsible for naming hundreds of new plants sent to him by early explorers.

John Muir came across the Snow Plant as he explored Yosemite and, after being moved by its strange form, wrote,

> "...it is a singularly cold and unsympathetic plant. Everybody admires it as a wonderful curiosity, but nobody loves it as lilies, violets, roses, daisies are loved. Without fragrance, it stands beneath the pines and firs lonely and silent, as if unacquainted with any other plant in the world; never moving in the wildest storms; rigid as if lifeless, though covered with beautiful rosy flowers."

Long before the Europeans came, Native Americans collected the Snow Plant, and, after drying and grinding it into a powder, used it to relieve toothaches or to heal sores in the mouth. The Washos at Pyramid Lake dried the whole plant and made a medicinal tea from it to bring relief from colds. The Snow Plant was thought to be of supernatural origin, because of its unique beauty and lack of green leaves, and thus it was greatly respected by native people.

A Flower with the Fragrance of Plumeria

As you continue along the trail, past sunny openings in the trees, look for the bright yellow blossoms of the Sierra Wallflower *(Erysimum perenne)*. This plant is an early bloomer, usually appearing here in late-May through early-June. Bend down and check out the detail of its lovely anthers; notice how their position changes after maturity. While you are down looking at the anthers, be sure to inhale the wallflower's lovely fragrance, which is as sweet as the Hawaiian Plumeria.

The wallflower is a member of the Mustard Family; notice its 4 petals, which are followed later in the season with long, thin seeds pods, as is typical of this family. Its name, wallflower, was given to this plant because it is often found growing on ledges backdropped by rock walls. The species name, perenne refers to the wallflower's perennial growth.

Rare Orchids Hide in the Shade of Alders

Within about 3/4 mile past where the trail previously split, begin looking for groves of large, shrubby alders growing down to the right of the trail in a wet area beneath the pines and firs. It is there, beneath the alders at the creek's edge, that you will find the rare flowers of a tiny orchid called Twayblade (*Listera convallarioides*).

The Twayblade blooms in mid-July with green flowers that look like delicate birds flying above the 2 oval-shaped leaves. It grows on stems from about 4 to 8 inches tall. This is the only place at Tahoe where I have found it growing, although Gladys Smith mentions in her book, *A Flora of the Tahoe Basin and Neighboring Areas*, that it grows on the trail to Grass Lake, so you might want to look for it in that area also.

In dryer areas on the slope near the Twayblade, look for the white, star-shaped flowers of Star Solomon's Seal (*Smilacina stellata*). They usually bloom from late-May through June. The plants grow about 3 feet tall with stalks of flowers made up of 3 white petals and 3 white sepals. Its prominent white pistil sits atop the petals, while its white stigma glistens receptively in the sunlight.

The flower is completely white, except for bright yellow anthers which are hinged to the top of the fleshy filaments. If you look closely at the stigma tips, you'll be able to see if any of the tips have been dusted with the yellow pollen. On those with yellow dust, you might just notice a rosy glow emanating from the flower's face!

If you follow the creek downhill for a few hundred feet, you'll find another rare flower. Look for a shrubby plant that has toothed, maple-like leaves that give off a disturbing odor when crushed. The leaves grow in pinnate sets of 3 to 5. (Pinnate means the leaflets grow in parallel sets along the leaf stem.)

The Baneberry (*Actaea rubra*) is easy to identify by the terminal clusters of compact, fuzzy, white flowers that elongate as the flowers mature. The Baneberry begins blooming in mid-May and can sometimes be found in bloom as late as mid-June. Its white petals are spoon-shaped and cradle a pistil that is made up of a white style that rises above the green ovary. Its creamy colored anthers rest on white, thread-like filaments, while beneath the petals, you'll find sepals tinged red on their tips and backs. The flowers are followed in July with poisonous berries, which if eaten can paralyze the respiratory system, causing death.

Other plants, such as alpine lilies, veronicas, orchids and monkeyflowers, come into bloom about two weeks later by the stream near the Baneberry. After enjoying this lovely spot, wander down the hillside southwest through the woods to the open meadow. On your way, look for the purplish brown flowers of Spotted Mountain Bells (*Fritillaria atropurpurea*) that bloom in mid-June. The coloring of these lilies camouflages them as they grow out of the humus floor, but once you spot one, you'll see many growing throughout the woods in delicate beauty with their nodding flowers and linear, grass-like leaves. By July the mountain bells will have gone to seed with pods which are both lovely and distinctive.

Arriving at the Meadow

The large, main meadow opens up as you come to the edge of the woods. The meadow becomes purple in mid-June from the blossoms of penstemons and is soon followed by other flowers that last until August or September, as purple asters come into bloom. The meadow is a relaxing place in which to paint, sketch, picnic or to just take a nap on a lazy afternoon.

As you relax, you may want to look among the grasses for some of the "belly flowers" that we have discussed on other trips. One, that you'll find here, may be new to you; it grows only a few inches tall in small openings in the grass. Its branched stems carry clusters of tiny, white flowers with uneven petals. You can identify it as a member of the Purslane

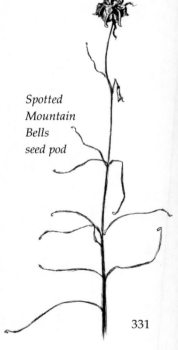

Spotted Mountain Bells seed pod

Family by its two sepals. The prettiest parts of the flower are the pink-striped sepals, that are most obvious before the flower opens. It is called Linear-leaved Montia *(Montia linearis)* and blooms in the meadow in late-May through early-June.

You'll usually find many birds in the meadow. The most common are the Mountain Chickadee *(Parus gambeli)* and Clark's Nutcracker *(Nucifraga columbiana)*, which were discussed on the Mt. Rose and Fontanillis hikes. If you leave the meadow after dark, you may hear the haunting hoots of an old owl that lives in the woods at the meadow's edge.

Ancient Horsetails Line the Creek

If you wander south through the meadow, you'll find a creek lined with aspens, alders and willows. In following the creek upstream, you'll discover hundreds of Horsetails *(Equisetum arvense)* lining its banks with their feathery, vegetative fronds. Horsetails are primitive plants, having appeared on this earth long before flowering plants. They are among the last representatives of a group of plants that grew abundantly when the dinosaurs lived.

Notice that these plants produce two types of jointed stems — one with whorls of horizontal, thread-like leaves and the other that ends in a cone. When mature, the cone releases spores that form separate plants that produce gametophytes. Gametophytes are tiny structures that produce sperm and ovum, which combine by traveling through water to produce the stalked plants that you see at the water's edge.

Silica in the walls of the outer cells of the stems of these plants made them popular with early colonialists as scouring pads. The Shoshones made whistles from the jointed stems, which, incidentally, is where most of the photosynthesis takes place. The Washos in nearby Nevada used the rough stems, as sandpaper, to smooth out their bows, while other tribes dried and burned the stems and then applied the ashes to heal sores in the mouth.

Creekside Slopes of Pinks and Purples

As you wander beneath lodgepoles and aspens near the stream, keep your eyes open for one of the prettiest pea flowers at Tahoe. It blooms in early- to mid-June in a gorgeous pink. Its angled, twisted stems carry narrow, pinnate leaves. Its wings are a paler pink and its reflexed banner is marked with pink veins. The white keel houses a green pistil, surrounded by stamens with white filaments that carry yellow-brown anthers. The united sepals are unevenly toothed and hairy. This lovely flower, which is called the Nevada Pea *(Lathyrus lanszwertii),* blooms alongside carpets of bluish purple lupines.

If you head up the slope along the creek, you'll arrive at the logging road. If you turn left, the road will take you back to the spot where you left the trail to find the Twayblade. Along the road, you'll find several species of lupines, gilias and paintbrushes and the white flowers of the Ox-eye Daisy *(Chrysanthemon leucanthemum).* This alien often moves into disturbed places. It can be found in wet areas growing up to about 3 feet tall with spoon-shaped leaves, that are toothed along the edges. Its white ray flowers surround a tight cluster of yellow disk flowers. This is one of the four flowers that Luther Burbank reportedly used to create the Shasta Daisy, a popular flower in home gardens.

Embracing Jeffrey

As you return along the trail, you'll arrive at an area covered with thousands of cones from the Jeffrey Pines *(Pinus jeffreyi)* which line the path. If you pick up one of the cones, notice that it does not prick your hands as does the cone of the Ponderosa Pine. Unlike the ponderosa, which also grows along the shores of Tahoe, the prickles of the jeffrey bend inward, which is a way to distinguish these similar-looking cones.

After checking out a cone, walk over to one of the Jeffrey Pines and bury your nose in the furrowed bark of its trunk. If it is a Jeffrey Pine, you will pick up the fragrance of vanilla. While you are there, why not put your arms around its large trunk and give the tree a hug?

After we grow up, we often forget how close we once felt to the plants and animals. As adults, our relationships with Nature often become more intellectual than connective, as we begin to relate to plants and animals as specimens. While the learning of names and the studying of processes is interesting, it can also be rewarding to sometimes forget about the intellectual approach for a while.

In growing up, although I didn't lose my joy in being around plants, I did lose some of that natural connection that I felt as a child. Then one day I was hiking in a wild storm and was so exhilarated at being alive and a part of the energy, that I reached out to embrace a tree. At first I felt a bit self-conscious, but then, since I was alone, and no one could laugh at me or think I was being affected, I closed my eyes and became very still and peaceful and waited until I felt its powerful energy flow into me and mine into it, in a mutual exchange.

It's easy to feel self-conscious about hugging a tree, especially if it is a new experience, because our culture looks upon such emotion as silly; but why be controlled by such a cultural bias when it feels so good to put your arms around a massive trunk, to rest your head against its fragrant bark and to inhale its rich fragrance. Why not feel the connection which is there all the time, patiently waiting to give and to receive, as soon as our hearts are open to the joy.

As you continue along the logging road, you will soon link up with the place where the trail originally forked. If you head right at the fork, you will return to your car. If you head to your left, the trail will take you to the shores of Lake Tahoe. Along this eastern side of the lake, the sunsets are often spectacular, so you may want to linger a while to watch the day draw to an end.

Highlighted Flowers

- Pinedrops
  (*Pterospora andromedea*)
- Brown's Peony
  (*Paeonia brownii*)
- Oregon Mallow
  (*Sidalcea oregana*)
- Great Polemonium
  (*Polemonium caeruleum*)
- Hoary Nettle
  (*Urtica holosericea*)
- Stephanomeria
  (*Stephanomeria lactucina*)
- Giant Collomia
  (*Collomia grandiflora*)
- Fireweed
  (*Epilobium angustifolium*)

Marlette Lake

Fall along a Golden Trail

🚶🏃♿ *(for the first few miles)*

One day	
One way	5 miles
Trail begins/ends	6950'/7823'
Net gain before dropping down to lake	1200'
Topo map Carson City, Nev.	
Wildflower Season	June through October

Marlette Lake lies nestled in the trees at the end of a flowery, creekside trail. Side trips to the creek reveal dramatic, vertical walls that cradle lacy blossoms, in tiny ledges, on the dark rock faces. The climb to the lake passes a broad meadow of wildflowers and an old funky shack near the meadow's edge. The warm, shallow waters of Marlette offer relief from the summer heat, while small flowers along the shoreline create random bouquets to brighten special picnic spots. By October, the color of flowers gives way to the rich hues of changing leaves that form swaths of orange and yellow, on the slopes above the blue waters, as if spilled from a giant paint bucket.

Trailhead Directions

Spooner Lake lies just north of Spooner Junction (where Highways 28 and 50 merge). The entrance to the Spooner Lake Picnic Area is well

Yarrow

marked on Highway 28.

The Trail Begins

After parking in the lot, to the left of the Spooner Campground entrance, head over to Spooner Lake to check out the flowers that bloom along its shores. In

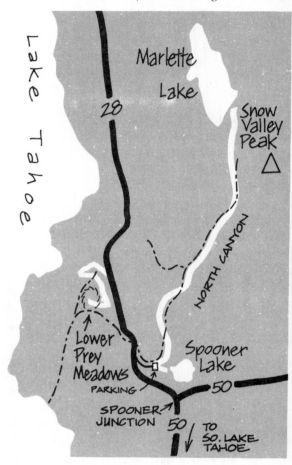

early-July the slopes along the lake are carpeted in yellow from the bright faces of monkey flowers. As you wander among the flowers, take care not to upset the nesting sites of Killdeers.

Killdeers are noisy, little birds that breed along the lake. They lay their spotted, pear-shaped eggs in shallow depressions, carved out of the gravel or soil

336

at the water's edge. The depressions are either bare or sparsely lined with grasses. The subtle nest and the mottled buff color of both the eggs and chicks help to conceal them from predators — a vital camouflage because of the strange and precarious nursery site selected by the parents.

Killdeers *(Charadrius vociferus)* are about the size of a robin and can be identified most easily by their repeating shrill cry, hence their name, vociferus. They can also be identified by the prominent black bands that mark the chest. They are common shore birds at Tahoe, swooping and flying above creeks or rapidly scurrying along the shore of lakes and streams in open, grassy meadows.

After checking out the lake, return to the parking area and head down the chained-off, black-topped road which drops a few hundred feet to the dirt trail. As you hike along the trail, keep your eyes open for the downward drooping flowers of Brown's Peony *(Paeonia brownii)* which appear in early-June. Look also for large clumps of reddish brown Pinedrops *(Pterospora andromedea)*, which bloom in July. Heading right on the dirt trail, you will soon arrive at the lake's outlet creek, while on your left will be the large, open meadow.

Heading up North Canyon

As you skirt the meadow, you'll pass through lodge-pole pines and August-blooming Fireweed *(Epilobium angustifolium)*, and soon arrive at the "Marlette Lake 5 mile" sign. At the sign, head left and continue for almost a mile, until you cross a creek and enter North Canyon. In this area of ample water, hundreds of Bog Mallow *(Sidalcea oregana)* bloom pink in July, in gorgeous contrast against the gray leaves of sagebrush.

You will also find the flat-topped, pink flower clusters of Yarrow *(Achillea lanulosa)*, which are more often found blooming in white. Its fern-like leaves, which are finely divided and very soft, were used by Native Americans to aid clotting or to heal abrasions.

A tea made from the plant was used for various medicinal purposes, from reducing the menstrual flow to encouraging the sweating out of a fever.

Look also in similar, damp areas near the meadow for the gorgeous, lavender flowers of the Great Polemonium *(Polemonium caeruleum)* which bloom in sweeping elegance along 3 to 4 foot tall stems. This flower was discussed on the Sagehen West hike but graces the creek along the trail as beautifully here as it does in Sagehen.

As you wander alongside the meadow, you will see large clumps of willows. Notice that at the base of the willows there are healthy groups of the Giant Red Paintbrush *(Castilleja miniata)*. Paintbrushes are interesting plants because, although they carry out photosynthesis, they also parasitize the roots of willows and other neighboring shrubs. Botanists have found that, while paintbrushes can exist without being parasitic, they are healthier with this added nourishment.

As you return to the trail, keep your eyes open for the Western Mugwort *(Artemisia ludoviciana)*. Mugwort is easy to identify by its tiny flower heads which grow in long, compact clusters and by its gray-green leaves which are downy white, due to the soft matted hairs that cover the lower surface. Its fragrant leaves were honored as a powerful plant by Native Americans and used for ceremonial incense in sweat lodges. They were also tucked in with clothing and grains to repel insects and seeped in boiling water to clear up congestion.

The genus was named to honor Artemisia, who was married to Mausolus, an ancient King in Southwest Asia Minor. When Mausolus died in 353 B.C., his heartsick wife built a magnificent tomb in his honor, which became one on the Seven Wonders of the Ancient World. It is from his tomb that the word Mausoleum is derived.

Artemisia was named in remembrance of Artemis, of Greek mythology, who was goddess of the moon, wild animals and hunting. Artemisia was highly re-

Mugwort

338

spected for her intelligence and courage. Herodotus, an historian of ancient times, wrote of her,

> "It seems to me a most strange and interesting thing that she — a woman — should have taken part in the campaign against Greece...Her own spirit of adventure and manly courage were her only incentives...not one of the confederate commanders gave Xerxes sounder advice than she did."

As you crush a leaf, to inhale the heady fragrance and power of this plant, imagine how special Artemisia must have been to have remained in our memories for over two thousand years.

Stinging Plants and Pink Dandelions

As you continue along the trail, keep your senses sharpened for a plant that I have found blooming along this trail in only one dampish spot. Its size will attract you; it grows about 5 feet tall. Its coarsely serrated leaves grow opposite one another and are lance-like to narrowly egg-shaped.

If you find it, don't touch the leaves for the Hoary Nettle *(Urtica holosericea)* is covered with stinging hairs that inject formic acid into the skin, with the pain lasting in some cases for hours. Its name comes from the word *uro*, which means "to burn." Each little hair is hollow and at the base there is a small gland that produces the stinging acid. When touched, the tip of the hair breaks off and the remaining stalk pierces the skin, acting as a conduit for the painful liquid.

Look closely and you will see that the nettle houses two different kinds of flowers. The female flowers grow at the top and are purple and clustered together. The white, 4-parted, male flowers grow below in droopy racemes that rise out of the axils of the leaves.

After leaving the nettle, look in drier areas nearby for flowers that look like pink dandelions. They bloom on a plant with linear leaves, called Large-flowered

Stephanomeria (*Stephanomeria lactucina*), which grows up to about 9 inches tall. Since this is a member of the Composite Family, that has ray flowers only, you will find that each petal carries both male and female reproductive parts.

Another plant, unusual for its color, also blooms in this area and is more common along the trail than the stephanomeria. Keep your eyes open for the lovely, salmon-colored, tubular flowers of Giant Collomia (*Collomia grandiflora*). Notice how exquisitely its blue anthers contrast with the salmon-colored petals.

One of most common flowers you will find in dryish areas is the Golden Aster (*Chrysopsis breweri*). Its name is confusing, because it is not an aster, for it lacks ray flowers. But it is a member of the Composite Family with disk flowers only. A small, compact golden head sits atop each leafy stem. The plant grows in a loose, shrubby manner and usually comes into bloom in July. Its bloom is followed a month or so later by bristly heads of tan pappus that will catch the wind to carry the tiny seeds far from the parent plant.

These and many other flowers bloom along the trail from late-June through August, with the height of the season usually lasting from mid-July through early-August. If you don't feel like taking a 10 mile round trip, you can hike up the canyon for whatever distance you choose, since there are flowers blooming all along the trail. The creek invites picnics in many places, along its accessible banks, and if you travel by wheel chair, the first mile or so is level and thus is easily accessible.

A Logging Operation at Nearby Spooner Summit
As you look out from the trail toward the white firs, lodgepole pines and aspens and out across verdant meadows of wildflowers, it will be hard to imagine what this area must have looked like in the 1870's. At that time the hillsides all around Tahoe were denuded of their magnificent virgin timber to serve the consumptive mining operations in Virginia City and the

Comstock Lode.

There were several lumber mills around the lake, and one major mill operated out of Glenbrook on the shore of Lake Tahoe, not far from where you now stand. Severe erosion occurred on the hillsides above the lake as logs were dragged overland by oxen or skidded down to the shoreline, where they were then floated across the water by steamer to Glenbrook.

After milling, the lumber was hauled up to Spooner Summit, just a mile or so southeast of Spooner Lake. It was transported by a narrow gauge railroad that ran from Glenbrook to a large receiving yard at the summit. At that point feeder flumes from Marlette Lake and from streams to the south brought water to the main flume, which was used to transport the lumber twelve miles and 3,000 feet down to Carson Valley to be distributed.

Such clear-cutting today would be unthinkable in the Tahoe Basin. Public outcry and present legislation would prevent it, but we must also be aware that the lake is still being threatened by over-building and by too many people and automobiles. It is vital that we put limits on our consumption and that we protect the health and clarity of this sacred body of water so that future generations can come to its shores for spiritual renewal and relaxation.

As you wander along the trail, you will parallel the creek for several miles, and after crossing the creek several times, you will begin the steep climb to the summit that sits just above Marlette Lake. Shortly before the summit, you will arrive at a split in the trail. At this point, you may want to take the short side trip to Snow Valley Peak, which offers magnificent views of Lake Tahoe.

The Descent to the Lake

Soon after this spot you will arrive at the ridge above Marlette before dropping a few hundred feet down to its shores. Along this part of the trail, lavender larkspurs, monkshoods and lupines and pink monkeyflowers bloom lushly in seeps next to the trail in

341

July, while in August, purple asters and yellow goldenrods come into full bloom.

In sunny, dryish openings in July, in this area along the trail, you will find a smaller flower that carpets the ground with its fuzzy, lavender blossoms. The Low Phacelia *(Phacelia humilis)* is an unassuming little Great Basin plant which is quite lovely up close. It grows in caterpillar-like coils above small, narrow leaves and only rises about 2 to 8 inches above the ground.

As you descend, you will catch glimpses of the blue waters of Marlette Lake through the heavy forest. When you reach the lake, you will find yourself in an open bowl surrounded by trees on gentle slopes that flow into the shallow, warm waters. Overnight camping is not allowed, as the water is stored for domestic use, but you may swim and picnic along its shores.

Fall's Golden Farewell

October at Marlette is a wonderful time to celebrate fall's arrival. It is then that hundreds of aspens line the trail in a blaze of yellow. Nowhere at Tahoe have I seen such a show of fall color in such lovely surroundings. As the leaves float downward from the trees, they carpet the trail in a wide ribbon of yellow. Other leaves float to the boughs of young fir trees along the trail, covering the branches like Christmas ornaments.

If the right cold snap hits in October, the trees around the lake turn yellow and orange in huge swaths of color that flow in unbroken splendor down the slopes to the lake's edge. It is a sight not to be missed. For those who would like the company of other good people, the Tahoe Chapter of the California Native Plant Society usually offers a hike to Marlette each fall to celebrate the color and to say goodby to the flower season.

The California Native Plant Society is a statewide, non-profit organization. It is made up of both amateurs and professionals who seek, through the activi-

Goldenrod

342

ties of the local chapters, to increase the understanding and appreciation of California's wildflowers so that this glorious gift of Nature will be preserved for future, as well as present, generations. Various chapters offer hikes throughout the state and guests are welcome. The Tahoe Chapter's hikes are usually offered from June through October. For further information, or to become a member, contact the Tahoe Chapter at P. O. Box 704, Tahoe City, CA 95730.

Saying Goodby

As our journey together comes to an end, I want to thank you for sharing it with me. After spending this time in Tahoe's gardens, I hope that you have enjoyed the richness of yourself as well as the beauty of Tahoe.

When our hearts are open, the study of wildflowers is not "just botany" and hiking is not "just exercise," but rather they become processes for self-discovery — a means to explore our inner selves to find wholeness. For as John Muir once said, "I only went out for a walk and finally concluded to stay out till sundown, for going out, I found, was really going in."

I too plan to stay out till sundown, and so if in a few decades from now you are out hiking and come upon an old woman with long grey braids and a scruffy red hat, joyfully examining a new flower, I hope you'll come on over and say hello!

Appendix
Suggestions for What to Carry on Body and Back

T he lighter your load the happier you'll be, in life and on the trail, so I recommend minimum baggage, but you may want to consider the following items:

• A Compass is important for orientation and can be critical to your survival if you are caught in a sudden snow storm that obscures vision.

• Topographical Maps (Topo maps) show elevations, trails, contour lines and major landmarks and are therefore excellent for cross-country travel. The problem is that some have not been updated for 20 years, so many of the trails may be missing or may have changed.

• U. S. Forest Service maps do not show contour lines, but are helpful because they are updated frequently and thus more accurately show trails and roads. These maps are available at the U. S. Forest Service station in Truckee, in Meeks Bay or at the Visitor's Center near Baldwin Beach.

• Wilderness permits are required for all hiking in Desolation Wilderness and can be picked up at the Forest Service stations listed above or in some cases, when designated, at the trailhead.

• Portable Water Filters are important because, sadly enough, many of the streams in the Sierra are now contaminated with giardia, a microscopic organism that can cause severe intestinal disorder. I still drink from many of Tahoe's high streams, but to be on the safe side I recently began using a small portable water filter. It's great because I can filter water in a minute or less. This is a far superior solution to boiling water or using chemicals for purification. I have used it in mighty suspicious waters with no after-effect! Such filters are available in many local backpacking stores.

• Insect Repellent frees us from unpleasant attack, but PLEASE don't use the poisonous ones readily available on the market. Let's not support companies that create products that are unhealthy or even dangerous to us and to the environment. I use "Green Ban," a plant product, which is available through many natural food stores. It smells good, is safe, and it works!

• A 10-Power Hand Lens can be purchased through universities or nature stores and is a real gift of love for yourself or someone you love. One look through it and you will be hooked on exploring the detail of every flower, leaf and insect you find. Be sure to buy a quality glass. Cheap magnifying glasses, often sold for this purpose, will only discourage you because of their lack of clarity and insufficient magnification. I use a Bausch & Lomb.

• Clothing Selection is personal, but I usually wear light-weight boots or tennis shoes, a hat, sunglasses, shorts, and I take warm clothing in case the weather changes.

• Wildflower Identification Books helpful for the Tahoe area, beside the Niehaus book, which was recommended in the Overview section, include: *A Flora of the Wright's Lake Area* by Judy L. Hutchinson and G. Ledyard Stebbins, with good illustrations and clear descriptions of Tahoe wildflowers; *Wildflowers 3, The Sierra Nevada* by Elizabeth Horn, with nice photography and descriptions — an inspiring starter book; *A Sierra Nevada Flora* by Norman F. Weeden, with broad coverage of flowers, trees and ferns and family, genus and species keys, good for those interested in more extensive field identification, botanical terminology is used; *A Flora of the Tahoe Basin and Neighboring Areas and Supplement*, by Gladys L. Smith, essentially an extensive plant list, includes a wonderful discussion of people who have botanized at Tahoe over the past 100 years.

Index

To Flowering Plants

347

349